BUSINESS ANALYTICS

THOMAS W. JACKSON AND STEVEN LOCKWOOD

BUSINESS ANALYTICS

A CONTEMPORARY APPROACH

 macmillan international
HIGHER EDUCATION

 RED GLOBE PRESS

First published 2018 by
RED GLOBE PRESS

Red Globe Press in the UK is an imprint of Springer Nature Limited,
registered in England, company number 785998, of 4 Crinan Street,
London, N1 9XW.

Red Globe Press® is a registered trademark in the United States,
the United Kingdom, Europe and other countries.

ISBN 978–1–137–61060–7 paperback

This book is printed on paper suitable for recycling and made from fully
managed and sustained forest sources. Logging, pulping and manufacturing
processes are expected to conform to the environmental regulations of the
country of origin.

A catalogue record for this book is available from the British Library.

A catalog record for this book is available from the Library of Congress.

SHORT CONTENTS

CONTENTS

LIST OF FIGURES

FOREWORD

Today information is everywhere. We're almost engulfed in it. From the non-stop nagging of social media, to the mega-sized billboard that leans in on the highways of the western world. No matter where you are or which way you turn, information will always be there. Its abundance has a nasty habit of putting us at ease, so much so that nowadays we almost take it for granted. Even worse, it lulls us into a false sense of security. We believe we know what it is. We think it's easy.

But make no mistake, understanding information is not easy. Far from it. And putting it to meaningful work is an even harder task. We have a word for that these days. We call it 'analytics', and most of the big companies around the world need it – not only to help turn a profit, but to literally help them survive. For them, information is a natural resource, like oil or water, and that elevates analytics to a particularly special position. Today not only is it essential for modern business, but its effects pervade our daily lives, almost like the nervous system of some vast creature. We influence it and it influences us. It is now an essential part of the human condition.

Nevertheless, very few really understand the tight bond between information and analytics and fewer still have a track record of real-world application to prove it. Few can walk the line between the rigour of academic study and the pragmatism of hands-on engineering. What is badly needed is a book that contains both, a book that not only tells you the important things to look for, but also tells you how to pull them apart and put them back together in useful ways. In many ways, we need a kind of car manual. A text that tells you what a gearbox is and tells you how and why to plug it into the back of the engine.

This is that much-awaited book. It has been written by two great friends of mine, one an academic and one an engineer. Both highly skilled at what they do, but in different ways and for very different reasons.

Professor Tom Jackson came to the door of information and analytics through his interest in helping people communicate better. His research centred on avoiding the information overload we so often experience when the tide of e-mails gets too much. Steve Lockwood was much more hands-on. He came across information, in the wild, early on in his career at IBM and has battled with it ever since. Over three decades he has helped build some of the largest and most successful analytics systems on the planet. Both Tom and Steve have looked analytics in the eye and survived to tell the tale. And what a tale it is!

I met with them both as they finished their writing and asked them firstly why they had chosen to team up and then what they wanted the reader to come away with. Their answer was both crisp and clear. They wanted to provide an appreciation of the subject matter, while avoiding the distractions that so often come with deep study. In simple terms, they wanted to provide a clear line of sight to success. They badly wanted to write that car manual.

So here it is, that rarest of things, a well-written and important book. No mess, no fuss, just good pragmatic insight and advice. As you read you will first be taken through the basics that lay out the components of importance to you. Next the various uses that these components can be put to when brought together is explained, with a slant on modern assembly practice. Then you will move on to understand how to manage and control information as it flows through the various analytics systems you might build over it. Here the book really starts to differentiate, as it begins to examine many of the challenges inherent to analytics that are often hidden from the casual consumer. This is perhaps the hardest climb in the book, but the effort is worth it, as once you reach the other side you will be well equipped to appreciate the material that comes next. This includes a view on how to harvest new forms of data as they start to come online and is followed by a discussion on the rights and wrongs of analytics in the modern world. This type of discussion is especially rare, as most experts in the field still choose to stay away from the gnarly subject of ethics. But not here. Instead the subject is treated with Jedi-like mastery, almost as if handing you the keys to the hypothetical car the manual has helped you build. Then out onto the open road and on into the future, as the authors explain what's just over the horizon and how the field of analytics is likely to change going forward.

This is more than a reference book aimed at students. It's a comprehensive and up-to-date accelerator to learning. What you will find in these pages, therefore, is a well-constructed attempt to walk you through an increasingly important discipline. It is focused, realistic and, in many ways, captures the views of a wide range of experts. I very much like this book and hope you do too. It deserves a wide readership.

Phil Tetlow, PhD, CTO Data Ecosystem IBM (UK), Adjunct Professor of Web Science, Southampton University

PREFACE

What is this Book About?

Imagine a factory that can identify when it needs additional stock or can recognise the potential failure of one of its machines; imagine a car that can recognise voice commands or manage self-diagnostics to predict its own failure; imagine a hospital that can predict and identify when available beds reach critical limitations and work with other hospitals to alleviate the risk; imagine being able to automatically analyse vast tranches of data on the web in order to evaluate the sentiments and emotions that people feel as they react to real-time events and take appropriate actions to respond to those feelings.

These solutions are not something for the future. With the rise of cloud-based solutions, the introduction of a wide variety of analytical techniques to grab data wherever it may reside, in whatever form it may take, and the rapid increase in sensor-based data streams, we have the means to monitor, move, analyse and draw conclusions and insights from most industries on the planet. From public sector to private sector, to charities and beyond, industries are making more informed business decisions to create new models, theories and hypotheses that disrupt current ways of thinking. Small businesses can also tap into these technologies because they can be purchased 'as you go' with little capital outlay, meaning that new ideas can be rapidly exploited with reduced financial risk and small companies are able to compete with larger ones.

In all this one thing rings clear: 'Data trumps everything.' Without access to data (depth of data and breadth of data) companies will stall in this new age. This data could be seen as the lifeblood flowing around an organisation's internal data; it is the data that flows across companies when they do business and all the external data that can now be obtained from open data sources (wikis, blogs, newsfeeds) and social media.

This book looks at the role analytics takes in such situations and especially how big data, managed in the cloud, plays a significant role in driving outcomes when analytics is used to inform and drive decision-making.

Who should read this book

Business Analytics should appeal to undergraduate, postgraduate and MBA students as well as a diverse business and technical audience, ranging from executive level to newcomers to the field. Whether you have a strong technical background or not, we hope you will enjoy reading the book and the guidance it offers, and that you will use it to further question yourself and others about this rapidly expanding field. In particular, we see our publication as a good way to 'on boarding' on a very diverse set of topics, requirements and thinking that need to be made around developing analytical solutions for the cloud.

What you will learn

Chapter 1 – 'Understanding the Big Data Landscape' – Why the term was used (it can be misleading); the key drivers of big data often referred to as the 5 'V's; and how to tackle big data problems and issues we face over the coming years.

Chapter 2 – 'Analytics: Descriptive, Predictive, Prescriptive and Cognitive' – The history of analytics and how we have moved from analysing the past to predicting and optimising future decisions. We use a specific approach to break down analytics into different 'styles' and discuss the use of those styles with some examples.

Chapter 3 – 'Building Analytics across a Hybrid Cloud' – How we need to think about data in today's world and the location of that data. This has a significant impact on how our analytic solutions are built and deployed to be most effective, efficient and economical. We describe an architectural framework for delivering these styles of analytics; explain why a hybrid cloud solution is often required; and consider some of the issues that must be addressed when developing solutions in this way.

Chapter 4 – 'Metadata Management' – How data is organised, defined and classified has always been a problem within most organisations. With poor metadata always comes poor analytics; simply put, no person or system knows what the data means when metadata is badly managed. This chapter looks at these problems and describes how they are being tackled in big data environments today, specifically considering Hadoop as a major platform in the big data world. It goes on to outline the various forms of metadata and their relationships with each other.

Chapter 5 – 'Governance: The Hardest Part?' – An often-forgotten element of design, considered last when it should be considered first (or very early on). This chapter looks at the differing forms of governance and drills down into Information Governance and the dimensions within that which must be considered to complete a successful information-centric programme.

Chapter 6 – 'Utilising the Promise of Open Data' – Open data is data that can be made freely available for use. Governments are using open data to empower end users and business to drive insights into performance or develop new business models. However, standards associated with open data are often poor, making the integration of such data difficult or unsustainable. This chapter offers but one approach to helping solve such a problem and is offered as a topic for debate. Without some approach to deal with these issues, the very rich promise of open data will fall by the wayside and may never achieve the huge benefits that could be accrued from it.

Chapter 7 – 'Ethics' – The proliferation of citizen, business and consumer data has resulted in many well-publicised breaches of data leading to loss of earnings, reputational damage and legal claims regarding privacy. This chapter outlines the ethical challenges companies face and the regulatory requirements that are being put in place by governments that companies will need to adhere to.

Chapter 8 – 'What Lies Ahead' – This chapter outlines the breakthroughs already taking place around analytics, such as applications in the fields of healthcare, manufacturing, government and finance. It's clear that the pace of change is still forever increasing and humanity needs to keep up with the advances in analytics, robotics and cognitive/artificial intelligence to make sure we exploit all the fascinating developments that lie ahead.

This book is intended to provide the reader with all the necessary background to enable them to start to make informed decisions about how to deploy analytics across public, private and legacy infrastructures. It not only describes a reference architecture to help you accomplish a logical view of a solution but also details the requirements to operate such a solution, including issues relating to metadata, governance, security, lifecycle management and privacy. It shows where past developments in analytics have led us to this new inflection point where we can begin to make sense of data that is diverse, large in volume and ever more quickly delivered. This enables business to make decisions faster, smarter and with more confidence than ever before. There are case studies and scenarios that describe solutions in a variety of industries to help you understand the context of the thinking described.

This book is *not* a detailed technical 'nuts and bolts' description of how to build hybrid cloud solutions, but it does help those who read it to develop a strong foundation on which to build their knowledge of this broad and deep subject area.

How to read this book

There are several ways to read this book. The most obvious way is to read it cover to cover to get a complete end-to-end story of the analytics journey that many companies have taken or are still taking over the last 20-plus years. The authors have organised the content in such a way that there are basic reading paths and appropriate deep dives into content within chapters that relate to business scenarios and the application of architectural patterns, so it's possible to 'dip' into various chapters for specific knowledge if required. Each chapter could work as a stand-alone piece but we've shown how there are four core sections to the book and each one could be its own separate focus area, although, of course, it's best to use the whole book!

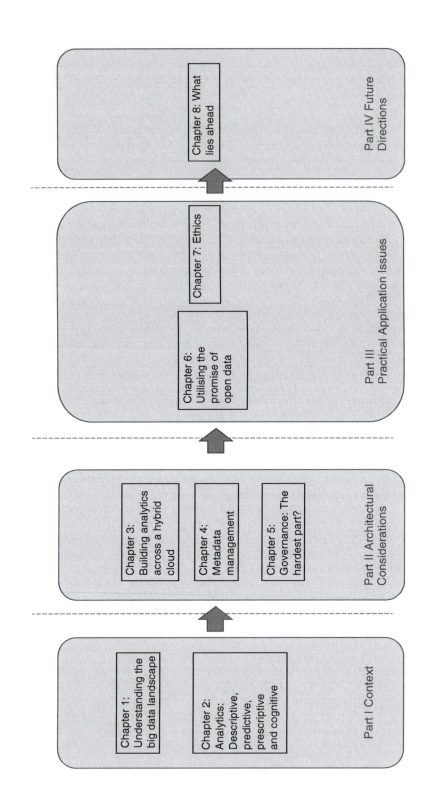

ACKNOWLEDGMENTS

The authors would like to thank the following people for the assistance and guidance in the development of this book:

- Dr Martin Sykora, Dr Suzanne Elayan and Geoff Smith for co-writing Chapter 8 on Ethics – they are the true experts in Ethics and General Data Protection Regulation (GDPR).
- Marcio T. Moura – an Executive Information Architect in IBM who has provided excellent, practical guidance on some of our chapters.
- Deepak Ranagarao – an Executive Information Specialist in IBM whose technical knowledge knows no bounds.
- Anthony O'Dowd – a Solution Architect who was instrumental in helping us push through the chapter on open data.
- Dr Philip Tetlow – for guidance and writing the foreword to this book.
- Katherine Van-Lopik – thank you for the wonderful graphics you created in the early part of the book.

And, of course, our families for their patience during the time we took to write this book. Steve Lockwood specifically thanks Vanessa (his wife) and family (Emma, Chris and Katie) for bearing with him over the past year! Tom would like to thank Lisa (his wife) and kids (Jess, Will and Ben) for holding the fort while he was writing this book with his mate Steve.

ABOUT THE AUTHORS

Thomas W. Jackson (BSc, PhD, FBCS) is a Professor of Information and Knowledge Management and is the Associate Dean Research in the School of Business and Economics at Loughborough University, UK. He has over 16 years' experience of research and industrial consultancy and secured over £14 million of research funding. His research areas are Electronic Communication and Information Retrieval, and Applied and Theory-based Knowledge Management, including his Natural Language Processing Email Knowledge Extraction system (EKE) that has the world's best f-ranking measure. In addition to this, his EMOTIVE project holds the world's best f-measure for fine-grained emotion detection. He is on a number of editorial boards for international journals and reviews for many more and has published more than 160 papers in peer-reviewed journals and conferences.

He has given a number of invited keynote talks throughout the world. Funding sources for his research include EPSRC, Royal Society, EU H2020, the private sector (e.g. SAP), the public sector (e.g. Leicestershire Constabulary, The National Archives); Knowledge Transfer Partnerships (KTPs) and the third sector (Amateur Swimming Association – predicting swimmer attendance); and he has won a number of prizes for his research, notably the research undertaken with Leicestershire Police and the implementation of Mobile Data Terminals in all police vehicles. He is currently working on the Robust Lifecycle Design and Health Monitoring for Fuel-Cell Extended Performance project; the Adaptive Informatics for Intelligent Manufacturing (AI2M) project; and the European Union (EU) H2020 Toxi-Triage project.

Steven Lockwood has been involved in all aspects of the development of information-related projects, covering Data Lakes/Business Intelligence, Information Integration, governance, metadata management and development of Master Data Management systems. Today he is more involved in the use of Big Data technologies deployed on hybrid cloud platforms (Hadoop, Data Lake, Spark, NoSQL, etc.) to solve a variety of analytical problems. These solutions have encompassed the entire life cycle for an Information Architecture from business discovery through to implementation, support and maintenance. His other focus area is cognitive solutions based on IBM's Watson services in the areas of chatbots, Natural Language Understanding (NLU), visual recognition and unstructured data analysis.

Steven's achievements have resulted in him being placed within IBM's Academy of Technology and the Academy Leadership team.

Steve has authored an IBM Blue Book – *The Art of Enterprise Information Architecture* – and an IBM Red Book on building large-scale SAP Business Warehouse (SAP BW) Data Warehouses, and he currently blogs on subjects related to analytics in the cloud.

He's also worked with Loughborough University, UK, on a variety of initiatives to bring business and the university closer together; and, finally, he is a Fellow of the British Computer society.

Part I

CONTEXT

CHAPTERS

1

UNDERSTANDING THE BIG DATA LANDSCAPE

1.1 Introduction

The speed of life seems greater than ever. Nowadays we are aided by the digital age, where the latest gadgets and gizmos keep us in touch with what is going on 24/7. Thanks to this, we are probably the best-informed generation ever. However, with digital technology there is a continuous battle to try to harness it and make it work for us rather than allowing it to dictate our daily lives, as is so often the case. With so much data and information being generated – for example, every 60 seconds, 100 hours of YouTube video is uploaded, 433k tweets sent and 204 million emails sent, we also face the battle of how to cope with increasing volumes of unstructured data and what to do with it. The effective management and efficient use of data is a major challenge for government, academia and industry. The scale, diversity and distributed nature of current and emerging data assets are increasing, for example through the realisation of the Internet of Things (IoT) through landmark reports like Industrie 4.0, which we will cover in this chapter. What is clear from these big data developments is that the lines between social and enterprise data have become fuzzy. But has the possibility of providing better insights into how to make an organisation more successful been fully realised? Consider healthcare provisions, for example. Think about the Fitbits that many wear and which could connect you to your doctor for 24/7 monitoring. There is the potential for your doctor to provide early intervention to improve your lifestyle, which could change your life insurance premiums. Of course, the next step would be to remove the doctor from the process altogether, and it could all be controlled by the various analytic techniques discussed in Chapter 2. Clearly, we are not at this point yet!

These are very exciting times to be involved in big data and this chapter sets out the big data landscape by covering the very basic concepts of the building blocks of big data through to discussing the exciting new developments of the big data world that will change our lives.

1.2 World Wide Web underpins everything we do

Without the World Wide Web (WWW) none of the changes we see in our lives could have happened. When first used, the Web was seen as no more than a vast search engine, where users could find all manner of useful, or indeed useless, information. This is still a crucial aspect of the Web but other interesting uses for it were beginning to be identified and exploited around 15 to 20 years ago when all aspects of traditional services began to change under its influence.

The first real large-scale change was in the use of online banking and shopping. The idea for online shopping had been around since the late 1970s when an Englishman named Michael Aldrich invented videotext, a modified domestic TV that connected to other systems using a telephone line and modem. Even though crude in our thinking today, the WWW introduced a level of scale not previously seen and companies such as Amazon and eBay (originally known as AuctionWeb) were established and grew rapidly. In the UK, traditional outlets such as Argos and Screwfix also created online shopping experiences, as did the world's largest retailer Walmart, with many others swiftly following suit. Even shopping for holidays changed dramatically, from going to the travel agents to book a holiday, to shopping online for the best deal. For Christmas 2016 the estimates for sales over the period leading up to Christmas through online sales alone was around £126 billion. We are rapidly reaching a point where most sales will be online. These scenarios are driven by structured information, such as stock, sales and prices.

The next big change the WWW enabled was the growth in social interaction. Blogs, chatrooms, wikis, social websites such as Facebook and more recently Twitter, Snapchat and Instagram have all arrived. These scenarios are using unstructured data (text, video, audio, images). This has allowed for individuals, groups and things (think chatbot!) to be constantly digitally connected anywhere across the globe where the WWW can function. We can now extend our reach to a far wider audience than ever before.

The third big change is the use of the WWW as the medium to move sensor data around. We can now connect almost anything to the cloud and operate it through the cloud (Rittinghouse and Ransome, 2016). This creates the opportunity to be able to understand just about anything we wish to, whether it be migratory paths of geese, the environmental impact of pollution, the movement of goods across a factory floor or an individual's basic health characteristics (think about all the data obtained through something like a Fitbit – steps walked, distance travelled, calories burnt, sleep quality – and which could be merged with information from your smart-phone – your location for example). Sensors can be attached/embedded in all these scenarios and a wealth of useful data obtained for analysis to understand and hopefully improve things (Seth, 2016). The interesting point here is that when we start to bring all this data together we can use analytics to identify trends, predict future patterns, identify best- and worst-case scenarios, and suggest next best actions to individuals based on similar peer-clustered data.

Many of these changes have been inspired by business or social pressures using the technologies we have had around for the last 20 years or so, gradually increasing the scale and complexity of those solutions. For example, the rise of internet speeds has continued at pace, enabling businesses and citizens to partake in activities not feasible even five to ten years ago – streaming video and content in general is an obvious example here, but the general movement of large quantities of data is not feasible without broadband. Figure 1.1,

	Country/Region	Q4 Avg. Mbps	QoQ Change	YoY Change
–	**Global**	**5.6**	**8.6%**	**23%**
1	South Korea	26.7	30%	20%
2	Sweden	19.1	9.3%	30%
3	Norway	18.8	14%	65%
4	Japan	17.4	16%	15%
5	Netherlands	17.0	8.7%	20%
6	Hong Kong	16.8	5.9%	-0.4%
7	Latvia	16.7	15%	28%
8	Switzerland	16.7	2.8%	15%
9	Finland	16.6	12%	37%
10	Denmark	16.1	15%	36%

Figure 1.1   Global average broadband speeds

Source: Copyright © ISPreview.co.uk. Reproduced with permission.

from the ISPreview website, shows the top 10 global average connection speeds. It's worth noting the UK and the USA are *not* in that list. Browsing is no longer just a PC/laptop process; Wi-Fi hotspots, 4G and 5G mean we can go online just about anywhere. This ability is important in changing how we have evolved to use the WWW.

1.3   The building blocks of big data

The contemporary literature views the growth in big data as directly attributed to accessibility of technology and new forms of distributed data storage. Hashem et al. (2015) characterises a common view, attributing the growth of big data to 'social media, IoT and multimedia' (2015, p. 99). Both Chen (2014) and Hashem (2015) warn of a consistently greater exponential increase of data from the IoT, with Jara et al. suggesting 'unprecedented scenarios of interaction' (2014, p. 379).

In recent times the world has witnessed a dramatic increase in the amount of formal and informal information produced in a crowded 'information society', in which the amount of information being created every two days is equivalent to that which had been created from the dawn of civilisation until the year 2003 (Seigler, 2003). This means that one of the fastest growing quantities on this planet is the amount of data/information being produced. We could frame it as Clive Humby does, 'data is the new oil', and as with oil there are dangers ahead, as we now know that oil has proven to be a polluter. We need, however, to understand the building blocks underpinning big data, which can be broken down into five key categories: Data, Information, Knowledge, Understanding and Wisdom. These are represented by Figure 1.2, which shows the size of the categories and the level of difficulty to reach the top, wisdom. It is helpful to provide a definition of these five categories as founded by Russell Ackoff, a systems theorist and professor of organisational change (Ackoff, 1967).

> **Data** – In simple terms, characters which are symbols, numbers or letters that we might interact with but which have no context. An example of data is a spreadsheet that has no row or column information which provides the context on how to interpret the data.

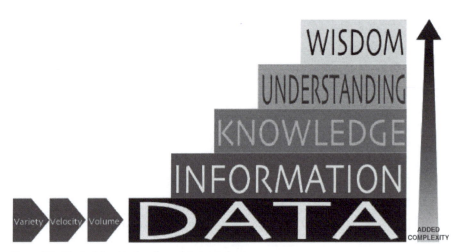

Figure 1.2   The building blocks – from data to wisdom

Information – Data that is processed to aid decision-making, i.e. provides answers to 'who', 'what', 'where' and 'when' questions. Therefore, once the context becomes sufficient to gain understanding of what the data is, we have information. For example, a spreadsheet that has data 090917 in one column and 10 in another means very little. However, if you add context of 'date' and 'temperature °C' you are provided with information that is usable, especially if the filename is titled 'Sydney Weather 2017'.

Knowledge – Application of data and information; answers 'how' questions. Knowledge is created by processing information and then applying it to create a feedback loop to further one's knowledge about the information. For example, if you lived in Sydney, Australia you would know that in September if the temperature was 10°C then that would be very cold. You would then question if the data was wrong or had global warming taken effect (which moves into Wisdom).

Understanding – Cognitive comprehension of 'why'. Understanding: the time that knowledge can be reasoned. It is the process by which one can take knowledge and synthesise new knowledge from the previously held knowledge. So this is more than memorising information; it is about learning. So if we knew the temperature in Sydney should be around 20°C in September and we know about climate change then we may have a better understanding of why it is so cold. Historically, machines have struggled to make this leap but deep learning is fast encroaching on this space and in the cognitive computing domain we are likely to see big developments as we approach and then transition into the next decade.

Wisdom – Evaluation of understanding. Unlike the four categories above, it's the ability to think about a question to which there is no (easily achievable) answer, and in some cases, to which there can be no humanly known answer, period. Wisdom is about our mental ability to determine – based on our knowledge and understanding – if something is a good or bad idea. For example, in the case of an autonomous car, what decision will it make when given the scenario the car has to crash and it can either injure the passenger or run over the pedestrian. This involves snap choices, ethics and morals which we will discuss in Chapter 8.

According to Ackoff, the first four categories relate to the past as they deal with what has happened or what is known. It is only the last category, Wisdom, that deals with the future as it incorporates vision and architecture. The 'Wisdom' category has the most value to society, and through the introduction of data analytics, organisations and wider society are able to understand why things have happened and in some cases predict what will happen next. Of course, there have been mixed results, and a good example of this is weather forecasting (meteorology) which dates back to 3000 BC. Although techniques have become much more accurate, the forecasts are still a hotly debated topic because they are still inaccurate, despite having improved significantly in the last 20 years. For example, predicting the minimum temperature on the first night of a forecast has improved over the years to the point where 86.5% of minimum temperature forecasts are accurate to within +/−2°C, over a 36-month average. Not surprising, then, that in 2017 a four-day forecast is more accurate than a one-day forecast in 1980 (Met Office, 2017).

With the building blocks in place, let's take a look at breaking down the Data category to aid us in understanding the different elements that need to be taken into consideration when dealing with big data. A popular classification of big data is defined by Laney (2001): Volume, Velocity and Variety, as shown in Figure 1.3. These three categories denote the size, speed and heterogeneous structures common across big data. Several definitions have since been applied to Laney's original classification, such as Veracity (Chen and Zhang, 2014), and more recently the cost or Value from the insights gained. So what do the 5 Vs mean and how do they interconnect?

Variety denotes the range and different formats of data available for use in today's world. Data today looks very different from data of the past. The enterprise needs of today are to manage this data as is, in its original format, or with extensive transformation tools to convert it to other desired formats for use in analytic solutions. We no longer have merely structured data (name, phone number, address, financials, etc.) that fits into a database table. Today's data is unstructured and 80% of all the world's data fits into this category, including photos, video sequences and social media updates (Cano, 2014).

Velocity refers to the speed at which vast amounts of data are being generated, collected and analysed. From a social media perspective, every day the number of emails, Twitter messages, photos and video clips increases at lightning speed around the world. There is a requirement to handle data arriving in large batches (e.g. sales data from a retailer arriving overnight), right down to low latency streams of data (e.g. stock market data arriving continuously or sensor data from a device attached to a human). Every second of every day data is increasing. Not only must it be analysed, but the speed of transmission, and access to the data, must also remain instantaneous to allow for real-time access to websites, credit card verification and instant messaging.

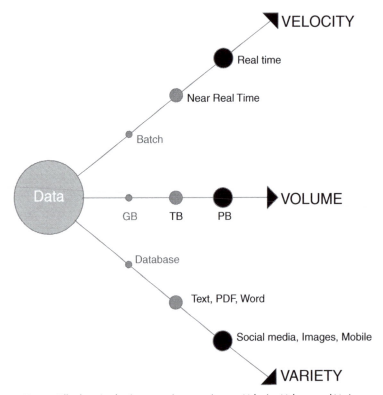

Figure 1.3   How rapidly changing business requirements impact Velocity, Volume and Variety

Volume refers to the incredible amounts of data generated each second from social media, mobile phones, cars, credit cards, sensors, photographs, video and so on (see Figure 1.3). Systems now create and consume more data than ever before. For example, 20 years ago a 2TB Data Warehouse at a large UK retailer was large; nowadays 20PB at a bank is standard. There is a requirement to handle ever-increasing volumes of data either at rest or even while in motion. The issue is the vast amounts of data have become so large that we can no longer store and analyse data using traditional database technology. The infrastructure has changed and we now use distributed systems, where parts of the data are stored in different locations and brought together by software.

Veracity refers to being able to identify and correct any uncertainty about the data being gathered, or show its results are not biased. Veracity is about the quality or trustworthiness of the data. For example, think about all the social media posts from all over the world with various hashtags, slang and typos, and the reliability and accuracy of all that content. Having lots of data is of little use if its quality or reliability is not accurate (Cano, 2014). Another good example of this relates to the use of Google Maps and GPS data. Google Maps will use Wi-Fi and GPS coordinates to identify your location, but actual GPS coordinates can become unreliable. Systems like Google Maps location have to fuse data with another data source such as road names, or data from an accelerometer to provide accurate data (Cano, 2014).

The **Value** of extracted data is critical, and an analogy could be drawn with the California Gold Rush which started in 1848. It was about deciding where to mine for gold to provide the best return on investment. Being able to understand the value of the data being used is critical, as we need to understand the costs and benefits of collecting and analysing the data to ensure that ultimately the data that is reaped can be monetised. This of course is much easier now as much of the data is now on the cloud (see Figure 1.4). However, a major stumbling block for big data solutions going forward is the inability to ingest and classify data without lots of manual effort which impedes progress. Chapter 4 on metadata management highlights this issue through the example of the open data problem.

Now we have the building blocks in place and know the data classifications, let's go back in history to look at the birth of big data and information in the next section.

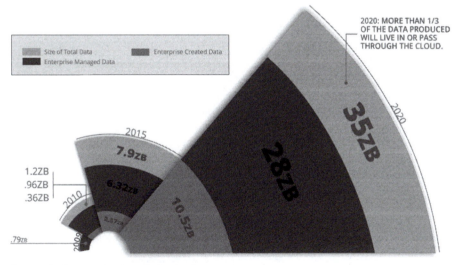

Figure 1.4   Data passing through the cloud

Source: Copyright © DXC Technology. Reproduced with permission.

1.4   Birth of big data and information

If we look back through history, at what point did data become 'big' data? McCartney locates the initial challenges of large volumes of data used by government in the development of computing architectures (McCartney, 1999). In 1890 Herman Hollerith's mechanical design automated the counting, categorising and summation of large volumes of census data, as the process had become beyond human capacity in the ten-year cycle. McCartney links the success of mechanical computing tools developed by Hollerith to the foundation of the Computing Tabulating and Recording Company, the forerunner of International Business Machines (IBM). It can be argued that big data has always been around and it is simply a race between what can be gathered and what can be analysed. One way to frame the context is that when data gathered is greater than the capability to analyse it, we refer to it as big data. What is big today is likely to be small tomorrow and big data is not just about the volume size. A good example of this is to look at information overload, where we have too much information to process in the time available and become overloaded by information. The term information overload is a common phrase used in today's society and one that is apparently seen as a recent addition to the vocabulary. However, the concept of information overload has been around for some time. Ackoff's research in 1967 looked at the abundance of irrelevant information (1967). Ackoff described one of the deficiencies with Management Information Systems as follows: 'Most MIS [Management Information Systems] are designed on the assumption that the critical deficiency under which most managers operate is the lack of relevant information' (1967).

In Edmunds and Morris's review of information overload in 2000, they claimed that the phenomenon dated back as far as the early 1800s, as Haynes recounts the rapid growth of case law (1996). The example provided was that in 1810 there were 18 volumes of reports and by 1845 there were 800. By 1885 there were nearly 3,800, demonstrating the expanding nature of information. Klapp stated that one of the first social scientists to notice this phenomenon was George Simmel who, in 1950, wrote of the overload of sensations in the urban world (Klapp, 1986). Karl Deutsch also noted that communication overload was a disease of cities (Deutsch, 1961) and in 1962 Richard Meier predicted a saturation in communications flow and crisis overload within the next half century (Meier, 1963). Long before the twentieth century, a French philosopher, Denis Diderot, noted in 1755 that: 'The number of books will grow continually, and one can predict that a time will come when it will be almost as difficult to learn anything from books as from the direct study of the whole universe' (Diderot, 1755).

In a world that is increasingly dominated by computer-mediated communication systems, it appears that the volume and pace of information can become overwhelming, as illustrated by early studies in the 1980s (Hiltz and Turoff, 1985; Kerr and Hiltz, 1982). Further studies have gone on to define information overload and the impact it has. For example, in the 1990s, Meglio and Kleiner looked at ways of managing information overload (Meglio and Kleiner, 1990). They considered time management, communication and the idea that individuals can reduce information overload because they are part of the problem (Meglio and Kleiner, 1990). The research showed that users of information all contribute towards information overload and if the mistakes can be realised, a conscious effort can be made to reduce the overload, thus improving the effectiveness of communication. A decade later, both Farhoomand and Drury showed that information overload affects managers in organisations on a daily basis and can have dramatic effects within an organisation (Farhoomand and Drury, 2002; Kirsh, 2000).

Information overload has clearly been around for some time, but it seems very similar to big data. Kaisler defines big data as 'the amount of data just beyond technologies'

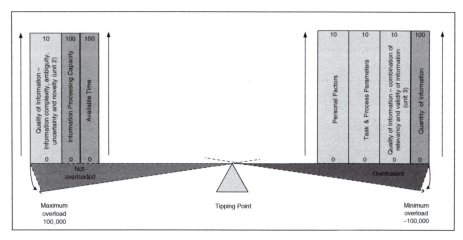

Figure 1.5   The elements that contribute to information overload
Source: Jackson and Farzaneh (2012)

capability to store, manage and process efficiently' (2013, p. 995). This is akin to someone trying to process all the information in the time available to complete a task. What is worrying is that as we try to turn data into useful information, we start to create a human bottleneck called information overload. Jackson and Farzaneh (2012) undertook research to determine the elements that contribute to information overload in order to develop a new theory-based model of factors that influence the phenomenon (this can be seen in Figure 1.5). Their research also provided a formula for calculating the extent of the overload, to aid the visualisation of complex issues. In a world of metrics their approach has helped quantify the information overload issues, which can now be addressed through the development of better data analytics techniques, to provide only the information that you require. However, the big question still remains: do we know what we are looking for in the data? In the next section we look at how the human bottleneck can be reduced by the use of the IoT to remove human intervention.

1.5   Sensors in the network: Internet of Things

This is where the big data landscape starts to get very exciting. The Internet of Things (IoT) refers to the rapidly growing network of connected objects that are able to collect and exchange data using embedded sensors without human intervention (Seth, 2016). As we saw from the previous section, human processing is usually the slowest part of the network and if there is too much to process the brain can become overloaded. In theory the software and techniques encapsulated by the IoT can reduce the need for human intervention by acting as an information broker, preparing all the data in a format that only requires a decision to be made by an individual. A simple example of this is Mimo, which uses proprietary sensor technology to give parents insight into their baby's sleep, helping them see patterns they never knew existed and develop plans to improve sleep routines. A wireless device built into the washable cot sheet communicates data to the parents' smartphone or tablet which converts the data into meaningful information about their baby's sleep activity and movement. By alerting parents throughout the night to changes in their baby's activity, it also produces large volumes of data to add to the vast amounts of data created worldwide every second (Mimibaby, 2018). Instead of parents having to monitor their baby 24/7, the software can act as an information broker to determine when to alert the parents that their intervention is required and to provide suggestions based on sleep patterns. However, this isn't a true example of the IoT, but rather an example of being able to remove the human element from some parts of the process. A more common example is a fridge-freezer with sensors that allow it to record which items have been placed in and removed from the fridge-freezer. The sensor can then connect to the system at your favourite super-market, or find the cheapest prices online, and re-order supplies as required to be delivered to your home, removing the need for human intervention. In addition, an application on your smart device can help you decide what to cook for lunch on the basis of the contents of your fridge-freezer. It can also help the supply chain better understand consumption so that the chain can be further optimised to reduce costs.

The IoT is a flexible architecture of interrelated devices, albeit mechanical and digital machines, objects or humans that are provided with a unique identifier. Their place in the system or architecture provides them with the ability to transfer data over a network with-out requiring human-to-human or human-to-computer interaction. It is fascinating that thermostats, cars, lights, refrigerators and other appliances can all be connected to the IoT to provide useful applications.

Within modular-structured smart factories, cyber-physical systems monitor physical processes, create a virtual copy of the physical world and make decentralised deci-sions (reducing the information overload processing discussed earlier). Over the IoT cyber-physical systems communicate and cooperate with each other and with humans in real time, and through the services and the internet both internal and cross-organisational services are offered and used by participants of the value chain. The growth in sensor data can be seen in Figure 1.6.

It is inevitable that the production world will become increasingly networked until everything is interlinked with everything else. In turn, this will mean that the complexity of production and supplier networks will grow enormously.

Currently, factories work independently of each other and do not share networks and processes. However, the vision of Industrie 4.0 is for the boundaries of individual factories to be removed through improved interconnectivity. Factories across the world will be

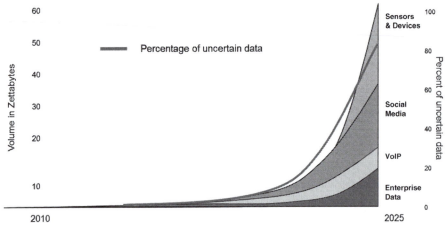

Figure 1.6   The rapid growth of uncertain data from 2010 to 2025

digitally connected to provide an integrated international supply chain. The current key performance indicators for factories are to provide high-end quality service or product at minimum cost. In most factories data is key to aid operating conditions and detect faults and failures. The step change created by Industrie 4.0 will see factories becomes much more intelligent. From machine level to component level, it will be possible to provide service management and monitoring (e.g. self-configuring, self-adapting, self-healing, self-optimising and self-protecting). Peer-to-peer networks will provide much improved service design and development (e.g. engineering of business services, versioning and adaptivity, governance across supply chains) through utilising the real-time data collected through the factory. This approach will see a leap in efficiency and effectiveness.

A good example of how new technology can create a connected intelligent supply chain can be found in the research undertaken at Loughborough University in the United Kingdom. In the past, cars had simple sensors and local 'dashboards' that were used to discover tolerance events (such as low oil pressure in the engine) and alert the driver. This only enabled the driver to decide to act or not and told the car manufacturers little about how their cars were operating at a global level. The sensors used generally only let a driver identify an issue when reaching levels that were serious and the manufacturers had no real knowledge of action taken by the driver beyond trying to establish what the sales of replacement parts might be. However, if we capture data about the engine in real time during its operation and begin to analyse it against similar engine types for all vehicles, we can begin to identify trends and predict events before they occur. We can then ensure preventative action is taken before any real damage to the engine can occur. For example, drivers can be contacted by SMS or a call to request they bring the vehicle in for preventative maintenance if an issue is identified early. To help make this vision a reality, engineers and scientists have created a chip that can be embedded into pretty much any car component. The chip can contain multiple sensors, such as temperature, vibration, motion direction, pressure, torque and electromagnetic. Once embedded within a component the chip can transmit readings via Bluetooth or Wi-fi to a computer on board the car that can process and interpret the data and upload it to the cloud. These readings can then be downloaded from the cloud in real time to aid the car manufacturers' production lines, the companies that provide the parts or the service department of a garage. This information is valuable in that it shows the overall car performance right down to how each component is performing across all cars manufactured.

This type of architecture would have helped with the recent recall of cars from worldwide manufacturers. The analyst would be able to review the component data and interpret the overall meaning to determine which cars are affected and which ones are likely to be affected and need to be recalled. It would have provided an early detection system so the issue with a component or design could have been determined much sooner than it was, saving the organisations billions of dollars. This would have been timely for the likes of Hyundai and Kia who have been ordered to recall thousands of cars by the South Korean government (Dean, 2017). Hyundai and its affiliate Kia have been ordered to recall around 240,000 cars after a whistle-blower flagged safety defects. The South Korean government issued its first ever compulsory vehicle recall over concerns that 12 different models were affected by the five flaws. The order came a month after Hyundai and Kia offered to fix around 1.5 million vehicles in the USA and South Korea because of an engine defect that was also brought to light by a whistle-blower.

A simple example of this architecture in practice is determining why a car crashed. Figure 1.7 shows some simple components (all with embedded sensors) of a car and how these components are connected. Along each line between each node a probability figure is given for the likelihood that a component has caused the crash. The cylinder nodes

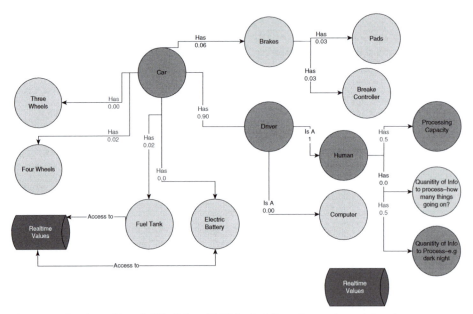

Figure 1.7 Ontology with probability links to highlight the failure of a car using real-time data

provide the real-time information from the sensors to help the system make these predictions. The shaded circles denote the likely components that caused the crash. Research at Loughborough University has been conducted into information overload to determine when a person can no longer deal with the vast quantities of information to process. As can be seen in Figure 1.7, it was likely to be a human fault that caused the crash. To provide context to this analysis, the driver was an elderly man driving at night along a country lane in icy conditions with snow falling (sensors determine weather conditions). The radio was on and there was noise from the back of the car, thought to be young children (sensors can determine this). The situation became too much for the driver and he crashed into a hedgerow on the country lane causing damage to the car. Although a simple example, it is a powerful one that highlights the importance of modelling data to provide the bigger picture. It is the ontology that provides the structure to make sense of the data to enable prediction or to determine why something happened. However, as systems start to build upon varying data sets, the question of data provenance governance is introduced. Data provenance refers to the process of tracing and recording the origins of data and its movement between databases. It is crucial to know where data has come from and how it was generated if it is to be validated and to be trusted. This is an added complexity for organisations to deal with when using intelligent systems based on the cloud. Throughout this book we will look at the technologies required to process such information and to create such an intelligent architecture and governance.

Another good and well-documented example is in the aerospace industry where Rolls-Royce developed their 'power by the hour' approach. This began 50 years ago for the de Havilland/Hawker Siddeley 125 business jet and has grown from there. Deep analytics across large data sets, using data from planes in use across the globe, allow Rolls-Royce to minimise downtime by predicting when components need servicing or replacing, reducing risk and making maintenance costs planned and predictable. This is essential in the aero industry – a plane that has unplanned downtime is a very expensive unused asset. This also enables Rolls-Royce to deploy a global network of authorised maintenance centres to ensure high-quality engineers and support are always available. The data they own prevents others from deploying similar services on their engines and gives Rolls-Royce another differentiator when it comes to servicing the engines.

In order for the devices to access each other's data, the data is usually stored on the cloud. The use of cloud services was originally designed for business applications and distributed storage management for big data but has now become popular among the general public. Cloud services were originally characterised as processes of enterprise architecture promoting migration from a high cost local data management service (Erl et al., 2016). A cost-effective virtual service doubled as either data storage or cloud virtual services, enabling cheap storage and/or processing, and of course, further promoting data growth (De Mauro et al., 2014). With the architecture in place that takes data from sensors and uploads into the cloud, the focus turns to how we structure the data. The predominant solution to uncontrolled exponential data growth of unstructured heterogeneous data, remains a continued process of management (Gandomi and Haiderand, 2015). A growing consensus from research indicates that between 80% and 98% of data can be defined as heterogeneous and unstructured, accounting for the highest proportion of data (Tsui et al., 2014, p. 1316). Heterogeneous data is also thought to have the greatest potential for providing the most valuable insight (Tsui et al., 2014). Now we know where the greatest potential is for the discovery of new information, but what techniques should be used to discover it? In the following chapters we will look at different techniques that have been used over the years and detail what the latest thinking is to unearth the secrets held within large volume data sets. Before we do that, however, we will look at the increase of data from human sensors in the next section.

1.6 Human sensors adding to the data load

We, of course, create large amounts of data in life's daily activities through systems of engagement, such as videos, audio, tweets and Facebook. All this adds to the vast quantities of data around the world (see Figure 1.8, illustrating what happens every 60 seconds worldwide).

Nowadays we all have a digital footprint. A digital footprint is all of the information online about a person, either posted by that person or others, intentionally or unintentionally. Filling out a form, leaving a blog comment, updating your status, checking into a location, emailing or snapchatting a friend, posting a photo, visiting a website, using a search engine ... everything you do online leaves a trail.

This trail is your digital footprint. You can determine the digital impact you have on the world by visiting the Dell EMC site and entering your details. Figure 1.9 shows one of the authors' digital footprints for 2014. When we repeated the exercise in 2017, the annual digital footprint had nearly doubled. This is sometimes quite hard to comprehend and for me it was quite striking when I visited the Tower of London (see Figure 1.10), when its grounds were covered in poppies to remember those who lost their lives in the war. I then thought back to 1914 and the analogue footprint a person would have had back then – medical records, ration book, bank details and so on. If you converted their whole analogue footprint it probably would have come to no more than 256k. A stark reminder of how far we have come in generating large volumes of data on a daily basis.

The International Data Corporation (IDC) is recognised by many sources (e.g. Raghavendra et al., 2008; Sharma and Mangat, 2015) as projecting a plausible prediction of an unprecedented growth data which will cause a deluge by 2020. Technological innovation is often a factor attributed to developmental growth, described as 'supergrowth' (Comin and Hobijn, 2011). Comin and Hobijn define growth across Western Europe and Japan,

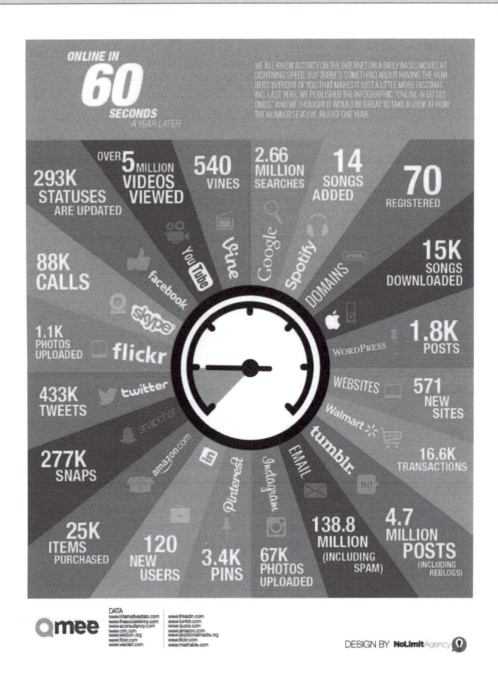

Figure 1.8 The volume of social media communication every 60 seconds

Source: Copyright © Qmee. Reproduced with permission.

to be 'driven by growth in Total Factor Productivity' (2011, p. 35) where the components of production, efficiency and technology are the nominal factors in growth. Despite the accepted position of technology and its central role in growth, contemporary sources generally attribute growth to the use of computing technology. Another possible reason for the large increase in data is due to the increase in the number of social media applications. Let us take an example of a large organisation that has 8,000 employees, and consider how much data, information, knowledge and wisdom the employees hold.

Figure 1.9 Author's digital footprint
Source: Copyright © DELL EMC. Reproduced with permission. EMC. (2018)

How many bytes do you think a human brain can hold? It's a tricky question to answer and maybe we should really think in terabytes. Based on number of junctions between neurons, the brain contains 100 billion neurons. Each has ~20,000 shared synaptic junctions and we assume each holds the equivalent of a binary 'bit'. Therefore, the storage capacity of a human brain is between 100 and 1,000 terabytes. To put this into context your brain is the size of a forest! 1TB = 50,000 trees cut down and made into paper and printed.

So our brains are the equivalent of 50,000,000 trees! There are 400 billion trees in the Amazon rainforest (1 billion = thousand million) which would equate to the brains of 8,000 people! When providing an analogy, it becomes easier to see how difficult it is to locate valuable data, information and knowledge held by employees in a large organisation. In the digital world it is assumed that it is much easier to discover what you are looking for, and when compared to eliciting information from colleagues, it probably is in terms of scalability. However, let us return to the original point that part of the reason for the increase in data is due to the number of increasing social media applications. As discussed above, we all have a lot of data, information and knowledge that we could share. In this day

Figure 1.10 Tower of London – Remembering those lost to war

and age there is a tendency for us to want to share everything on social media, from what we had for breakfast to what our plans are for tonight. We want to take pictures of nearly everything on our smartphones and share this with the world. It is this thirst to capture and then share material that is leading to the increase in data. Eventually, big data becomes about 'value' as we have a lot of data, but how do we aggregate, sift and combine it to make it valuable? Our brains are good at this, but this is where the computer struggles and this is the technological challenge that we need to address.

1.7 Conclusion

The proliferation of data available today opens up the opportunity to better focus resources where needed in an optimised manner. Although this goal is not new, the chance to move far beyond what we have seen before by analysing the vast sets of data available and understanding what are the best approaches to take, whether they be in manufacturing, healthcare, government, retail and so on, is without precedent. However, history also teaches us that those with the greatest power (and data is power in today's world) can cause great harm as well as great benefit. How we elect to use the data available will shape how citizens and society see the benefits of big data in the years to come. With countries, governments and bodies like the European Union legislating around security and privacy regarding personal information, the warning signs are there even today. In addition, there are very loud alarm bells sounding around the rapid growth of 'mis-information'. Again, this is nothing new – propaganda in various forms has been around for centuries – but the volume and velocity of sending such mis-information out to huge numbers is without precedent. How society deals with these problems will probably spawn several books over the coming years.

However, through the evolution of better data analytics techniques, it could be argued that we have greatly reduced information overload. The next generation of machine learning systems are enabling humans to make better sense of what is out there by enabling improved interaction with computers and by providing information that requires less sifting to obtain what is required. To significantly reduce information overload we need the role of the computer systems to act as 'another trusted advisor' to aid navigation through the sea of information. There is, however, a constant battle in our thirst to turn data into information. Turning data into information can have unwanted consequences in that we generate too much useless information that will eventually lead to information overload.

Thanks to technology and clever marketing we've turned into a 'want' society rather than thinking about the 'need'. A good example is the tablet market, where suppliers try and fit more and more gizmos onto a device hoping the consumer will figure out how to best utilise them and give them a competitive edge. However, in the business world there is no room for investing on a whim – reality must strike, and every investment into an information system or data process should be thought through carefully to justify the benefits of the investment. What specifically should it do? How should it draw valuable links between unconnected information? What value will it bring to the company? Although we have many more algorithms at our fingertips to analyse data, we still need to think about what we are ultimately trying to achieve before setting off on our data journey.

As you read this book you might already be in the analytics industry or are planning to work in the industry. It is therefore our collective responsibility to think about our actions and the impact they will have on society.

Study area

To test your understanding of the chapter please attempt to answer these questions, either by debating them in the class with colleagues or by writing them down to help formulate your answers.

Questions:

1 What are data, information, knowledge, understanding and wisdom and what are their main differences?
2 In relation to data, what are volume, velocity, variety and value?
3 What is the Internet of Things (IoT) and how will it affect you?
4 What is a digital footprint?
5 What key changes of the last 20 years have driven the growth of digitisation?
6 What other challenges beyond technical has this rapid growth in data storage and use through analytics brought?
7 How will the collection of all forms of data potentially affect citizens' and customers' lives – this has many, many ramifications – think of just three and explore them.
8 How might analytics impinge on our daily lives even further than has occurred to date (consider the examples above and try to extrapolate where they may lead – or look for new, disruptive solutions that may arrive in the next five years)?

Further reading:

Please use additional resources to further your understanding of the following:

- Security, privacy and the Internet of Things
  ○ Li, S. and Da Xu, L. (2017). *Securing the Internet of Things*. Cambridge, MA: Syngress.
- Industrie 4.0 – German trade and invest, 2016, INDUSTRIE 4.0 Smart manufacturing for the future.
  ○ GTAI (German Trade and Invest). (2016). INDUSTRIE 4.0 – Smart manufacturing for the future. [Online.] http://www.gtai.de/
- Semantic technology
  ○ Mora-Rodriguez, M., Atemezing, G.A. and Preist, C. (2017). Adopting semantic technologies for effective corporate transparency. In: E. Blomqvist, D. Maynard, A. Gangemi, R. Hoekstra, P. Hitzler and O. Hartig (eds), *The Semantic Web: 14th International Conference, ESWC 2017, Portorož, Slovenia, May 28–June 1, 2017 technologies for effective corporate transparency*, (pp. 655–670). Cham: Springer.
- Data provenance
  ○ W3C. (2013). An overview of the PROV family of documents. [Online.] https://www.w3.org/TR/prov-overview/
- The Web's Awake
  ○ Tetlow, P. (2007). *The Web's awake: An introduction to the field of Web Science and the concept of Web life*. Hoboken, NJ: John Wiley & Sons.

References

Ackoff, R.L. (1967). Management misinformation systems. *Management Science*, 14(4), pp. 147–156.
Bellinger, G., Castro, D. and Mills, A. (2004). Data, information, knowledge, and wisdom. Available at: www.systems-thinking.org/dikw/dikw.htm, last accessed 27 June 2018.

Cano, J. (2014). *The V's of Big Data: Velocity, Volume, Value, Variety, and Veracity*. XSNet. [Online.] https://www.xsnet.com/blog/bid/205405/The-V-s-of-Big-Data-Velocity-Volume-Value-Variety-and-Veracity, last accessed 1 August 2017.

Chen, P.L., Zhang, C. and Yang, C. (2014). Data-intensive applications, challenges, techniques and technologies: A survey on Big Data. *Information Sciences*, 275, pp. 314–347. Available at: http://dx.doi.org/10.1016/j.ins.2014.01.015, last accessed 31 August 2018.

Comin, D. and Hobijn, B. (2011). Technology diffusion and postwar growth technology diffusion and postwar growth. *NBER Macroeconomics Annual*, 25, pp. 209–259.

Dean, S. (2017). "Hyundai and Kia ordered to recall thousands of cars by South Korean government", *Telegraph*, http://www.telegraph.co.uk/business/2017/05/12/hyundai-kia-ordered-recall-thousands-cars-south-korean-government/, last accessed 3 August 2017.

De Mauro, A., Greco, M. and Grimaldi, M. (2014). What is Big Data? A consensual definition and a review of key research topics. Paper presented at the 4th International Conference on Integrated Information, Madrid, Spain, 5–8 September.

Deutsch, K.W. (1961). On social communication and the metropolis. *Daedalus*, 90(1), pp. 99–110.

Diderot, D. (1755). The definition of an encyclopedia. [Article translated from Diderot's L'Encyclopédie]. In: K.M. Baker (ed.), *The Old Regime and the French Revolution* (pp. 71–88). Chicago, IL: University of Chicago Press, 1987 (University of Chicago readings in western civilizations, 7).

Edmunds, A. and Morris, A. (2000). The problem of information overload in business organisations: A review of the literature. *International Journal of Information Management*, 20(1), pp. 17–28. doi: 10.1016/S0268-4012(99)00051-1.

EMC. (2018). Personal Footprint Ticker. Available at: https://www.emc.com/digital_universe/downloads/web/personal-ticker.htm%20, last accessed 27 June 2018.

Erl, T., Khattak, W. and Buhler, P. (2016). *Big Data Fundamentals Concepts, Drivers & Techniques*. Upper Saddle River, NJ: Prentice Hall.

Farhoomand, A.F. and Drury, D.H. (2002). Managerial information overload. *Communications of the ACM*, 45(10), pp. 127–131. doi: 10.1145/570907.570909.

Gandomi, A. and Haider, M. (2015). Beyond the hype: Big data concepts, methods, and analytics. *International Journal of Information Management*, 35(2), pp. 137–144. Available at: http://dx.doi.org/10.1016/j.ijinfomgt.2014.10.007, last accessed 29 July 2018

Hashem, I.A.T., Yaqoob, I., Anuar, N.B., Mokhtar, S., Gani, A. and Ullah Khan, S. (2015). The rise of "big data" on cloud computing: Review and open research issues. *Information System* 47: 98–115.

Haynes, S.L. (1996). Too much information can leave you powerless: Is today's information? In: M.E. Williams (ed.), *Proceedings of the 17th National Online Meeting 1996* (pp. 127–135). Medford, NJ: Information Today Inc.

Hiltz, S.R. and Turoff, M. (1985). Structuring computer-mediated communication systems to avoid information overload. *Communications of the ACM*, 28(7), pp. 680–689. doi: http://doi.acm.org/10.1145/3894.3895, last accessed on 31 August 2018.

Jackson, T.W. and Farzaneh, P. (2012). Theory-based model of factors affecting information overload. *International Journal of Information Management*, 32(6), pp. 523–532.

Jara, A.J., Genoud, D. and Bocchi, Y. (2014). Big data for cyber physical systems: An analysis of challenges, solutions and opportunities. In: *Proceedings of the Eighth International Conference on Innovative Mobile and Internet Services in Ubiquitous Computing (IMIS)*, pp. 376–380.

Kaisler, S., Armour, F., Espinosa, J.A. and Money, W. (2013). Big data: Issues and challenges moving forward, System Sciences (HICSS), 2013. In: *Proceedings of the 46th Hawaii International Conference on System Sciences (HICSS)*, pp. 995–1004. Available at: http://ieeexplore.ieee.org/lpdocs/epic03/wrapper.htm?arnumber=6479953, last accessed on 31 August 2018.

Kerr, E.B. and Hiltz, S.R. (1982). *Computer-Mediated Communication Systems: Status and Evaluation*. Orlando, FL: Academic Press.

Kirsh, D. (2000). A few thoughts on cognitive overload. *Intellectica*, 1(30), pp. 19–51.

Klapp, O.E. (1986). *Overload and Boredom: Essays on the Quality of Life in the Information Society*. Westport, CT: Greenwood Publishing Group.

Laney, D. (2001). 3D Data management controlling data volume, velocity, and variety. *Application Delivery Strategies*, 949(February 2001), p. 4.

McCartney, S. (1999). *ENIAC: The Triumphs and Tragedies of the World's First Computer*. New York: Walker & Company.

Meglio, C. and Kleiner, B. (1990). Managing information overload. *Industrial Management & Data Systems*, 90(1), pp. 23–25. doi: 10.1108/02635579010003405.

Meier, R.L. (1963). Communications overload: Proposals from the study of a university library. *Administrative Science Quarterly*, 7(4), pp. 521–544.

Met Office. (2017). The nature of probability. http://www.metoffice.gov.uk/about-us/who/accuracy/forecasts, last accessed 28 February 2017.

Mimobaby. (2018). New Technology. http://mimobaby.com/, last accessed 25 January 2018.

NIST (The National Institute of Standards and Technology) (2017). Big Information. [Online.] https://www.nist.gov/el/cyber-physical-systems/big-data-pwg, last accessed 28 February 2017.

Raghavendra, R., Ranganathan, P., Talwar, V., Wang, Z. and Zhu, X. (2008). No power struggles: Coordinated multi-level power management for the data center. *ACM SIGARCH Computer Architecture News*, 36(1), pp. 48–59.

Rittinghouse, J.W. and Ransome, J.F. (2016). *Cloud Computing: Implementation, Management, and Security*. Boca Raton, FL: CRC Press.

Seigler, M.G. (2003). Every two days we create as much information as we did up to 2003. [Online.] Available at: http://techcrunch.com/2010/08/04/schmidt-data/, last accessed 31 August 2018.

Seth, A. (2016). Internet of Things to smart IoT through semantic, cognitive, and perceptual computing. *IEEE Intelligent Systems*, 31(2), pp. 108–112.

Sharma, S. and Mangat, V. (2015). Technology and trends to handle big data: Survey. In: *Proceedings of the 2015 Fifth International Conference on Advanced Computing & Communication Technologies* (pp. 266–271). Available at: http://ieeexplore.ieee.org/lpdocs/epic03/wrapper.htm?arnumber=7079091, last accessed 31 August 2018.

Tsui, E., Wang, W.M., Cai, L., Cheung, C.F. and Lee, W.B. (2014). Knowledge-based extraction of intellectual capital-related information from unstructured data. *Expert Systems with Applications*, 41(4), pp. 1315–1325.

2

ANALYTICS: DESCRIPTIVE, PREDICTIVE, PRESCRIPTIVE AND COGNITIVE

2.1 Introduction

This chapter introduces the challenges of big data and looks at the methods used to understand what the data means through the lens of descriptive, predictive, prescriptive and cognitive computing. The contemporary challenges of big data are presented along with the predominant approaches to address data growth and the variety of unstructured data types requiring extra real-time processing.

By applying the right set of tools, we can pull powerful insights from seemingly unconnected data, but where should you begin? In this chapter we start by taking a look at the different classes of analytics outlined below – Descriptive, Predictive, Prescriptive and Cognitive – as well as discuss the merits of each and the techniques used to create the analytical method.

Descriptive – Manipulates data to provide insights into what has happened.

Predictive – As the name suggests, this uses analytical methods to provide forecasts. An example of this is the EMOTIVE system which used social media to predict the outcome of the UK General Election in 2015 and the US Presidential Election in 2016. EMOTIVE is used as a case study in this chapter.

Prescriptive – A type of predictive analytics. In simple terms it looks at what we should do by using optimisation and simulation algorithms. For it to work it requires the construction of a predictive model that takes actionable data as an input and the output of the model provides feedback which also loops back into the model (Information Week, 2017).

The next stage of development in analytics comes from the emerging field of **cognitive analytics** or computing (Hwang, 2017). A good example of this is IBM Watson. Watson accesses vast amounts of data offline and then applies machine learning algorithms to determine the connections and correlations. Once Watson has this knowledge bank it can be interrogated and used as a decision support system. The main appeal of cognitive analytics is it can aid the end user to make informed decisions. It does this by creating a probabilistic set of models that will provide a range of solutions. The user can then determine which solution to go for by using the associate scores of confidence and precision against each solution, which helps determine how that answer was reached.

2.2 So what has changed?

In the past, relational databases and the like have managed 'systems of record' to aid in the tracking of transactions of a variety of types to enable understanding of historical events. Computers driving On Line Transaction Processing (OLTP) systems generate much of this information automatically across the globe every day. Over time we have taken these systems and grown them with ever-increasing volumes of data and developed solutions that can trawl through this data at increasing speeds. Such systems that tend to drive analytical solutions we know as Online Analytical Processing (OLAP) and are often in the form of data warehouses, which these days are tens or even hundreds of terabytes in size (even more in some specific cases). Relational Online Analytical Processing (ROLAP) works on a relational database performing dynamic multi-dimensional analysis and the other uses a multi-dimensional database known as Multi-dimensional Online Analytical Processing (MOLAP) which is another kind of OLAP that, like ROLAP, uses a multi-dimensional data model to analyse data.

Historically, organisations have used structured information to make many of their decisions, and these data sets are traditionally the ones that have fed enterprise systems for many years. However, with the onset of social media and mobile apps, and the wealth of unstructured information we see today, enterprises are turning to this new, rich source of data to gain additional insight and knowledge about their business and customers. When we start to fuse the traditional 'system of record' with the newer 'system of engagement' data sets we begin to identify a very powerful proposition: not only do we understand what is happening (e.g. by viewing sales of product over time going up or down) but we also start to begin to understand why it is happening (by seeing customer sentiment from blogs or customer complaints through e-mails). When these two domains come together we find ourselves in what can be termed a 'system of insight', in that we finally have the information we need to make informed decisions. Figure 2.1 offers a visualisation of this way of thinking. (We expand this a little in chapter 3 to include the Internet of Things as a specific system area).

Today, we find ourselves with masses of unstructured information (e.g. web pages, video, audio, blogs) and data sources (e.g. e-mail and electronic documents) that have the

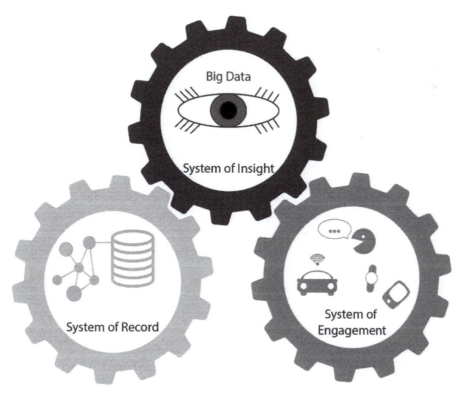

Figure 2.1   System of insight

capacity to augment more traditional data sets and enable a whole new set of insights to be gained. The systems which support these forms of data tend to encourage peer interaction of some kind – e-mail, of course, is an obvious one, but the social sites through mobile connectivity highlight the direction in which things are heading. We refer to these solutions as 'systems of engagement' – primarily because they often have some form of peer-to-peer interaction between humans involved. These data sets grow very large and require new techniques to manage and use them.

Viewing sales of a product is a very simple example, but how about if we could bring together historical records of a hospital patient (their age, ethnicity, sex, weight, blood pressure and other measured data) who has a genetic disorder with historical written notes on that patient, along with x-rays, ultrasound, CAT scans and so on. This information could then be combined with that of similar patients from around the world and with their treatment history, based on expert clinicians' previous experiences to identify different forms of treatment for different types of patients. This approach would provide personalised treatment based on a number of data sets collected from across the world. This example starts to highlight the power of such systems and the benefit they can offer.

What if the computer could interact with us in a natural way (through speech for example)? We (humans) could ask it (the computer) questions and the computer would use the information from such a 'system of insight' to gather and identify answers. If the computer could use all the information available to it and make these decisions in a reasonable period of time to give the user insightful options to consider this would surely help in any decision-making process. The challenge is for this to happen in seconds or minutes compared to the weeks and months it takes today. The following sections review the current techniques used and how future developments might realise the potential of the examples outlined in this section.

2.3 Descriptive analytics

Descriptive analytics is all about providing greater meaning, so taking raw data and presenting it to the end user in a readable format that is easier to interpret. Descriptive analytics processes the data by analysing past events for insights into how to approach the future (Deng et al., 2016). Descriptive analytics is about analysing past performance and it does this by mining historical data to look for the reasons for past success or failure. This post-mortem method is used by almost all management reporting systems, including finance, sales, operations and marketing.

Descriptive models are created to quantify relationships in data in a way that is often used to both identify and classify customers or prospects into lists (Deng et al., 2016). The difference with this approach compared with predictive models is the focus: predictive models look at single customer behaviour, while descriptive models identify many different relationships between customers or products. However, descriptive models do not rank-order customers by their likelihood of taking a particular action as predictive models do. Descriptive models can be used, for example, to categorise customers by their preferences and lifestyle given their current age. What is good about this method is that descriptive modelling tools can be utilised to develop potentially better models that can simulate large numbers of individualised entities and make predictions. For example, descriptive analytics examines historical gas usage data to help plan power needs and allow gas organisations to set optimal prices. The descriptive approach is considered the foundation of research. Its logical design is based on statistics of the research analysis. However, this analysis does not explain the cause of results, so it cannot take into account the validity of research results.

2.3.1   Techniques

Usually, the underlying data is a count or aggregate of a filtered column of data to which basic mathematics is applied. For all practical purposes, there are an infinite number of these statistics. Descriptive statistics are useful to show things such as total stock in inventory, average dollars spent per customer and year-on-year change in sales.

- Observation technique: Data is observed in both natural and artificial ways to draw meaningful conclusions. It is an effective way of inferring from natural observation since we can obtain original results.
- Case study technique: This involves an in-depth study on all the problems discussed. It makes us assess a situation more closely. This technique becomes even more powerful if case-based reasoning is used, where a number of cases are studied to gain a better insight into what has happened.

2.4   Predictive analytics

Predictive analytics has become more prominent with the emergence of big data systems. Organisations have turned to their enterprise systems to collect larger and broader pools of data for their big data platforms, for example Hadoop clusters. By doing this, it has increased the potential to mine the data for predictive insights. So, what's a Hadoop cluster? It is a special type of computational cluster that has been designed for storing and analysing large amounts of data in a distributed computing environment. Hadoop clusters are best known for increasing the speed of data analysis applications as they are highly scalable, and if a cluster's processing power is overwhelmed by the volume of data, additional cluster nodes can be added to increase throughput. This is known as horizontal scaling.

Predictive analytics is the use of data, statistical algorithms and machine learning techniques to identify the likelihood of future outcomes based on historical data (Williamson, 2016). The aim is to provide insights into what will happen in the future. Predictive analytics software applications analyse the data to predict likely behaviour of individuals, machinery or other things, like events. For example, when you come to renew your car insurance, an analytical software application will determine how likely it is that you will be involved in an accident and price the premium accordingly. It will use variables such as age, gender, location, type of vehicle and driving record when pricing and issuing auto insurance policies. These multiple variables are combined and used to build a predictive model that can determine the future probabilities with an acceptable level of reliability. The software relies upon techniques like logistic regressions, time series analysis and decision trees.

- **Logistic regressions** are used to explain the relationship between variables, for example, one dependent binary variable and one or more nominal, ordinal, interval or ratio-level independent variable. For example, how does the probability of getting emphysema (yes vs. no) change for every additional pound of excess weight and for every pack of cigarettes smoked per day?
- **Time series analysis** looks at sets of data that have been taken over time (series) and tries to determine the characteristics of the data using statistical methods. Time series *forecasting* uses a model to predict future values based on previously observed values. For example, it can be used in the area of Time Series Analysis for many applications, including economic forecasting, sales forecasting, budgetary analysis, stock market analysis, yield projections, process and quality control, inventory studies, workload projections, utility studies and census analysis. Well-known supermarkets use it to predict what you will buy to ensure they have enough products on the shelf, taking into account the

time of year, weather conditions, typical time of the month when salaries are paid and so on.

- A **decision tree** is a schematic and is a tree-shaped diagram. Each branch provides a statistical probability of that event happening. The tree is structured to show how and why one choice may lead to the next, with the use of the branches indicating each option is mutually exclusive. A similar example of a decision tree can be found in Chapter 1 of this book (determining why a car crashed).

Although predictive analytics has been around for decades, it is a technology whose time has come (Williamson, 2016). Increasingly, organisations are turning to predictive analytics to improve the performance of their organisation. Organisations have started to invest in this technology for several reasons, such as growing volumes and types of data; greater interest in using data to produce valuable insights; cheaper and faster computers; accessible software; and a greater need for competitive differentiation (SAS, 2017).

Predictive analytics can be used in a number of areas and here are just some examples:

- **Risk reduction** – It can be used to provide credit scores, for example: if you apply for a credit card, the company will determine your credit score rating before offering you the card. The score assesses a buyer's likelihood to default on payment, and so a person's creditworthiness. Other risk-related uses include insurance claims and collections.
- **Fraud detection** – Through combining multiple analytics techniques it is possible to improve pattern detection. By understanding patterns it is then possible to prevent criminal behaviour. If you have ever had your credit card blocked when trying to pay for an item then that is an example of predictive analytics in action. For example, the item you are trying to purchase or the location you are using the card (or combination) may not fit your 'usual' purchasing pattern. As cyber-security becomes an increasing concern, behavioural analytics analyses all actions on a network in real time to spot abnormalities that may indicate fraud. Note that this is done in near real time as the activity must be tracked and scored while the purchase is ongoing. This normally means building models from past data in advance and applying those models to the transaction under review at the moment of interaction.
- **Improved marketing campaigns** – If you've ever purchased anything from Amazon you will have seen predictive analytics in action. When you purchase an item from the site it will also promote cross-selling and up-selling opportunities. It will also use your purchase history to determine your future responses or purchases. Predictive models help businesses attract, retain and grow their most profitable customers.
- **Operations optimisation** – An increasing number of organisations turn to predictive models to forecast inventory and manage resources. For example, airlines such as British Airways use predictive analytics to set ticket prices. Hotels try to predict the number of guests for any given night to maximise occupancy and increase revenue.

(SAS, 2017)

Predictive analytics is increasingly being used in different domains. The next section is an example that discusses how it can be used to make sense of the increasing volumes of data emerging from the social media sphere in predicting the outcome of the next riot or political election. It also looks at the complexity of mining such unstructured data.

2.4.1   Predictive analytics: EMOTIVE case study

The Extracting the Meaning Of Terse Information in a Geo-Visualisation of Emotion (EMOTIVE) system was researched and developed at Loughborough University in the Centre for Information Management in the School of Business and Economics (formerly the

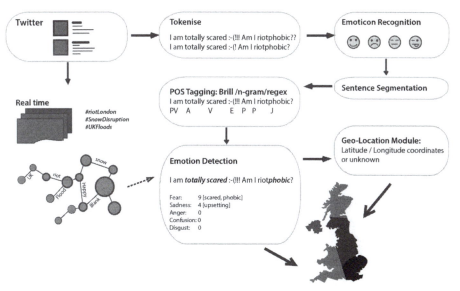

Figure 2.2   The EMOTIVE pipeline to determine emotions

Information Science department) (Sykora et al., 2013). EMOTIVE captures tweets and analyses them to extract the emotion using its own proprietary technology, a complex natural language processing ontology, as shown in Figure 2.2. The system provides organisations with a world through which they can know instantly what their customers feel about products and services. It was originally developed for military use, as the ability for ordinary people to express and exchange their opinions and feelings had dramatically increased beyond all expectations in the past ten years of internet expansion and availability. To the military and national security agencies this has provided both opportunities and challenges. Opportunities have emerged in the sense of readily available awareness of discontent and oppositional movements and initiatives. Recent urban disturbances have illustrated the key role played by social networks in fast-moving events – for example, the London riots of summer 2011. The challenges have escalated due to the sheer number of sources of social interaction and public communication media. The key challenge is to take data from social media streams and use predictive analytics to determine events such as (say) the next London riot.

Sensitive words and phrases which may be of concern to the military and national security agencies, and especially emotionally charged words and phrases, are extracted by EMOTIVE using a Natural Language Processing technique (NLP). The team developed an ontology (a rule-based linguistic database) in which the extracted words and phrases can be semantically filtered and restricted to a manageable set of agreed terms. The ontology is trained to recognise the words and phrases, making semantic links between them and delivering one or more accepted descriptors to the analysts. EMOTIVE monitors the traffic of sensitive words and phrases filtered through the ontology when applied to specific incidents, individuals and groups. Increased activity is indicated by frequency of occurrence or severity, which is presented visually through a graph with a colour-coded indication of the strength of emotion attached to the language-based terms (see Figure 2.3). The fine-grained, explicit emotions that EMOTIVE is capable of extracting from sparse, informal messages are anger, disgust, fear, happiness, sadness and surprise (Ekman's six basic emotions), as well as shame and confusion. This is considerably more specific than much of the existing work in the sentiment analysis domain, where most techniques tend to focus on overall document polarity (negative, neutral, positive scales) or bundle together emotions with states and opinions, rather than focus on real and basic emotions.

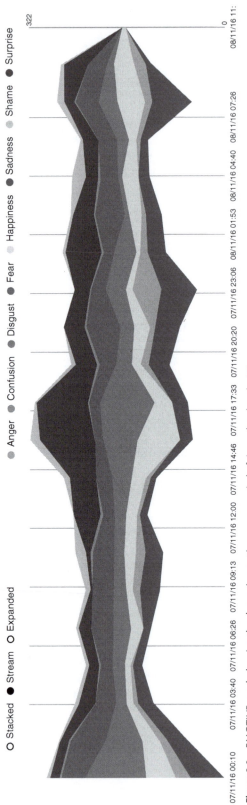

Figure 2.3 EMOTIVE graph showing the change in emotions over a period of time related to the US Election. Emotions towards the Trump camp

EMOTIVE has been designed to detect these emotions based on well-defined and tested theories of emotion and uses a computational linguistics engine, with a novel underlying semantic model (Sykora et al., 2013). By detecting emotional content, EMOTIVE can analyse the types of emotions expressed and the strengths (i.e. activation levels) of various emotive expressions. The output of EMOTIVE can be used to further understand and model emotional discourse and can be used to produce rich emotional visualisations (as a graph) at either the individual user level or at group level. EMOTIVE has been used in a range of settings including national security, election prediction and more recently for mental health. In the latter, the emotional output of geo-tagged Twitter messages was analysed in relation to post-traumatic stress during the Paris terror attacks from 2015 in France (Gruebner et al., 2016). The results suggested that EMOTIVE would be a useful and viable systems approach for monitoring public mental health following major natural or man-made disasters (ibid.). This work provides encouraging evidence for applying EMOTIVE to improve understanding around mental health and emotional expression. Although the system was developed for a particular domain, it has morphed over time to be able to provide different insights for different domains, which could raise ethical issues (see Chapter 8 on Ethics). However, what it does show is the power of analytics and that creating the right analytical architecture can lead to a versatile tool that can be reused. Who would have thought that the emotions found in tweets could predict the outcome of the US Presidential Election in 2016?

2.5   Prescriptive analytics

Although the term first appeared in 2003, and it is based on predictive analytics, it goes further by providing rules directly applicable to the business (Shi–Nash and Hardoon, 2016). This enables decision makers to take immediate action based on probabilistic forecasts. An important feature of the prescriptive analytics models is their ability to analyse the feedback coming from using the rules. They can then take action based on the effects of the results into account, as shown in Figure 2.4.

As already mentioned, prescriptive analytics models are also part of the predictive analytics family, but the advantage of them is to explain the reasons behind a certain

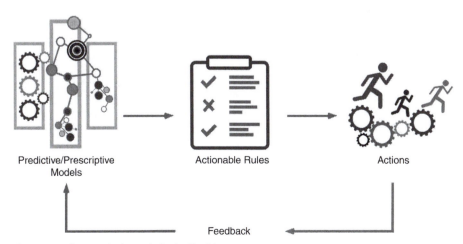

Predictive/Prescriptive Models   Actionable Rules   Actions

Feedback

Figure 2.4   The prescriptive analytics feedback loop

event. Predictive models tell us what is likely to occur while the prescriptive models seek to determine the best solution or outcome among various choices, given the known parameters, and will explain the reasons by using a set of rules (Wang at al., 2016).

Predictions are not valid forever, and therefore the clues the model provides should leave enough time to act or they would end up being of little use during the decision-making and implementation process. If the rules produced by the model are simple and easy to interpret, then the time necessary for the action to take place will be short, allowing decision makers to fit them into the time frame of the prediction's validity (Shi-Nash and Hardoon, 2016). Behind the predictions are three classes of algorithms:

- **Fuzzy rule-based systems** – are the best from the predictive viewpoint but are not very common, possibly because they are harder to use than decision trees. Fuzzy systems try to mimic the human mind in its ability to reason in fuzzy terms (de Barros et al., 2017). To help the computer address the imprecision of the input and output variables, 'fuzzy' numbers can be expressed in linguistic variables. Fuzzy logic was developed by Professor Lotfi Zadeh in 1965, at the University of California in Berkeley, and since 1965 has been used extensively for household and entertainment electronics, controlling industrial processes, diagnosis systems and other expert systems. Fuzzy logic is basically a multi-valued logic enabling intermediate values to be defined like yes/no, true/false, black/white and so on. More importantly, intensifiers like 'pretty cold' can be formulated mathematically and algorithmically processed (Elkano et al., 2016). This provides the computer with a more human-like way of thinking in the programming of computers.
- **Decision trees** – are widely used because they are simple to build and they produce their own rules, yet they do not have a brilliant predictive performance. However, a Switching Neural Network (SNN) algorithm was implemented in Rulex, and claims to present a very high predictive ability. A neural network, more properly referred to as an 'Artificial' Neural Network (ANN), is usually organised in layers. The layers are made up of a number of interconnected 'nodes', which contain an 'activation function', which contain some form of 'learning rule', which modifies the weights of the connections according to the inputs. Inputs are fed into the network via the 'input layer', which communicates to one or more 'hidden layers' where the actual processing is done via a system of weighted 'connections'. The hidden layers then link to an 'output layer' where the answer is output.
- **Switching Neural Networks** – Rudimentary Artificial Neural Networks have been used for over 50 years to simulate the brain's approach to problem solving. ANNs are versatile learners that can be applied to nearly any learning task, classification, numeric prediction and even unsupervised pattern recognition. Where input and output data are well understood, mainly because they are simple, yet the relationship between input and output are more complex, a black box system like ANNs can perform well. A black box problem can be viewed in terms of its inputs and outputs, and without knowledge of its internal workings. The 1990s saw the introduction of the SNN method to overcome the issues with black box methods such as multi-layer perceptron and support vector machine. Although these approaches had good accuracy they lacked the insight required by most. In contrast to this, decision trees provided good insights but lacked accuracy. The SNN built sets of intelligent rules using Boolean algebra to gain improved performance. An efficient version of SNN was developed in 2014 and implemented in the Rulex suite with the name Logic Learning Machine (Muselli, 2006).

2.6   Cognitive computing – understand, reason and learn

Cognitive computing involves attempting to simulate the human thought processes and involves self-learning systems that use data mining, pattern recognition and natural language processing to mimic the way the human brain works. The aim is to create an IT system that is capable of solving problems without human intervention. A cognitive computing solution is one which can learn from a corpus of previous knowledge (Hwang, 2017). For this to happen it would need to be trained using subject matter experts to guide its decisions, but would be able to learn as it progressed from previous decisions it made based on the evidence presented to it. It would be limited to the corpus of information it held (just as a human can only make informed decisions based on the information available to him/her) and would be capable of distinguishing the decisions it made with appropriate reasoning based on how confident it was that the answers it derived were correct. It should also be capable of explaining what it thought were NOT correct answers with the reasoning as to why. Such systems that deal in the 'question and answer' style could help many different industries to quickly identify potential solutions, and even identify new options from the information available to the system.

To be able to build such systems there are many things that are different or require assembly of new and old techniques. This is illustrated by information retrieval and data ingestion for any form of data, natural language processing, machine learning and interfaces that humans can use beyond a simple keyboard and mouse (direct speech being an obvious interface). This sounds a little like something from 'Star Trek' but these systems are within our grasp and will become more mainstream over the next five to ten years. To build such a system, think how a human may do this, firstly listening to the question, sifting through many potential options (in parallel maybe) and then applying reasoning in some form, based on the users' knowledge to date. The answers are nearly always better if we use multiple people (the assumption is they understand the domain they are being questioned on) and a consensus is reached as to the likely answer to a problem. So, what are the things a computer must do to act in a similar manner:

1 Must be able to exploit the body of information available to it and understand the question asked of it (act as an expert). This means being able to identify simple and complex relationships, the shallow and deep natural language processing we have already mentioned.
2 Be able to develop a set of answers that the computer can describe levels of confidence to. Rather like a group of experts coming to a joint agreement of likely solutions. This requires that each candidate answer that is discovered is analysed alongside all the others to identify evidence that supports or disproves the potential answer to that question. Each answer must be weighed against the others to give a final ranking for the total set of answers under review.
3 Do this all very quickly – requires parallelism of many of the hypotheses and confidence estimates to do things in a reasonable time frame.

A cognitive system applies human-like characteristics to communicating and manipulating ideas, which is important when trying to determine the relevance of something rather than retrieving the popularity of some trend, word or image, which is not the prime indicator. For example, how many people have 500+ Facebook friends but really only have five strong close friends? How could you identify these from the other friends? A cognitive computing approach, coupled with the scale associated with current trends in computing, can help users deal with problems not easily managed today, especially with higher levels of accuracy and precision than has been the case. Cognitive computing brings together a host of techniques and technologies – such as statistical techniques, unstructured data analysis, natural language processing – with the context of big data to underpin the results obtained (Seth, 2016). One domain that is seeing a number of techniques being developed is that of the artificial intelligence (AI) domain. It is emerging as a feasible technological solution for the likes of IBM's Watson or Amazon AI. AI techniques are being used to search unstructured data to find patterns and reach answers (Niccolai, 2015). It is likely that cognitive computing could be the answer for many businesses wanting to access consumers in the most customised way. When applying this to employees, unstructured data (e.g. Twitter feeds) could be analysed to identify when people are disengaged at work, predicting when people might leave. Organisations could use these insights by recognising the early signals of dissatisfaction and taking action to resolve issues before losing employees to competitors.

The approach to cognitive computing described in this book uses full disclosure, as used by IBM Watson. The key point here is to identify ALL the potential answers, rather like a human having a perfect memory that can recall everything that might be related to the question asked of him/her. So we attempt to identify 'snippets' (small chunks of information from the corpus) as candidate answers.

One of the first problems to solve is how much data should we process to gather a wide enough net of answers that the one we are looking for has a high chance of being within that set, without taking far too long to do it. We can achieve this goal by setting some simple parameters that gauge the confidence we have the right answer within the set against a target number of ranked answers. This could, for example, be that we are 90% confident the answer is somewhere in the top 100 ranked answers we have found using relatively simple techniques such as Indri and Lucene document search engines to derive results or SPRQL queries to find relationships based on triple stores and others. By setting such parameters we get a balance between things to trawl through (the 100 candidate answers) to get our final well-researched answer and the confidence we have the answer in the first place versus time to do it all.

The next step involves the system taking the 'first pass' answers and delving more deeply into building a candidate set of answers that can then be rigorously reviewed. We now take each 'first stage' answer and begin to analyse it in depth against the corpus of information available and the related documents within it. We start to see if any of the 'first stage' answers have many related documents. For example, this step can also potentially yield more answers if the related docs are relevant to the question being asked. We are scanning the first quick pass of answers to try and identify if there are any others we should be considering (a bit like 'jogging' our own memory) to ensure that we don't miss any potentially strong answers. If we miss something at this stage we cannot hope to answer the question later.

Filtering is also introduced to augment the set of answers using a variety of techniques such as the Lexical Answer Type (LAT) or relation detection for question resolution to reduce the number of answers to a reasonable level. LAT and relation detection are used to identify the key focus of the question. LAT looks for words such as 'this', 'that', 'what', 'how' and their fitness to identify the nature of the question being asked. Relation detection looks for subject-verb-object type groupings of words (can be described in triples) or semantic links between entities (people for example) and is used to help further understand the nature of the question. There is, of course, a variable time limit based on how long we give the computer to solve the question being asked. The longer it gets, the more candidate answers it could review. Clearly there is a trade-off between precision and resources here.

Even after all these steps, involving attempting to understand the question and then building a candidate list, we have only now reached a point where a very rigorous approach to ranking the final set of potential answers takes place. This part consumes the greatest resource as it uses a multitude of approaches to try to identify the likely best answer from all the candidates available.

2.6.1   What are the requirements of a cognitive system?

The following pages describe in general how such systems are being considered today. Please note that there is no one 'magic bullet' to this problem; to arrive at an answer from such a system, many different techniques are adopted (potentially hundreds or even thousands) for analysing language, generating hypotheses, scoring evidence to support hypotheses and so on. As the technology improves, new techniques will surface and things will morph over time to improve approaches to dealing with this style of processing. Let us break down the goals we set ourselves above into a formal set of requirements to be able to describe what we need from a cognitive computing system. Let us consider the things we have mentioned:

1 The system will interact through the use of human language.
2 The system needs to be able to sift through all forms of data available to it to generate hypotheses regarding any questions asked of it.
3 It needs to be able to rank these hypotheses using advanced analytics evaluated on relevant evidence to supply answers that are confidence based (rather like humans sifting through what they know to identify an answer they have confidence in).
4 It needs to be able to learn based on whether its answers were correct or not and new information supplied to it.

So what can we infer from these requirements?

1 The system will have to be taught based on existing expertise and knowledge in the area of analysis it is going to be used in to be able to generate hypotheses and rank them (build models).
2 The data sets used will be wide and potentially ambiguous, utilising all the range of structured, semi-structured and unstructured data sources available (***ingest data*** – see Figure 2.6).
3 The system must be able to understand the nuances of the spoken word (***natural language processing*** – see section in this chapter).
4 We are no longer simply looking at programmatic answers driven from structured data sets to find an answer that is always the same (***hypothesis and evidence-based scoring*** – see section in this chapter).
5 Answers will no longer be absolutes but driven by probabilistic techniques (***ranking*** – see section in this chapter).
6 All this must happen over a period of time that is useful to the humans using it – this could be seconds but may be minutes or longer.

Looking at the requirements mentioned and what they infer we now find ourselves with a number of problems that must be overcome to be able to create a cognitive computing solution, as shown in Figure 2.5. We will consider each one in turn.

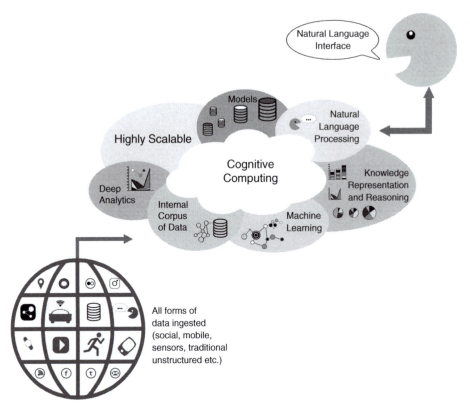

Figure 2.5 The factors that need to be addressed to build a cognitive system

2.6.2 Data ingestion

Any cognitive system needs to be able to take various information sources (of multiple formats) and process them in such a way that they can all be made available in a consistent manner for later use when attempting to answer questions asked of it. For written language a series of annotators will be required to pre-process and classify relevant parts of documents that will need to be ingested. These annotators are stored in some common structure. Once this step has been completed, two further steps are usually undertaken: first, a generic process that will look over any document supplied and gather language-related information associated with that document; the second process is built to be domain specific and therefore is driven by the areas of interest that the knowledge base is being built around. It is used to extract specific meaning, relationships and concepts for the data associated with that domain.

All this processed data is stored in a final repository that has the knowledge amassed in a consistent manner for use at 'run time' when questions are actually asked on the system, as shown in Figure 2.6.

The final consideration is that we want any answer to have a good level of confidence the system is correct, so a key difference between cognitive systems and traditional ones is the ability for the computer to decide on an answer based on its confidence (rather like a human would – we hope!) In other words, if the computer cannot find enough supporting evidence it will either not answer or show the user a list of all the answers with its confidence of them being correct or not. We could have scores that are highly ranked here, but low confidence because, for example, there are only small pieces of evidence available to support that answer.

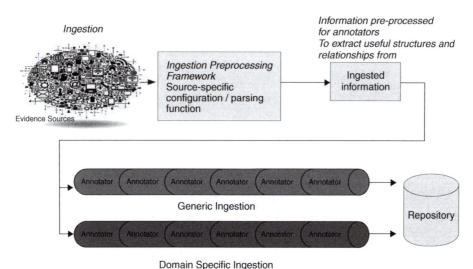

Figure 2.6 The process of data ingestion

2.6.3 Natural language processing

How do we understand what we say to each other every day? Consider this problem for just a moment. We as humans seem to have very little difficulty understanding each other but we do have moments of confusion when cultural and contextual differences in language cause us to think. For example, we can have 'feet that run' and 'a runny nose'; we can have a 'smart person' and a 'smart Alec'; and 'brain storms' and 'weather storms'. These examples show how we as humans, with a lifetime of experience of language, can decipher different meanings from these statements. However, this is a huge challenge for a computer. A computer must manage issues such as context, temporal issues, spatial issues and potentially slang terms to make sense of questions asked of it in a language such as English. Humans tackle these anomalies with a great degree of accuracy – most of the time we understand what each other is saying!

Most natural language systems tend to be precise, which means they can perform complex rules that allow a document or passage of text to be broken down into its constituent parts without really understanding what the text really means. For example, a word count of different words in a document falls into this category. If we wish to go further we need to go deeper and analyse the context of the passage. This is done using the passage itself and is also tested against a corpus (also known as a knowledge base) of available information to try to gather meaning for the passage in question. It is worth adding that the EMOTIVE system discussed earlier in this chapter works using the same natural language technique to understand what the text means.

Note that in the paragraphs above we used the terms 'precise' and 'accurate' – these are key to understanding how our language works and can be broken down. As we have already said, most natural language systems tend to be precise – they can find words or similar words (often from look-up tables) to do specific things. Of course, this is what computers have been good at for many years. However, humans can do this and be accurate, therefore understanding the context of a phrase or passage to convey obvious and non-obvious meaning in the words used. This is the step that moves from what is termed **shallow natural language processing** (precise) to **deep natural language processing** (accurate) (Zhao et al., 2017).

A clear distinction between the two types of processing begins to emerge. If we have a large enough sample which can be used to identify trends (so statistically false positives and false negatives can be factored out), analysis that lets us observe trends, such as sentiments against particular products, people, locations and the like, can be managed with a shallow, natural language-processing approach. Many statistical and rule-based systems can enable this sort of approach to process massive amounts of (often) unstructured data. If, however, we are searching for a nugget of information that is bounded by tight considerations (a concise context) then deep, natural language processing is needed to ensure that each piece of information supplied is thoroughly understood with regard to its meaning. To attach contextual meaning to any chunk of information it cannot be analysed in isolation; the information has to be tested against other similar pieces of information that have been gathered in advance to enable meaning to be extracted. This requires some degree of pre-population of a knowledge base (or corpus) of information that supports the areas of research or interest that is being undertaken. It is worth noting that our problem space becomes bounded by the amount of relevant information we have at our disposal. For example, a deep natural language system that offers answers related to healthcare in Europe may well offer different diagnoses to that offered in Asia because differing knowledge bases may be used to 'seed' the engine. This in itself raises an interesting problem: 'how wide a net' must we cast with our knowledge base to gain the maximum accuracy we would desire for our answers? In theory, the ultimate would be to take ALL information available, and if we ever get to the point of having infinite processing power, bandwidth and storage this might be an option! As we do not have this we must work out how to generalise the data we use for best accuracy, which is a daunting challenge we need to consider when building these forms of systems.

After any corpus has been developed (or seeded) with standard things like dbPedia (structured information extracts from Wikipedia), WordNet (primarily helps with identifying synonyms), subject related databases, content stores and the like, the system makes sense of all of this using algorithms that identify co-referenced terms, relationship between terms, named entities and semantic role labels – to name but a few (WordNet, 2018).

Finally, we can use techniques such as LAT and relation detection to identify the key focus of the question.

These steps allow the computer to classify and analyse the corpus of information available to enable a question to be set in context and understood. Later steps can now build on this to use that deep understanding of the question to look for the right answer.

2.6.4 Hypothesis and evidence-based scoring to aid model building

2.6.4.1 *Evidence retrieval*

One particularly powerful technique here is to add the potential answer to the primary search (done earlier) for the question being asked of the system (Gani et al., 2016). This effectively shows where the answers match contextually to the original question asked. If no results are returned it is highly likely that the answer is less probable than others that do return results. We can also use graphing techniques (triple stores) to see if the answers are linked in some way to the question being asked. The results from these steps are then used in the final ranking and scoring models where the majority of processing is performed.

2.6.4.2   *Scoring*

The scoring algorithms are what really determine which answer is seen as the 'best' one. This requires many different approaches that have to be amalgamated to produce a final set of results, for example, probability analysis, simple counts, category grouping. It may be that for certain forms of question one technique is more appropriate than another, therefore the ways in which the scoring algorithms can be weighted and tuned is of great importance here. Remember, at this point we may have hundreds of potential answers that all have to be sifted, sorted and ranked with potentially thousands of algorithms to yield a suitable set of scored answers. This is where scalability and parallelism play an essential part in delivering results in a meaningful amount of time. For a moment let us consider what the challenge is here. We need to analyse structured, semi-structured and unstructured data by a variety of means, taking into account spatial, temporal and contextual context. This needs to be done alongside gauging the quality of the underlying evidence and the overall correlation of the answer to the question being asked, using a variety of approaches to link answer(s) with questions. What should be noted is that none of the algorithms dominate, but a blend is used, for example, popular hits on a web-based search may not be sufficient to justify an answer having a high confidence rating dependent on its sources and other supporting evidence. After each answer has been scored within its own right, each answer is considered against the others to identify if answers can be merged. This helps to identify similar answers that have resulted from different algorithms but have essentially returned the same answer. For an example, we might have two answers that return the results 'New York' and 'The Big Apple', and we could merge these if the underlying relationships and hypotheses suggest they are the same thing.

2.6.5   Ranking

The final step is to determine the ranking and confidence level estimates. With the reduced list of potential answers we now use machine learning techniques to map these answers against a set of trained answers. The training is absolutely critical to

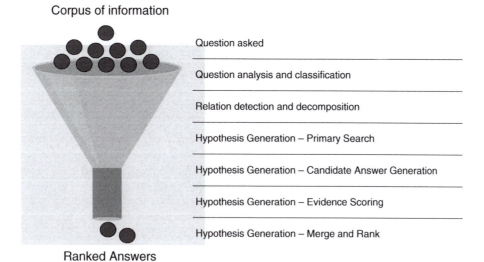

Corpus of information

Question asked

Question analysis and classification

Relation detection and decomposition

Hypothesis Generation – Primary Search

Hypothesis Generation – Candidate Answer Generation

Hypothesis Generation – Evidence Scoring

Hypothesis Generation – Merge and Rank

Ranked Answers

Figure 2.7   Illustration of how answers are ranked

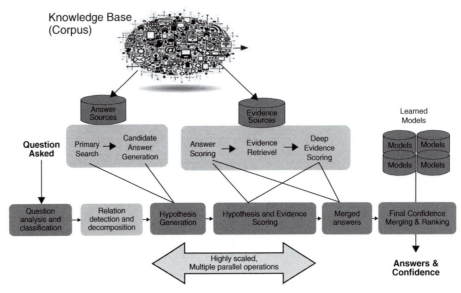

Figure 2.8 Components of a cognitive system

gaining reasonable responses, just as in training an infant/child. If the wrong lessons are taught at an early age it becomes much harder to work out right from wrong later. The ranking and confidence levels generated from testing the results against similar learned answers are seen as separate exercises and a metamodel that can be used to assess an answer against a question based on what has gone before is needed. This is extracted and developed from the learning phase. One very important feature to note here is that the models are **not** static. If the answer generated is used to help build a better model on subsequent iterations, then if the original model was good, lessons can be learnt from subsequent questions and answers to further enhance the model. If the model originally developed was below a certain threshold it may be difficult to train it to be better by simply using the answers the system returns. Figure 2.7 is a very simple illustration that attempts to simplify a complex process into a set of steps used to move from an initial question asked to answer(s) being supplied that are ranked and given confidence levels.

Figure 2.8 shows the end-to-end operation of a cognitive system as described in this chapter. The narrative is based on the Watson architecture developed within IBM.

2.7 Conclusion

In this chapter, we have discussed a range of methods (descriptive, predictive, prescriptive and cognitive computing) that can be used to better understand data to provide us with valuable information. With complexity usually comes costs and therefore it is important to determine the business requirements before investing in a method. A major challenge is to address data growth and the variety of unstructured data types requiring extra real-time processing. Moving forward it is likely that cognitive computing can help meet this demand, but currently it is still in its infancy. However, when it does finally arrive, it could certainly be a game changer that provides us with more intelligence, but with an ethical dilemma to contemplate – could it reduce the number of white-collar worker jobs?

Study area

To test your understanding of the chapter, please attempt to answer these questions, either by debating them in the class with colleagues or by writing them down to help formulate your answers.

Questions:

1 What are Hadoop clusters and what are their benefits?
2 What is a predictive model and how is it made?
3 What is shallow natural language processing?
4 What is deep natural language processing?
5 What are the limitations of cognitive computing?
6 Socially, where might software like the cognitive systems discussed in this chapter lead to regarding job redundancies?

Further reading:

Please use additional resources to further your understanding of the following:

- What is distributed computing and what is the relationship to Hadoop?
  - White, T. (2015). *Hadoop – The definitive guide: Storage and analysis at Internet scale*, 4th edn. Sebastopol, CA: O'Reilly Media.
- What are logistic regressions?
  - Welc, Jacek and Esquerdo Pedro J. Rodriguez (2018). *Applied regression analysis for business: Tools, traps and applications*. Cham: Springer.
- Deep machine learning
  - Arel, I., Rose, D.C. and Karnowski, T.P. (2010). Deep machine learning: A new frontier in artificial intelligence research [research frontier]. *IEEE Computational Intelligence*, 5(4), pp. 13–18.
- Neural networks
  - Schmidhuber, J. (2015). Deep learning in neural networks: An overview. *Neural Networks*, 61, pp. 85–117.
- Cognitive computing
  - Demirkan, H., Earley, S. and Harmon, R.R. (2017). Cognitive computing. *IT Professional*, 19(4), pp. 16–20.
- Quantum computing
  - Hassanien, A.E. and Elhoseny, M. (2017). *Quantum computing: An environment for Intelligent Large Scale Real Application (Studies in Big Data)*. Cham: Springer.

References

de Barros, L.C., Bassanezi, R.C. and Lodwick, W.A. (2017). Fuzzy rule-based systems. In: *A First Course in Fuzzy Logic, Fuzzy Dynamical Systems, and Biomathematics* (pp. 79–111). Berlin: Springer, Berlin, Heidelberg.

Deng, X., Lin, W.H., Tai, E., Eric, K.Y.H., Salloway, M.K. and Seng, T.C. (2016). From descriptive to diagnostic analytics for assessing data quality: An application to temporal data elements in electronic health records. In: *2016 IEEE-EMBS International Conference on Biomedical and Health Informatics (BHI)*, pp. 236–239.

Elkano, M., Galar, M., Sanz, J. and Bustince, H. (2016). Fuzzy rule-based classification systems for multi-class problems using binary decomposition strategies: On the influence of *n*-dimensional overlap functions in the fuzzy reasoning method. *Information Sciences*, 332, pp. 94–114.

Gani, A., Siddiqa, A., Shamshirband, S. and Hanum, F. (2016). A survey on indexing techniques for big data: Taxonomy and performance evaluation. *Knowledge and Information Systems*, 46(2), pp. 241–284.

Gruebner, O., Sykora, M., Lowe, S.R., Shankardass, K., Trinquart, L., Jackson, T., et al. (2016). Mental health surveillance after the terrorist attacks in Paris. *The Lancet*, 387, pp. 2195–2196, doi: 10.1016/S0140-6736(16)30602-X.

Hwang, K. (2017). *Cloud and Cognitive Computing: Principles, Architecture, Programming*. Cambridge, MA: MIT Press.

Information Week. (2017). Big data analytics: Descriptive vs. predictive vs. prescriptive. *Information Week*. [Online.] http://www.informationweek.com/big-data/big-data-analytics/big-data-analytics-descriptive-vs-predictive-vs-prescriptive/d/d-id/1113279, last accessed 07/03/2017.

Muselli, M. (2006). Switching neural networks: A new connectionist model for classification. In: Apolloni B., Marinaro M., Nicosia G. and Tagliaferri R. (eds) *Neural Nets. WIRN 2005 and NAIS 2005, Lecture Notes on Computer Science* (Vol. 3931, pp. 23–30). Berlin: Springer, Berlin, Heidelberg. Vietri sul Mare, Italy, June 8-11.

Niccolai, J. (2015). *A New API Called Visual Insights Can Analyze Images and Videos on Social Networks*. [Online.] Available at: http://www.computerworld.com/article/2986113/high-performance-computing/ibm-watson-will-know-what-you-did-last-summer.html, last accessed 21 October 2015.

SAS. (2017). Predictive analytics: What it is and why it matters. [Online.] https://www.sas.com/en_gb/insights/analytics/predictive-analytics.html, last accessed 15 March 2017.

Sheth, A. (2016). Internet of things to smart IoT through semantic, cognitive, and perceptual computing. *IEEE Intelligent Systems*, 31(2), pp. 108–112.

Shi-Nash, A. and Hardoon, D.R. (2016). Data analytics and predictive analytics in the era of big data. In: Hwaiyu Geng (ed.), *Internet of Things and Data Analytics Handbook* (pp. 329–345). New York: John Wiley & Sons.

Sykora M., Jackson, T.W., O'Brien, A. and Elayan, S. (2013). EMOTIVE ontology: Extracting fine-grained emotions from terse, informal messages. *IADIS International Journal on Computer Science and Information Systems*, 8(2), pp. 106–118.

Verostek J. (2014). Black box methods – Neural networks and support vector machines. [Online.] http://www.johnverostek.com/wp-content/uploads/2014/06/Chapter-7.pdf, last accessed 17 August 2017.

Wang, G., Gunasekaran, A., Ngai, E.W. and Papadopoulos, T. (2016). Big data analytics in logistics and supply chain management: Certain investigations for research and applications. *International Journal of Production Economics*, 176, pp. 98–110.

Williamson, B. (2016). Digital education governance: Data visualization, predictive analytics, and 'real-time' policy instruments. *Journal of Education Policy*, 31(2), pp. 123–141.

Wordnet. (2018). What is Wordnet? *Wordnet from Princeton University (website)*. http://wordnet.princeton.edu/ Last accessed 25 January 2018.

Zhao, L., Feng, Z., Xu, K. and Weng, F., Robert Bosch Gmbh. (2017). Speech recognition of partial proper names by natural language processing. U.S. Patent 9,589,563.

Part II

ARCHITECTURAL CONSIDERATIONS

CHAPTERS

BUILDING ANALYTICS ACROSS A HYBRID CLOUD

3.1 Introduction

In this chapter we review the data we have at our disposal in the cloud(s) alongside traditional solutions. It considers where data should be deployed to maximise the benefits of analysing that data to a company, bearing in mind that the newer data sources found on the internet are not under the control of many companies wishing to exploit it. It considers what 'hybrid cloud' solutions are and offers some recommendations on how to deploy your analytic solutions across a hybrid cloud to deliver maximum flexibility and economy.

Consider the forms of data we have at our disposal today; we do this to describe the entire landscape of differing data we can make use of in any analytics solution, as shown in Figure 3.1.

We can see, from Figure 3.1, that there are multiple differing forms of data now available for use beyond the formal, structured data sets businesses have relied on for many years.

- Systems of Record (SoR) – Traditional OLTP systems such as ERP, asset management, financial data and master data all reside in this area.
- Systems of Engagement (SoE) – These systems fundamentally differ from the SoR as they focus on people rather than transactions. This is where we find the end user-driven data – blogs, web pages, social media. The SoR often works with the SoE to enhance the contextual aspect of the user interaction and give the user the latest information from those systems.
- Systems of Automation (SoA) – This is a new domain we are using to describe the data derived by machines, known as the Internet of Things (IoT). This is being driven from the Industrial Internet of Things (IIoT) for manufacturing, sensors and devices that, for instance, control and monitor factories' production and scheduling, and Consumer Internet of Things (CIoT) solutions, such as devices and sensors in the home or wearables (as discussed in Chapter 1).
- Systems of Insight (SoI) – This can use all or some of the data in the SoR, SoA and SoE to analyse, derive insights and potentially drive new business processes. This is our area of concern for this chapter.

As we are focused on analytics we will only look at the relationships into and out of the SoI; however, each system can interact with any other system (as a system of systems), moving data as and when required. Any data being accessed for use can have a number of core characteristics that can be summarised by the 5 Vs, which have been covered in Chapter 1: *Variety*, *Velocity*, *Volume*, *Veracity* and *Value*. Other Vs that are sometimes considered are the *variability* and *visibility* of the data sets to be used.

As we are focusing on analytic solutions we need to describe how to successfully build an SoI landscape. We consider what logical components we will need to build a comprehensive

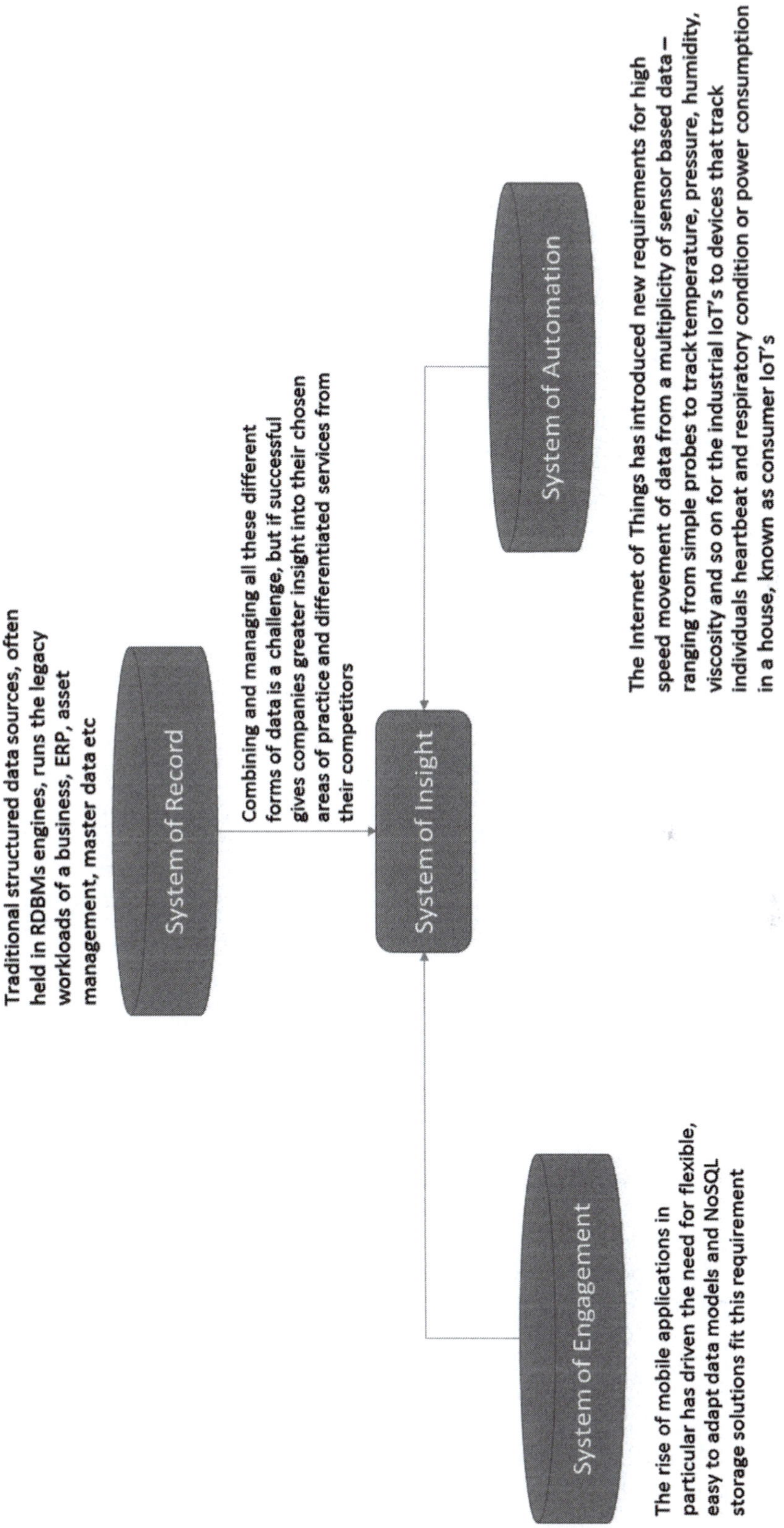

Traditional structured data sources, often held in RDBMs engines, runs the legacy workloads of a business, ERP, asset management, master data etc

System of Record

Combining and managing all these different forms of data is a challenge, but if successful gives companies greater insight into their chosen areas of practice and differentiated services from their competitors

System of Insight

The Internet of Things has introduced new requirements for high speed movement of data from a multiplicity of sensor based data – ranging from simple probes to track temperature, pressure, humidity, viscosity and so on for the industrial IoT's to devices that track individuals heartbeat and respiratory condition or power consumption in a house, known as consumer IoT's

System of Automation

The rise of mobile applications in particular has driven the need for flexible, easy to adapt data models and NoSQL storage solutions fit this requirement

System of Engagement

Figure 3.1   System of systems

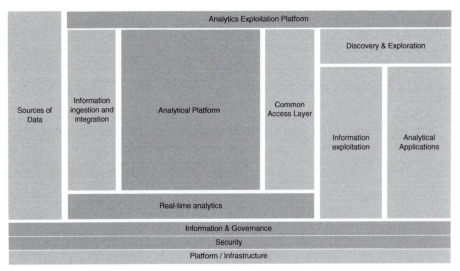

Figure 3.2 The basic building blocks needed to support a Big Data platform (a system of insight)

framework to satisfy analysing all forms of data, anywhere, at any time, and presented in the most appropriate manner. Below is a typical high-level logical architecture that could be used to deploy such a solution; we refer to this as a Big Data Analytics Platform as it covers all forms of data that may need ingesting and managing to build a comprehensive analytics platform, as shown in Figure 3.2.

The Big Data Analytics Platform needs to be supported by an infrastructure that is scalable and capable of being deployed in a traditional environment, or a private or public cloud. For example, this offers flexibility as to where development and test environments could be set up, utilising a private or public cloud to share resources easily. In addition, the public cloud resources capability can be bought as needed on a month-by-month basis with some provider to maintain maximum cost-effectiveness. For production, a more traditional on-premises solution could still be used where control and governance are currently easier to deal with.

This chapter will deal with the core capabilities as shown in dark grey in Figure 3.2 to set some context as to what a hybrid cloud needs to be able to accomplish regarding the storing of data types and the analytical actions placed upon those data types. A summary of the other components can be found in Appendix 1.

3.2 Analytical platform

The Analytical Platform component consists of several differing data platforms to form a polyglot data store, as shown in Figure 3.3.

Hadoop – This is a framework based on Java that can support vast volumes of any form of data, and process it using a distributed, scale-out environment. Hadoop is very flexible in that data can be stored in a Hadoop File System (HDFS) before any schema is defined. This ensures that no models need to be developed. This makes it very easy to capture data for all forms of analytics use. For example, an area to simply land raw data (structured or unstructured) could be created and, in this form, can act as a historical record. Hadoop could also be used to explore the data through querying and analytics of the detailed data in its raw form.

Hadoop uses MapReduce to enable processing and generating big data sets with a parallel, distributed algorithm on a cluster of servers.

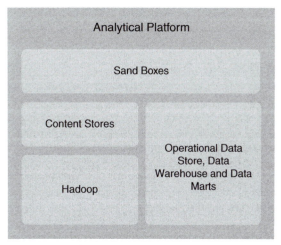

Figure 3.3   The analytical platform for cloud computing

The 'Map' part of MapReduce will take a set of data and convert it into elements that are key/value pairs (think: 'Product' as key; 'Computer Part' as value – a very simple way to define all the data). The 'Reduce' aspect takes the output from the mapping process and combines the data across those mapped key/value pairs to some smaller set (say, total count of all products that are called 'computer parts' in the data set) thus reducing the original data set to a smaller (reduced) one.

Utilising MapReduce and annotators to connect to different data sets, queries can be run on many file types (e.g., video, audio) that may not have been considered in the past.

MapReduce can be slow in many instances, though, as it is a batch-based process that uses disk to split data up and recombine. This is not the fastest way to query data but can be an excellent way to trawl through vast amounts of data looking for new insights and opportunities. Another good use for HDFS could be as a long-term but accessible archive, due to the low cost of storage. For example, data that is no longer required except for regulatory and compliance reasons could be held in there.

In this book, we will assume that any 'flavour' of Hadoop we describe is based on the Open Data Platform initiative (ODPi)[1] which specifies how Apache components are installed and configured to allow interoperability between different distributions of Hadoop and big data technologies. We do this as it's the most 'Open' way of ensuring differing technologies operate well together. Apache Hadoop is an open source framework for distributed storage and processing of large sets of data on commodity hardware. More on Apache Hadoop can be found at http://hadoop.apache.org/.

Operational Data Stores, Data Warehouses and Data Marts – These forms of databases have been around for over 20 years. These data stores analyse structured, transactional data that is held within relational databases. We include the core Data Warehouse – a normalised structured data store which holds a cleansed, transformed record of each business transaction from traditional SoR solutions. We also include other stores such as Operational Data Stores (to monitor near real-time analytics) and Data Marts (highly summarised data that is generally focused on specific lines of business). Products such as Teradata, Oracle, DB2 and SQL server are legacy platforms; Postgres SQL is an open source example (Erl et al., 2016).

Content Stores – These data stores contain unstructured data within a content management repository. For example, this could be where you store business documents, legal agreements and product specifications in their raw form. It might also include documents to

---

1 https://www.odpi.org/

publish externally to a website or a rich media store. These rich media data types can include audio and video such as educational material, announcements and podcasts (Dumais et al., 2016). All these sources of data are then available for subsequent processing within the Data Lake. Examples of content stores are FileNet, Documentum, Lotus Notes and SharePoint.

Sand Boxes – These are areas where users can 'play' with data sets extracted for their own, or a small group's, use. Sand boxes are created and deployed, torn down and redeployed more often than other data repositories (Hunt et al., 2016). The data associated with the sand box is taken from a number of areas from the rest of the central analytical platform. The purpose is exploratory in nature, with users trying to quickly identify new patterns within the data.

3.2.1 Real-time analytics

- The real-time data ingestion component is used to enable small delta (changes) in data to be loaded in an incremental fashion; message queuing and real-time replication are approaches that are commonly used.
- The Stream Computing component, is designed to analyse data in motion while providing huge scalability and processing of multiple concurrent input streams. A stream is a potentially infinite sequence of data elements (tuples) ordered by time, that is made available one at a time (Sun et al., 2016). Streams are processed differently from batch data, where all the data required for processing is immediately available. As data arrives in a stream, processing of the stream must happen in an incremental fashion, either on one data element at a time as soon as it arrives or on relatively small windows of data elements. Windows of data have to be held in some form of interim cache to enable different widowed sets to be worked upon (Youn et al., 2017).

Stream processing is generally required for handling a number of the 'Vs' we described above, in particular:

- o *Volume* – the amount of data arriving per unit time is typically too large to collect all the data over a period of time and apply batch processing techniques. For example, in an IoT-type architecture we could be gathering very large volumes of sensor-derived data and may not be able to (or wish to) store all this data over time (Endler et al., 2017). We could process each packet as it arrives in memory and reduce the volume of data through filtering, aggregation and other analytics before storing to disk.
- o *Velocity* – when we need insights from the data as soon as it arrives, stream computing is essential. There is simply not enough time to store data to disk and apply batch processing techniques. For example, in the stock market, we could have huge volumes of data arriving each microsecond and need to apply models/algorithms to predict movement of stock and make buying decisions in real time, something only a streaming solution can offer (Hendricks, 2017).

- Complex Event Processing is a huge topic in its own right. It links with streams in that the various streams of data processed can be analysed in some manner to identify a pattern in the data arising (maybe a stock is about to fall, maybe using weather data and social media

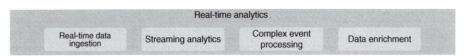

Figure 3.4 Elements of the real-time analytics component

feeds predict it's about to rain in some area, maybe using sensors to detect flows of people or traffic identify if bottlenecks in traffic/people flow are going to occur). This may also use previous history and/or algorithms trained from that history to help predict the future state.

● Data Enrichment processes the incoming raw data to make it fit for purpose – for example, simple things like fixing data formats to be a consistent approach, or combining data for a particular purpose (join first, last name with a space in between from data in a database). Or much more complex situations where empty data items could be derived from the overall sample set to build a new data set that is fit for purpose in downstream processing (a technique often used by data scientists to help build data sets that are fit for purpose).

3.2.2 Analytics exploitation platform

In-memory processing   Analytics Exploitation Platform

This layer allows a wide range of *in-memory* processing performed on the data residing within the central analytical platform. It can be used to process data as it enters the system and load data from source systems into the analytical platform area, or more commonly to shift data into memory from the analytic platform where a variety of analytical techniques can be applied. This component often uses the Apache Spark toolset against data in motion or at rest.[2] This approach is rapidly becoming/has become a standard approach to helping drive decision science style tools.

Apache Spark is split into four capabilities (Figure 3.5):

Spark SQL – Allows users to use the familiar SQL language to query all forms of data. There are at least three variations to being able to build SQL-like queries: using resilient distributed datasets (RDD); DataFrames; or DataSets with differing versions of Spark. Please see the Apache Spark guides for more information.[3]

Spark Streaming – Similar to the streaming mentioned earlier but is actually 'micro batches' which enable streaming-like functions until data becomes very fast-flowing (Wang et al., 2016).

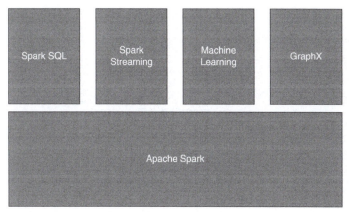

Figure 3.5   Spark platform

Source: Copyright © Apache Foundation. Reproduced with permission.

---

2 http://spark.apache.org/

3 https://spark.apache.org/docs/1.6.1/sql-programming-guide.html

Machine Learning – A set of machine learning libraries which offers data scientists a very rich set of analytical functions to work with (classification models, regression, clustering, etc.) (Shmueli and Lichtendahl, 2017).

GraphX – Enables graph-style structures to be built in memory for novel approaches to querying data that allows relationships between data to be more easily navigated (Malak and East, 2016). Basically, GraphX extends the Spark RDD to create a graph-style structure with properties attached to each vertex and edge. GraphX has basic operators to manipulate the graph models built, such as join vertices, aggregation and create subgraph. It can be used with all forms of data but often sits over persistent data stores such as Titan which is a graph database.

Python or Scala are commonly used to build out sets of functions that can be stored as notebooks (a simple file that holds the code written). This can be shared and extended, allowing common analytical techniques to be shared across communities of similar interest.

3.2.3 Information integration and governance

> Information and Governance

This layer provides governance and trust for big data by using capabilities such as security controls, tracking data lineage, lifecycle management to control big data growth and master data to establish a single source of truth. This is a huge topic but here are a few thoughts to consider:

- Can we measure what we are governing? – if not we can't improve
- Can we understand as much of our data as we need to? – if not we can't effectively use our data
- Is information governance baked into our processes? – if not we can't adapt and change

For many years this layer has been poorly constructed in many solutions because of the need to integrate metadata to enable users to understand what data is available within the big data platform and who can use it (Kune et al., 2016). A comprehensive and well-structured metadata layer is essential for good governance.

The metadata has been locked within various vendors' proprietary tools but recently the idea around adopting an open metadata repository and standards for metadata such that all vendors could share and integrate their metadata data sets is becoming a reality (O'Connor, 2016). Apache have defined a set of core foundational governance services which should grow over time.[4] Governance is considered in more detail in Chapter 5.

3.2.4 Security

Any architecture would not be complete without a security component. It is essential. The core objective is to protect data from internal or external threats and a number of key subcomponents are shown here:

- Data masking – This component enables data to be masked while potentially still retaining its integrity with other pieces of data across the Analytics platform. The masking uses a consistent approach to enable this and can be applied at a very granular level (i.e., a data element such as a single column in a single row in a table of data) (Ali and Ouda,

4 http://atlas.incubator.apache.org/

2017). This approach is often used if data from production systems needs to be used for testing, as this enables complete testing to be done on data that exhibits the same properties but does not share confidential data to those testing. It can also be used to simply prevent users from seeing confidential data in the production system if their level of authority permits access.

- Data encryption – Encryption involves the use of public and private keys to encrypt the data under question. Users will see a scrambled set of data that is unintelligible without having the key to decrypt. Masking does not do this but rather alters the data to something else that is understandable by humans or simply 'overwrites' the data with a predefined template such as 'XXXXXXX'. Encryption is used to protect data when being moved from site to site or shared among a group of users who have the same rights to the data.

- Data assurance – Prevents access to the data in the first place. This requires knowing who can access your systems (authentication) and who has permission to the data within the systems (authorisation), and with this knowledge track, block and report access to that data. This forms the ability to know where your sensitive data is in both structured and unstructured text and the ability to monitor, block and report upon access and usage of that data.

3.3   What is a hybrid cloud?

Now that we have the high-level view of a big data platform let's step back and consider what the hybrid cloud actually means, as shown by Figure 3.6.

Firstly, our definition for hybrid cloud for this book is '*The connection of one or more clouds to on-premises systems and/or the connection of one or more clouds to other clouds*' and here are our definitions for each component above:

- On-premises – the traditional IT landscape where the technical resources are built on specific hardware assets (this can be virtualised and managed in the same way as a public/private cloud to form a *dedicated cloud* and even managed externally by a third party but the data remains behind the company's firewalls).

- A private cloud is exclusively operated for a single organisation and is deployed and hosted externally. Private clouds can take advantage of clouds' efficiencies, yet some of the elasticity of a public cloud may be limited as multi-tenancy is not employed but does enable more control of those resources in a highly secure environment.

- Public clouds are owned and operated by companies that offer rapid access over a public network to computing resources, from bare metal to complete software solutions with supporting layers. With public cloud services, users often simply pay on a 'pay as you

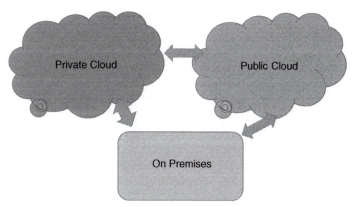

Figure 3.6   The hybrid cloud architecture

go' basis, eliminating the need for capital expenditure and enabling great flexibility to try things out with little risk associated with the infrastructure and application software used.

The cloud is generally seen as an environment that offers two main benefits, one being the chance to *reduce costs* by having someone else manage the environment and accessing resources on demand in a revenue-driven model. Historically all hardware and software were bought as capital expenditure and if not used were simply wasted expense (Pahl et al., 2016). Secondly and probably more importantly is *flexibility*. The cloud offers the chance to try to build new solutions and test them out very quickly with little or no risk and only minimal cost. To some degree this allows for agile development as new environments can be deployed almost instantaneously for developers to use.

For each element described above we *could h*ave differing systems running, for example take a look at Figure 3.7.

Note that the dark grey describe where *typically* we would find each system type, that is:

- SoR on Premises – This is generally the data an organisation has on traditional OLTP systems, and can be difficult to move to another platform or for privacy/security/regulation and compliance it felt better to leave them on site (Ailamaki et al., 2017). These systems host processes that record transactions as part of the core business.
- SoE in a public cloud – This data is often driven from and consumed by mobile phones and notepad devices, being the preferred route by many to access such systems. They cover newsfeeds, blogs, wikis, social media sites and tweets, and are focused around interactions with people. Unstructured data sources such as document and key/value pair databases play a significant role here.
- SoA in a private cloud – Sensor-based data fuels this element. Maintaining such data in a private cloud means (certainly for the industrial users of such data) better flexibility and control of what may be very sensitive data. Note that for customer-focused IoT solutions, such as devices and sensors in the home and wearables, a public cloud may be the best option.
- SoI in a private cloud – A private cloud for a business's critical analytical data is becoming the preferred option to enable relatively easy scaling (bandwidth, capacity and processing) of any solution while retaining control of metrics/analyses that describe the 'heartbeat' of the company in an environment that is seen as more secure than a public cloud.

Figure 3.7 shows the way in which a hybrid cloud connects multiple IT environments managed or accessed by the enterprise, including on-premises IT, private cloud and public cloud.

3.4   So why is a hybrid cloud a good idea?

A hybrid cloud leverages the best from each environment it has to offer (public, private, on-premises). This provides greater flexibility for users to locate and access different types of data and services to ensure analytics is delivered at the right place, at the right time, at the right price, to the right person and to meet business needs (Bibani et al., 2016). It is important to have this choice of hybrid cloud deployment because location is one of the first architectural decisions for building an enterprise-wide analytics solution. In particular, where should the data be stored and where should the analytics processing be located relative to the location of the data? Moving data is always expensive, and non-functional requirements (performance, cost, security, etc.) all impact the choices to be made. In addition, legal and regulatory requirements also impact where data can be located. Many countries have data sovereignty laws that prevent data about individuals, finances and intellectual property from moving across country borders; this forces

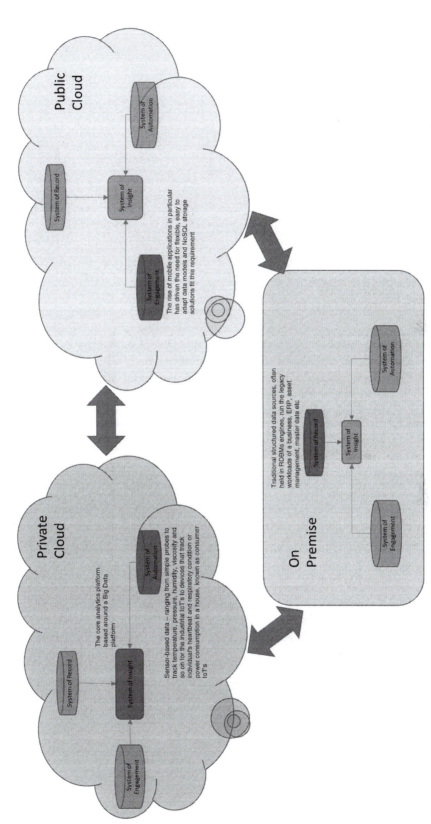

Figure 3.7   Hybrid cloud with *typical* location (in dark grey) for systems overlaid

data to be located within a country/regional borders and impacts the architectural decisions to be made. If it's such a good idea, what is stopping businesses from adopting hybrid cloud faster?

Here are some key areas that need consideration to deliver on the promise of a hybrid cloud environment.

3.4.1   Integration across each cloud environment

Each cloud platform needs to be connected to users such that they have an understanding of where their data is being provisioned from. This means strong integration across the data stored in each environment (Jayaraman et al., 2017). A typical use case is an organisation that needs to integrate data from:

- SoE (social media, news feeds, wikis, blogs, content stores, open data sources, weather data from third-party suppliers and so on) in a public cloud with
- SoA (sensors – industrial and personal, such as IoT devices for the home, business and individuals) in a private cloud with
- SoR (data from mission critical applications and databases stored on servers in its internal data centre)

Today, the reality is that most organisations have many sets of data silos across business units. Each business unit may be using differing platforms and services to deliver its own services to its own customers. Some business units are managing critical data in Software as a Service (SaaS) environments (for example, a human resource management solution). These are often run in public cloud instances and companies sign up to the service as a complete package run on behalf of them and their users. Each business unit may sign up to a specific SaaS solution for a variety of applications. Other business units may manage mission-critical systems such as transaction management and customer-facing applications on-premises for security, governance and regulatory reasons. Yet others may be building PaaS-style (or Platform as a Service) applications on a private or public cloud to reduce costs and increase speed of development deployment (Bassiliades et al., 2017).

None of these are easily brought together to fuel their analytics (SoI solution), as differing standards; vendors; non-functional limitations such as network capability, security models, availability, disaster recovery and failover; performance; operations support; and so on are all fragmented, which makes the task of consistently and continually bringing these data sets together difficult.

Organisations must be able to integrate data across these platforms in order to service their customers effectively and unlock the data across the platforms to identify what customers are asking for and potentially thinking, and bring new innovations to them. A single sign-on (SSO) for end users and single console for operations regardless of the location of data or processing would make things much more attractive for hybrid cloud progress.

To accomplish this goal, it is essential that companies solve the integration challenge to fully realise the cost-saving and long-term benefits of the hybrid cloud (Jones et al., 2017). Data integration is not a one-time process. Data integration requirements will change depending on many factors, not least the most attractive place to store data commercially, the volume of data to be stored and the non-functional requirements for that data.

3.4.2   Workload management

Traditionally, clouds have been designed for general-purpose workloads (such as middleware, application servers and databases) and work on the principle of consolidation and resource sharing where there are relatively predictable workloads. However, big data and analytics workloads require special consideration as big data solutions stretch the limits of elasticity provided by a traditional cloud. Historically, Data Warehouses that dealt with structured data had good solutions to deal with this that enabled fine-grained prioritisation of workloads by the user and/or optimisation costs. We know specific workloads can have dramatic consequences for the resources available around memory, CPU and bandwidth. These are not easily predicted and one or two individuals can create very intensive workloads that even with 'elastic' cloud capability can cause operational problems with the time needed to provision new resources and/or be costly to run. Big data systems only make the issues of the Data Warehouse more extreme, and we can now have situations where many Virtual Machines (VMs) may need to be provisioned quickly. This is a normal 'BI/analytics' pattern; start of week, month end, year end, seasonal events and ad hoc analysis by business users and/or data scientists often create huge spikes in demand on the system – completely different from a normal application.

An organisation needs to determine where its data should reside based on workload requirements, economics and regulatory pressures. Different workloads have different requirements for security, speed, energy and storage. Many organisations are driven to hybrid cloud because they want the option to place data and applications in the most sensible place based on workload requirements.

3.4.3   Easily moving applications between environments

If we are to easily move data around the cloud platforms, we must also be able to move, when necessary, the applications that make use of this data. Docker,[5] a container technology, is gaining traction as a preferred approach to ensuring portability across clouds. Docker is used to create an encapsulated environment for applications without requiring a separate Operating System (OS) to be supplied to each application in the virtualised environment you are building, making it simpler to deploy the application in either public or private clouds (Figure 3.8).

3.4.4   Networking must be optimised

An efficient network is crucial for a big data cluster. Networks in a cloud must be designed to provide resiliency with multiple paths between computing nodes for rapid data transfer, and they must be able to scale to handle the larger data volumes and throughput required to support big data. Dedicated network paths might be required for different types of data. For example, separate paths might be required for the interchange of user data, big data and management data. In addition, third-party cloud providers may need to invest

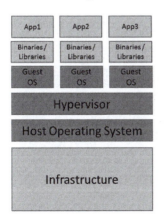

Containers share the operating system and only need to isolate some parts of that Operating System for writes that are needed back to the OS
So docker doesn't need to replicate the whole OS each time a new instance is created – this saves on space and enables new containers to be started and stopped very quickly … At the expense of complete isolation of resources
Each guest OS shown in the VM stack could be different – for the containers they all share the same OS

Virtual Machines   **Docker Containers**

Figure 3.8   Docker containers vs. Virtual Machines

5 https://www.docker.com/

in expanding access networks to allow faster rates of data ingestion, and new tooling to guarantee that they meet their Quality of Service/Service Level commitments.

3.4.5 Security is paramount

Security has been and continues to be the number-one concern with the adoption of public cloud, and the same challenges are also present in a hybrid cloud scenario (Hussein and Khalid, 2016). Compliance with security requirements is crucial because if cloud deployments are not compliant with industry regulations or government legislation, companies could face monetary fines and sanctions. Meeting this challenge requires a shift in local IT focus away from pure technology management and to a larger-scale view that is focused on ensuring compliance across both public and private clouds.

Privacy regulation associated with data sovereignty may limit certain workloads from crossing geographical boundaries. In addition, regulatory requirements such as the Health Information Portability and Accountability Act (HIPAA)[6] and the Sarbanes-Oxley Act (SOX)[7] require that the infrastructure where data resides for a specific application has been deemed compliant. The EU General Data Protection Regulation (GDPR)[8] is only set to make things even more difficult for IT providers.

When dealing with assuring the identity and authentication privileges of users it should be clear that any rules deployed in an on-premises or private cloud solution must also be strictly replicated in any public cloud solution.

At a minimum, software and tooling in all the environments should support cryptography and data protection requirements associated with company and legal needs; this includes ensuring aspects such as virus and malware protection are kept up to date.

A common framework to enable security across all the platforms is highly desirable. If data is moved from one platform to another it should automatically have the same set of rules and processes applied to it through a common governance model that support *all* the environments in question.

Sometimes it is easy to fall into the trap of rapid deployment with easy access and focus on usability for end users rather than the 'back-end' security needs. This must be avoided at all costs. Security breaches on the cloud can ruin a company's brand for both the company using the service and the vendor providing the service. Good governance and data classification (access rights, lifecycle management, data definitions) are paramount to ensuring this is successful. The European legislation on users' data access rights and companies' use of data (i.e. GDPR) will undoubtedly highlight some shortcomings in the near future.

3.4.6 Data movement is a challenge

Copying large volumes of data to the public cloud can take too much time and a lot of bandwidth. After the first copy/load, how is data then, if needed, synchronised?

The current available data movement options between on-premises and public cloud or between private and public clouds suffer from the speed of the wide area network (WAN). Moving to a hybrid model where data can exist across different cloud platforms and large volumes of that data needs moving around to satisfy analytic needs can be challenging. This often runs into WAN speed and high latency issues. Latency can reach milliseconds, compared with the microseconds expected on-premises and in the private cloud, and this means public instances can be inefficient and slow if care is not taken to manage this appropriately.

---

6 http://www.dhcs.ca.gov/formsandpubs/laws/hipaa/Pages/1.00WhatisHIPAA.aspx
7 http://www.soxlaw.com/
8 http://www.eugdpr.org/

There are a few possible ways to improve on this scenario. The simplest way is to use a dedicated, private network that connects the public cloud to the private or on-premises environments. Often a paid-for service, it can prove expensive so other techniques can be applied to simplify things.

1 Try and keep similar data within geographical boundaries – this simply reduces latency associated with the distance data needs to travel over the network.
2 Apply caching wherever possible – once a slowly changing data set has been moved, cache that data locally, this reduces the need to move data that hasn't changed. This technique is used in many data-centric problems so is well known and relatively easy to apply.
3 Data compression – compression techniques that pack and tag identical data to prevent it from needing to be sent more than once within a data packet can considerably reduce overall network traffic (Tu et al., 2017).

It is worth noting that the problems identified above are not new; they have been dealt with before but on a much smaller scale when networks were first being installed and client/server-style solutions were put in place (actually this goes as far back as the first mainframes). All that has happened is that volume, variety and velocity have all increased as technology moves on and the same problems now manifest themselves at a grander scale. No doubt infrastructure will improve again, but no doubt also that new bottlenecks will arise. The capacity to manage data through the IoT is probably the next large hurdle to overcome as the data from these new sources of information extends across the globe (and beyond – satellites, drones and planes all create data that is being consumed and will increase) (Erevelles et al., 2016).

Alongside the technology challenges there are always business challenges to consider. Two critical areas are:

- Managing the culture change – One of the biggest challenges in moving to a hybrid cloud infrastructure is less about the technology and more about management being able to accommodate a more collaborative, service-oriented approach for the provision of automated, self-service IT capabilities via the cloud. Moving to hybrid is driven by being able to deliver the right information to the right people at the right time. This will mean new skills being adopted throughout the business to exploit the information available and even entirely new roles being created, such as a data scientist. Such an individual has the skills to explore and gather different data sets and build new insights that drive new business models and ways of working.
- Varying levels of hybrid sophistication – A hybrid cloud strategy can have different levels of sophistication: deep integration between public cloud and private/on-premises environments or more simplistic, static, point-to-point connections designed to serve a particular functional need. A business needs to understand its level of maturity and where and when it needs to evolve to greater levels of sophistication. This should be a relentless reinventing of itself to make the most of the hybrid cloud over time.

3.5 Building the hybrid cloud platform

We arrive at a key point. Hybrid Cloud can be hard to enable in the real world, but the benefits can be large. If we can define some good working practices/architectural disciplines before we go on this voyage we may help to alleviate a great deal of pain later!

If we consider the typical solution outline described in Figure 3.7, we can start to think about this as a good 'best of breed' example. Why? Well how does an organisation decide where to put data on a hybrid cloud and how to use it? What's the best strategy to balance sharing and mobility with the need for privacy and security on a hybrid cloud? Analytical insights (and the data associated with it) are such a valuable form of intellectual property that organisations are naturally concerned about moving it (Missbach et al., 2016). Best-in-class organisations[9] use the 80–20 rule by moving 80 per cent of their data to the cloud with only 20 per cent retained on-premises under the following three categories of data:

1 Data that the business wants to deploy externally on a public cloud – for example, SaaS applications to simplify costs, management, and so on. Of course this data is still managed in a secure manner, but in a multi-tenancy model it is possible that it could be accessed by the unscrupulous more easily than in a private or on-premises model. In addition there is the data they don't own but make use of – for example, the weather, government, news feeds, open data sets, social media data and so forth.

2 Data that the business wants to share across the enterprise on a private cloud – for example, the analytics solution we are considering in this book including all the repositories mentioned and additional functions to enable smooth operation of the analytic solution – for example metadata, master data and so on – or maybe a content management system that holds business guidelines that everyone in the company needs access to.

3 Data that resides on legacy solutions that cannot be moved for compliance, regulatory or cost reasons – this covers data that is highly sensitive, for example highly confidential customer data, financial metrics not for general exposure, intellectual property and data that is simply too expensive to migrate away or run on another platform at the current time.

The first two categories make up 80 per cent of data for most companies. Data in the second category needs to be protected by authentication restrictions and an understanding of the privacy settings offered in the most appropriate cloud platform. The third category comprises the remaining 20 per cent of data for most companies.

Using Figure 3.7 and focusing on just a typical deployment model, a simplified model can be seen in Figure 3.9.

Figure 3.9 describes the location of typical systems, but we now need to delve deeper and identify more detailed components that describe how our typical hybrid cloud solution could exist. Figure 3.10 describes a best-of-breed approach and a typical reference architecture to support this scenario.

We've built a simple first pass highly genericised solution defined in Figure 3.10 from publicly available information from the IBM Cloud Architecture Centre.[10] We can map this architecture to Figure 3.9 where the public cloud primarily supports SoE, such as the social media, wikis and open data sets we have mentioned earlier. It may seem odd at first glance not to include sensors out in the public cloud, but we assume such devices have their data gathered to some readily available open sourced and open data platform for sharing, so these fit in the data sources icon. Private cloud supports local sensors and the analytics solution, and finally on-premises holds the legacy solutions. Of course reality is more complex than this and there are generally many more systems to consider. Although not a detailed diagram of every potential component, this view describes our best-of-breed approach in sufficient detail to clarify the major elements in the reference architecture. Let's describe each component in more detail:

- **User** – A role that describes a user within the business or a third party.
- **Application** – A software solution that has some function that a user exploits. This is the way in which a user interacts with the system(s) they have access to.
- **Sensor** – A device that collects information that can be used on the device itself or transmitted to another agent for analysis at real time or at a later point in time. These devices create the data that are associated with the **SoA** we described earlier. Examples could be your

9 https://msdn.microsoft.com/en-us/library/mt422890.aspx
10 https://developer.ibm.com/architecture/

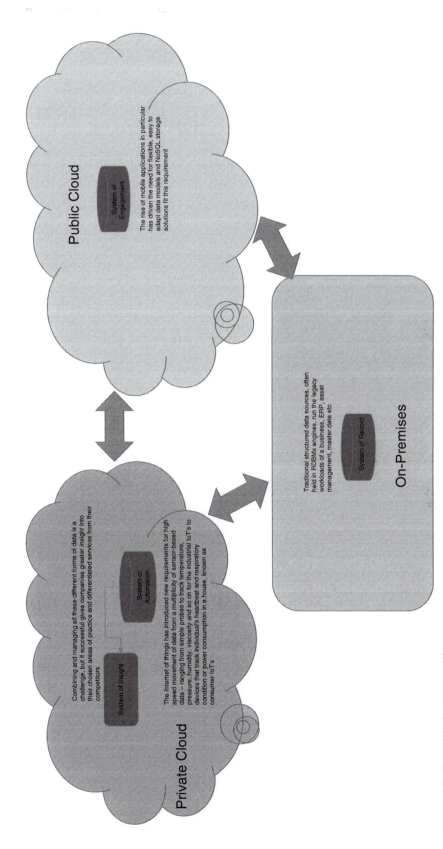

Figure 3.9 Typical deployment model

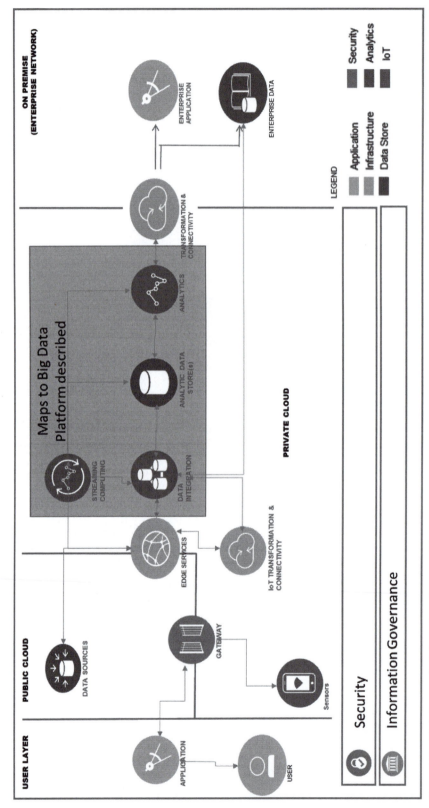

Figure 3.10 Typical enterprise information reference architecture

mobile phone or any sensor that can be used to monitor physical characteristics of some end point – pressure, humidity, temperature, frequency, light, voltage, current and so on.

- **Data sources** – Data that exists publicly for consumption, for example social media, weather, government open data, blogs, wikis, web pages and so on. These data sources are associated with the **SoE**.
- **Gateway** – An intelligent network point that can route data to edge services or enable 'analytics at the edge' to provide specific, local analytics close to the point of creation of the data. An intelligent router in the home could be an example of such a device.
- **Edge services** – Provide capabilities to move data across boundaries to the internet (domain name services, firewalls, load balancing, etc.).
- **IoT transform and connectivity** – Messaging and connectivity through an enterprise service bus that enables rationalisation of data to standard formats and some limited manipulation of data if necessary (standardising dates/times and reference coding may be good examples). Can handle sensor device management and authorisation of those devices.
- **Transformation and connectivity** – An enterprise service bus to allow secure connections between services running on data/applications on-premises.
- **Enterprise application** – Simply an application that resides within the enterprise rather than on any cloud platform. For example, core banking transactions that reside on a mainframe or sales data that is gathered from a set of retail outlets.
- **Enterprise data** – The data created by the enterprise applications, namely the **SoR** and metadata about the data for enterprise applications.
- **Big data platform** – the **SoI**.

  - Streaming computing
  - Data integration
  - Analytics store(s)
  - Analytics

- **Security** – A comprehensive security layer needs to be put in pace that enables a consistent approach across the public, private and traditional layers.
- **Governance** – Information governance is the most critical component to ensure consistency of information and information use; the key to this is the use of metadata that allows a business to view all their assets across all the platforms. Governance is discussed in much more detail in Chapter 5.

The goal of this architecture as with any analytics solution is to provide an organisation with actionable insights for smarter decisions and better business outcomes. Different types of analytics, however, provide different types of insights. There are three principal types of analytics, as discussed in Chapter 2: descriptive ('What has happened?'), predictive ('What could happen?') and prescriptive ('What should we do?'). Descriptive analytics has been used for at least 20 years to enable businesses to understand customers' previous purchases. This is often referred to as 'looking into the rear-view mirror' as it can only state what has happened. Predictive analytics takes this information and begins to analyse it to understand what might happen next. This often requires new data sources to help with the prediction, for example the weather could be used to predict sales of ice cream (geography and culture may also be other useful data sets – selling ice cream to Eskimos might not be useful!). Prescriptive analytics takes one further step to describe possible 'next best actions' based on the analysis, so for the ice cream example the next best action could be to buy a different set of flavours of ice cream for a particular demographic or location, because the predictive analysis has offered insights into flavours of ice cream most often chosen by particular demographics and locations.

Some further examples across all industries to more efficiently deploy predictive and prescriptive analytics use cases include:

- Retail – create personalised marketing campaigns using real-time actionable insights into customer shopping behaviour across all channels including sentiment analysis.
- Healthcare – analyse clinical, identify trends, detect patterns and predict outcomes; help healthcare organisations to anticipate change – so that they can plan and carry out strategies to improve patient outcomes.
- Financial services – allow more efficient and faster fraud detection at the point of sales (POS).
- Telecommunications – allow more efficient network optimisation and network failure detection.

One of the most challenging question companies will face is deciding what data to place where on a hybrid cloud. How are decisions around cost, performance, robustness, security, data movement and so on taken? Each company's sets of data will have differing value in the way they are used, the competitive advantage it brings, the cost if lost and recovery needed, and the loss of reputation should it be accessed by those who shouldn't.

The future of the hybrid cloud strategy for most of the traditional organisations is still unclear. Industries are still trying to figure out the best use cases to move to the cloud and they have not started a hybrid cloud strategy yet (Carlson, 2016). The best-case scenario for the *traditional* organisations in the future will probably be a 50/50 rule where 50 per cent of the workload is still found on-premises and the other 50 per cent will be moved to the cloud, and aim for the 80/20 split discussed earlier in this chapter over time. But the real question for the traditional organisation is with SoE and SoA on the cloud and where does the SoI go? This will really depend on where the source system data is. Alternatively, the internet-born organisations are using the 80/20 rule by moving 80 per cent of their data to the cloud (private and/ or public), with only 20 per cent retained on-premises, including the highly sensitive data.

One of the most important considerations on the hybrid cloud strategy for most of the organisations is the concept of *data gravity*. The term data gravity has been coined to describe how, as data accumulates over time, it becomes larger and denser, or has a greater mass. As the data density increases, the data's *gravitational* pull increases. Services and applications also have mass but generally much smaller than the data. As data continues to build mass, services and applications are more likely to be drawn to the data, rather than vice versa.

As the data stored on public and private clouds continues to grow at a rapid rate and includes large sets of as yet untapped useful information in unstructured form, the data gravity will inexorably move to those platforms. Simply moving this data around will become one of the greatest expenses so processing and applications will gravitate to that data rather than the other way around. In this way building an analytics data hub where as much data can be held local to the needs is often useful. This does *not* mean building one huge analytics data hub, but rather building out data hubs that are suitable for groups of users at say a regional or functional level and then judiciously moving the most important data as copies between each data hub to extend its capabilities.

3.6 Managing the hybrid cloud platform

Hopefully this chapter has shown the reader how a hybrid cloud can offer real flexibility, positioning different capabilities on differing cloud platforms to maximise effectiveness, efficiency and economy. In terms of effectiveness, this is achieved by exploiting the best of each cloud platform style to suit requirements; with efficiency, by only developing solutions in virtualised environments to share resources in a way that is better than in the past; and with economy by exploiting each platform to drive down the overall cost of supporting that environment.

But this comes at a cost – we could conceivably have multiple cloud providers providing different elements of the solution outlined here. This enables us to choose the right platform/price point/service but means we need to integrate across provider solutions and keep track of the services we use. Where in the past we had only internal systems to support and understand, we now must track (at least) the different services we use and the various connections between those services. This has driven the need for cloud management services to track what we have in our extended enterprise and the need to drive standards still harder, if we wish we can swap services between suppliers to obtain the best approach at any given point in time. For example, having the capability to build a simple virtual environment that can redeploy a single application from legacy to the cloud is one thing; moving several thousand applications across differing cloud providers that require integration points that could become broken is another; and ensuring the cost is controlled/optimised across providers is yet another.

Hybrid cloud is already with many large enterprises where different systems are used in public/private and on-premises solutions and different providers supply solutions in each area (Montero et al., 2016). This has complicated things somewhat and though the benefits of these solutions are seen by almost all companies (primarily, it must be said, through cost reduction and later flexibility) the management and tracking of all these solutions needs to be thoroughly considered. The authors have seen many instances where 'shadow IT' projects have been started (that is lines of business-building solutions on a cloud provider with little or no thought to overall strategy or standards) that are causing duplication of effort, difficulty in integration, hidden costs and raised complexity.

This cycle of requiring rapid development and flexibility versus the need for good IT governance and control so costs do not spiral is nothing new and is probably in its third iteration over the last 25 years in IT. However, the need to understand the overall landscape and govern the solutions in place has never been greater. With the integration of 'born on the cloud' solutions and their respective data sets the opportunity for using data that is not appropriate or in some cases simply bad becomes greater (Oliveira et al., 2016). The need for security and control over a company's systems needs to be very carefully managed alongside the cloud providers used, service level agreements and commercial consideration when/if data leakages occur are critical (loss of data resulting in weakening the brand of a company keeps CIOs awake in the twenty-first century).

It is for those with strategic and tactical control to ensure this does not happen and is controlled through good governance and tooling.

3.7 Conclusion

Hybrid cloud offers a future for business that is highly flexible, optimised and low-cost to deploy. This will enable a 'fail fast' culture to be built that enables companies to get to new novel solutions by rapidly iterating through options to reach the best one. Having a hybrid cloud architecture which can provide access to multiple new technologies as they emerge without requiring internal IT departments to learn, install or support them can be a significant accelerator for business analytic solutions. SaaS offerings are targeting specific subject areas such as churn detection as a service, fraud detection as a service or marketing campaign as a service. These tend to improve business outcomes much faster than solely in-house efforts.

However, to make good on this, a strategy to manage this new world will need to be considered and put in place that manages the pitfalls we have discussed. The list below suggests some areas that will need to be addressed and controlled in an appropriate manner as each business will have (at least some) unique needs.

1 Use of data and analytics – New tools that are 'self-service' and require minimal programming will need to be developed that can deploy the complex analytical models out to end users in an easy to consume manner. This effort is ongoing and will need better classification of data through metadata and possibly new approaches to easily create metadata in an automatic or semi-automatic manner.

2 Data movement and replication – Deploy new approaches to enhance movement of data through compression techniques, caching and the use of in-memory databases.

3 Data preparation and integration – Either move the transformation closer to the data to prepare data in advance or build pipelines of data in-memory to rapidly wrangle and transform data to fit best needs. Basically, process data where its most appropriate to do so based on available compute resource and requirements.

4 Data ownership, governance and compliance – Enable hybrid cloud environments with solid governance models and tools to support. This is already taking shape and can be seen in the next generation of data science toolkits such as IBM's Watson Studio[11] which can build an enterprise (and beyond) catalogue of assets that all authorised users can access. Implement improved cloud environments compliant with all industry and government regulations.

5 High availability and disaster recovery – Two approaches to ensure business continuity. Some cloud providers do not yet manage this in a robust manner; things like Cloud Object Storage helps at the data layer with comprehensive replication across regions but application resilience can still be suspect, especially on the public cloud. This is critical because if solutions are moved to the cloud, the business has far less control over service levels and can only resort to financial penalties with the vendor which may not help if a system is down at peak usage time!

6 Network configuration and latency – Software-defined networks with simple configuration are a very low-level task that is key to ensuring performance and resilience at a very low level in the overall infrastructure. Approaches that optimise location of data, using dedicated connections where performance must be assured, cloud caching to prevent repetitive reads and writes to the back-end systems, network traffic optimisation and workload optimisation are needed in the overall landscape of the solution.

7 Workload and portability – The use of docker containers is becoming a preferred approach to enable portability and agility across the hybrid cloud. A container can easily be migrated from one cloud environment to another, preventing 'lock in' to a vendor's resources.

8 Management control and dashboards – These allow the cloud resources in use to be tracked, allowing a business to predict their costs and shift resources to the best platform easily as and when required.

It's clear that cloud computing is disrupting and transforming the way organisations work in the digital world. However, confusion remains about the true potential of the hybrid cloud. Most companies have not yet developed a hybrid cloud strategy, and many are simply using the cloud infrastructure to run existing applications. There are huge gaps when comparing the solutions available on the public cloud with the solutions available on the private cloud and on-premises.

For hybrid cloud to be successful, any company will need to ensure the choice of tooling and placement of data are considered within any design. Today the complexity of the application, data stores, networks and lack of governance make this difficult to achieve. One area that must be addressed to enable a hybrid cloud is that of metadata. If consistent metadata across all environments can be shared, everything can at least be catalogued at a global level and the business can begin to identify where its resources should be focused to maximise their returns now and in the future.

These problems will be overcome over time but cannot be tackled without such a global metadata management approach. Companies that adopt a hybrid cloud platform will improve

---

11 https://www.ibm.com/cloud/watson-studio

their ability to respond to changing circumstances, keeping costs under control, improving flexibility by placing data and analytics on the most appropriate platform and ensuring data use is maximised by bringing analytics to bear quickly at the right point in the business.

 Study area

To test your understanding of the chapter please attempt to answer these questions, either by debating them in the class/among colleagues or making notes to formulate your answers.

Questions:

1 What are the 5 Vs that describe data in today's world?
2 Name the key benefits of a cloud platform.
3 Can you describe the core elements of the Big Data Analytics Platform? This underpins a lot of the thinking in this chapter.
4 What do you consider to be the benefits of a hybrid cloud for an analytics strategy?
5 What might be some of the pitfalls of adopting a hybrid cloud for an analytics strategy and what can be done to control such issues?
6 Is it a good thing that there are most likely only three or four global providers of cloud services in the foreseeable future? How will this impact company's services who use those cloud providers? Can you see any conflicts of interest (Hint: Think about Amazon Web Services and then Walmart using those services)?

Further reading:

- Weapons of math destruction: How big data increases inequality and threatens democracy
  - O'Neil, C. (2017). *Weapons of math destruction: How big data increases inequality and threatens democracy*. New York: Broadway Books.
- Understanding big data: Analytics for enterprise class Hadoop and streaming data
  - Zikopoulos, P. and Eaton, C. (2011). *Understanding big data: Analytics for enterprise class Hadoop and streaming data*. McGraw-Hill.
- Hybrid cloud for Dummies
  - Hurwitz, J., Kaufman, M., Halper, F. and Kirsch, D. (2012). *Hybrid cloud for dummies*. New York: John Wiley & Sons.
- Mastering Apache Spark 2.X
  - Kienzler, Romeo. (2017). *Mastering Apache Spark*, 2nd edn. Birmingham: Packt Publishing.
- Apache Spark in 24 Hours, Sams Teach Yourself
  - Aven, J. (2016). *Apache Spark in 24 hours, Sams Teach Yourself*. Indianapolis, IN: Sams Publishing.

References

Ailamaki, A., Porobic, D. and Sirin, U. (2017). Performance and energy analysis using transactional workloads. In: *8th TPC Technology Conference on Performance Evaluation and Benchmarking. Traditional-Big Data-Internet of Things, TPCTC 2016, New Delhi, India, September 5–9, 2016, Revised Selected Papers* (Vol. 10080, p. 159). Springer.
Ali, O. and Ouda, A. (2017). A content-based data masking technique for a built-in framework in Business Intelligence platform. In: *2017 IEEE 30th Canadian Conference on Electrical and Computer Engineering (CCECE)* (pp. 1–4). IEEE.

Bassiliades, N., Symeonidis, M., Meditskos, G., Kontopoulos, E., Gouvas, P. and Vlahavas, I. (2017). A semantic recommendation algorithm for the PaaSport platform-as-a-service marketplace. *Expert Systems with Applications*, 67, pp. 203–227.

Bibani, O., Yangui, S., Glitho, R.H., Gaaloul, W., Hadj-Alouane, N.B., Morrow, M.J. and Polakos, P.A. (2016). A demo of a PaaS for IoT applications provisioning in hybrid cloud/fog environment. In: *2016 IEEE International Symposium on Local and Metropolitan Area Networks (LANMAN)* (pp. 1–2). IEEE.

Dumais, S., Cutrell, E., Cadiz, J.J., Jancke, G., Sarin, R. and Robbins, D.C. (2016). Stuff I've seen: A system for personal information retrieval and re-use. In: *ACM SIGIR Forum* (Vol. 49, No. 2, pp. 28–35). ACM.

Endler, M., Briot, J.P., De Almeida, V., Dos Reis, R. and Silva, F.S.E. (2017). Stream-based reasoning for IoT applications–proposal of architecture and analysis of challenges. *International Journal of Semantic Computing*, 11(3), pp. 325–344.

Erevelles, S., Fukawa, N. and Swayne, L. (2016). Big Data consumer analytics and the transformation of marketing. *Journal of Business Research*, 69(2), pp. 897–904.

Erl, T., Khattak, W. and Buhler, P. (2016). Big data fundamentals: concepts, drivers and techniques. Prentice Hall Press.

Hendricks, D. (2017). Using real-time cluster configurations of streaming asynchronous features as online state descriptors in financial markets. *Pattern Recognition Letters*, 97, pp. 21–28.

Hosseinian-Far, A., Ramachandran, M. and Sarwar, D., eds. (2017). *Strategic Engineering for Cloud Computing and Big Data Analytics*. Springer. Greenwich, CT, USA ©2016

Hunt, T., Zhu, Z., Xu, Y., Peter, S. and Witchel, E., 2016, November. Ryoan: A Distributed Sandbox for Untrusted Computation on Secret Data. In OSDI (pp. 533-549).

Hussein, N.H. and Khalid, A. (2016). A survey of Cloud Computing Security challenges and solutions. *International Journal of Computer Science and Information Security*, 14(1), p. 52.

Jayaraman, P.P., Perera, C., Georgakopoulos, D., Dustdar, S., Thakker, D. and Ranjan, R. (2017). Analytics-as-a-service in a multi-cloud environment through semantically-enabled hierarchical data processing. *Software: Practice and Experience*, 47(8), pp. 1139–1156.

Jones, R.D., Cooke, M., Hinchliffe, J., Morley, J. and Barry, S.T. (2017). Developing PreDICT– a fully integrated data platform for preclinical in vivo data: learning from experience. *Drug Discovery Today*.

Kitchin, R. and McArdle G. (2016). What makes Big Data, Big Data? Exploring the ontological characteristics of 26 datasets. *Big Data & Society*. [Online.] http://bds.sagepub.com/content/3/1/2053951716631130, last accessed 18 May 2018.

Kozielski, S., Mrozek, D., Kasprowski, P., Małysiak-Mrozek, B. and Kostrzewa, D., eds. (2016). Beyond databases, architectures and structures. Advanced technologies for data mining and knowledge discovery. In: *Proceedings of the 12th International Conference, BDAS 2016, Ustroń, Poland, May 31–June 3, 2016* (Vol. 613). New York and London: Springer.

Kune, R., Konugurthi, P.K., Agarwal, A., Chillarige, R.R. and Buyya, R. (2016). The anatomy of big data computing. *Software: Practice and Experience*, 46(1), pp. 79–105.

Malak, M. and East, R. (2016). *Spark GraphX in Action*. Manning Publications Co.

Missbach, M., Staerk, T., Gardiner, C., McCloud, J., Madl, R., Tempes, M. and Anderson, G. (2016). The hybrid cloud. In: Missbach, M. et al. (ed.), *SAP on the Cloud* (pp. 153–164). New York and London: Springer, Berlin, Heidelberg.

Montero, R.S., Massonet, P., Villari, M., Merlino, G., Celesti, A., Levin, A., Schour, L., Vázquez, C., Melis, J., Spahr, S. and Whigham, D. (2016). BEACON: A cloud network federation framework. In: *Workshops of ESOCC 2015 Advances in Service-Oriented and Cloud Computing, Taormina, Italy, September 15–17, 2015, Revised Selected Papers* (Vol. 567, p. 325). New York and London: Springer.

O'Connor, M.J., Martínez-Romero, M., Egyedi, A.L., Willrett, D., Graybeal, J. and Musen, M.A. (2016). An open repository model for acquiring knowledge about scientific experiments. In: *20th International Conference on Knowledge Engineering and Knowledge Management, EKAW 2016, Bologna, Italy, November 19–23, 2016* (pp. 762–777). New York and London: Springer International Publishing.

Oliveira, F., Eilam, T., Nagpurkar, P., Isci, C., Kalantar, M., Segmuller, W. and Snible, E. (2016). Delivering software with agility and quality in a cloud environment. *IBM Journal of Research and Development*, 60(2–3), pp. 10–11.

Pahl C, Jamshidi P, Weyns D. (2017). Cloud architecture continuity: Change models and change rules for sustainable cloud software architectures. *Journal of Software Evolution Process*. 29, e1849.

San Murugesan, Irena Bojanova Carlson, E. (2016). eds. Enterprise cloud computing strategy and policy. *Encyclopedia of Cloud Computing* (Vol. 1, p. 363). Wiley

Shmueli, G. and Lichtendahl Jr, K.C. (2017). *Data Mining for Business Analytics: Concepts, Techniques, and Applications in R*. John Wiley & Sons.

Sun, D., Tang, H., Gao, S. and Li, F. (2016). A strategy to improve accuracy of multi-dimensional feature forecasting in Big Data stream computing environments. In: *International Conference on Web Information Systems Engineering* (pp. 405–413). Springer International Publishing.

Tu, C., Takeuchi, E., Miyajima, C. and Takeda, K. (2017). Continuous point cloud data compression using SLAM based prediction. In: *2017 IEEE Intelligent Vehicles Symposium (IV)* (pp. 1744–1751). IEEE.

Wang, X., Liu, C. and Zhu, M. (2016). Instant traveling companion discovery based on traffic-monitoring streaming data. In: *2016 13th Web Information Systems and Applications Conference* (pp. 89–94). IEEE.

Youn, J., Choi, J., Shim, J. and Lee, S.G. (2017). Partition-based clustering with sliding windows for data streams. In: *International Conference on Database Systems for Advanced Applications* (pp. 289–303). Cham: Springer.

4

METADATA MANAGEMENT

4.1 Introduction

Metadata management is a topic that often does not get the focus it deserves. Think of metadata as the 'library' of all your information assets. Without that library, there is no guidance as to where data resides in the organisation, how it is classified (Sci-fi, History, Geography, Travel, etc.), what it consists of (chapters in the book and glossaries), the condition of the assets in the library (books are in mint, excellent, good, fair condition, etc.) and so on. Our data within our systems needs to be managed with as much rigour, if not more.

We find ourselves in an age when we are awash with data but have very few good, accurate, repeatable and easy to access mechanisms to understand and make use of all the data at our disposal. The advent of big data has only exacerbated the problem, making classification of metadata harder still. We need to address metadata as a holistic, global resource that can be used to work as our 'library' of data for all sources of data, internal and external to the business or indeed anywhere. With many differing environments and systems, such as cloud, public/private, on- and off-premises, databases, data movement tools, forms of metadata repositories, operating systems and so on all confuse the landscape. Imagine if there was just one way of doing something! Being able to manage a single all-encompassing repository of metadata that covers everywhere an organisation touches is simply not possible, especially as much of the data may not even be under the control of the organisation that wishes to use it. Marketing data, other supplier data, open data, news feeds, weather and IoT-related data are all possible candidates in this space. We must somehow work with all these new feeds of data and still create a complete picture of all our data assets.

This chapter will explore differing forms of metadata that are required to give a complete and accurate view of the data within the business and enable anyone who is authorised to do so to access and use that data easily, potentially through a form of 'self-service'. This is where data can be identified, understood and used in manners that are much easier than is currently the case.

4.2 The metadata problem space

Traditionally we have loaded metadata at periodic intervals, sometimes as slow as changing every week or even monthly for business metadata, although extracts from traditional database systems could be daily. This can lead to loss of faith in the accuracy of that metadata. The rapid change of data structures that NoSQL engines bring to bear and external data feeds means we must accommodate ways in which we can build metadata in a manner that can be changed quickly as the data changes (Ueda et al., 2016).

Using a specific model created by any one party is difficult to maintain. Currently vendors all use their own proprietary models and build adaptors to try and extract metadata from each other's solution where it's possible to do so (Verma et al., 2016). A more open approach is needed that everyone can adhere to based upon open standards for metadata and open APIs to build metadata (Davison et al., 2017).

Let us consider how we create metadata today to try to envisage how we *could create* metadata in the future and the benefits that would accrue. Today we capture metadata through a variety of tools or simply create by hand (Pal, J.K. 2016). For example, building a business glossary can be very time consuming, requiring manual tasks working with a governance team and the data stewards to work through all the different terms a business creates. Then the business would need to define the semantics of that term, ownership of the data item and other details such as security classification, rules associated with the data, policies it is linked to and so forth.

Technical metadata often has to be laboriously extracted or even created by third- party tools to glean some insights into data structures and the processes that are used against it when moving data from operational systems to analytical ones. It becomes harder still when trying to extract metadata from unstructured sources (Vaduva and Dittrich, 2001). For example, who created the document, what revision dates does it have, what are the key terms it is associated with, who is permitted to read/write to the document? All this information is often copied from templates or other documents and is never updated, leaving a very poor audit trail of what has actually happened to that document. This is seen time and again with other forms of unstructured data and open data – no standards are in place and the people who create/use this data don't keep the metadata fresh (Vaduva and Dittrich, 2001). This had led to countless problems when trying to understand and make best use of that data.

Let's consider one particularly good example with unstructured data where automation has been employed to make things much simpler: when a photograph is taken with your camera, at the time of creation a host of useful metadata is created automatically, as shown in Figure 4.1.

Figure 4.1   Photo and metadata created

Figure 4.1 shows some of the metadata created at creation time, which includes:

- Phone type
- Camera model
- Exposure time
- ... much more on actual photo metrics/parameters
- Name of file
- Location of file
- Data created/modified
- Owner and computer picture originates from

This is a wealth of useful metadata with the user having to take no action at all to generate it. In addition, the metadata is in a standard format that other picture viewing and processing tools can use to read and then manipulate the photo with a wide variety of tools available. This is an excellent example of open standards and automatic metadata generation available today to show how simple things could be (Park and Tosaka et al., (2010).

The above example shows how it is possible to easily create technical metadata at the time of data creation. Let's now consider what forms of metadata can be identified in a typical business where metadata comes from many sources and in multiple forms. Here are the main sources and classifications for metadata we use in this book.

4.2.1   Sources of metadata

It may be difficult to specify a comprehensive list of all potential metadata sources. Nevertheless, you may identify metadata in the following organisations, IT systems and other parts of the enterprise:

- **Operational systems** – these are, for instance, industry specific systems, such as core banking systems, Operational Support Systems (OSS) in the Telco industry, or Claims Processing Systems in the Insurance industry.
- **Middleware software** – metadata is contained in almost all middleware software, such as Enterprise Information Integration (EII) and Enterprise Application Integration (EAI) software, but also Enterprise Content Management (ECM) systems.
- **Database systems** – all database management systems do contain metadata, such as descriptions on tables, indexes and other database objects. This metadata is not only used for maintenance but also performance optimisation purposes. These can be structured or non-structured sources (NoSQL db's) such as HBase, Titan, Cassandra, Hive and so on.
- **Applications** – this includes packaged applications (for instance ERP, CRM, SCM and PLM systems), other industry specific applications such as anti-money laundering (AML) or fraud prevention applications, mobile applications, web applications and so forth.[1]
- **Data Warehouses (DW)** – this includes metadata contained in the DW and also in the Data Marts. An example of metadata in this context is the specification of OLAP cubes.[2]
- **Unstructured sources of data** – including NoSQL databases and file systems such as HDFS or object storage. These are rapidly gaining in popularity.
- **BI reporting tools** – This metadata is associated with the generation of BI dashboards, KPI measurements and other analytical reports including those for performance management purposes.

---

1 See http://www.investopedia.com/terms/a/aml.asp for more information on AML.
2 Online Analytical Processing (OLAP).

- **Other tools** – metadata (e.g. best practices, rules, guidelines, patterns) is contained, for instance, in development tools, business processes modelling tools and data modelling tools, and is an essential part in the modelling tasks.
- **Documentation** – this could be spreadsheets, requirement and specification documents, EIA deliverables and documents.
- **Policies and procedures** – policies themselves or at least certain parts or attributes of policies may be considered as metadata. Procedures, for instance to back up a database or to perform other maintenance tasks to any IT system or application, can be viewed as a description or set of imperatives that need to be followed.
- **Processes** – this applies to business and technical processes alike. They are characterised through attributes and detailed specifications. Business processes, for instance, may also be linked to regulations that they need to comply with.
- **People** – this may sound a bit odd, but people (project managers, solution architects, business partners and also customers) are one of the best sources of metadata, and their knowledge about data still influences the execution of business processes.
- **Open data** – for example, the UK's Gov.uk and Data.gov.uk or the USA's data.gov and usopendata.org

All these forms of metadata need to be managed in some manner and can be classified in the following areas described below.

4.3   Metadata classification

4.3.1   Business metadata

Business metadata defines data used in the business in a way that spans all the systems that a business uses and possibly external data sets too. For example, the business term 'Party' might be used as a generic term for 'customer', 'patient', 'person', 'user' that is used in various systems as a technical metadata term for the data in those systems.

This can now be used to set a whole group of rules and definitions against the business metadata once. This should be adhered to across all the technical metadata terms and therefore the data within those systems should remain consistent. Examples of such rules are defining data quality metrics, whether a field is null or not, the data retention policy and so on.

In addition, the business metadata is used as the way in which data is presented to the end users through dashboards, using key performance indicators (KPIs) and other metrics, such as for financial planning, supply chain monitoring, personnel statistics and more.

One other very useful application for the business metadata is to create a business glossary for all the data which is the single reference point for all the data vocabulary used in the business. In theory, this means everyone can speak the same business language if the business glossary is complete and accurate (which has proven difficult for many organisations).

4.3.2   Technical metadata

Technical metadata goes hand in hand with business metadata, it defines the data sets and fields in the data sets as defined within each database used. For example, within a traditional relational database a schema-on-write approach would be developed with the technical metadata for each term defined up front – this should be driven from the business metadata described above. In more modern forms of data storage systems that use schema-on-read the data is still defined as a particular *thing* as in a key/value pair – within the database itself – but the modelling and use of the data is done when it is used rather than up front.

With these two approaches, the technical metadata encompasses all the data – internal and external (that the business may wish to exploit and have access to). Systems such as Master Data, Data Lakes, Data Marts and Cloud Object Storage will all have some form of technical metadata that lets developers and users understand and make use of the data when required.

But it doesn't stop here; as well as defining the data structures, in some manner technical metadata also can be used to define things like:

- Operational metadata – data associated with the running of the systems in use, for example, how many rows have been loaded to a table today, how many failures occurred? Logs form databases on performance, accesses made etc., in fact any operation on data can be of use and logged. This is sometimes referred to as the 'digital exhaust' or 'footprint' of a system (Dong et al., 2016; Veneberg et al., 2016).
- Deployment metadata – describe application components that have been used in an SOA, or probably a dockerised environment (in today's world). This metadata describes the use of the artefact or service, what its inputs are expected to be and what outputs will be generated. It forms a core component of any modern microservices architecture. This metadata is held in some form of (often separate) repository that developers can use to reuse services that have previously been created (Pillay et al., 2016).
- Report and dashboard metadata – metadata that is created from the reports and analytics developed for the business, this takes the form of information in reusable reports right through to services based on REST APIs that can be invoked through a simple get or post statement, once again promoting reuse of analytics in this case.
- Security metadata – used to control who can access the metadata created and can be thought of as a meta-metadata layer that gives authentication and authorisation controls for any given user of that metadata (Renners et al., 2015).

4.3.3   Information governance metadata

Information governance metadata deserves special attention as it lays out the governance requirements for the use and management of data, how it will be implemented and how it will be measured (Rasouli et al., 2016).

Specifically, these include:

- Policy, rule specifications, classifications, measures and metrics. These definitions define the requirements and expected results of the governance programme. The governance team maintains these definitions and then tracks how well different parts of the organisation are meeting the requirements. The classifications are linked to the technical metadata, business attributes and business objects to show where the governance actions need to be applied.
- Governance actions and processes – links to the implementation(s) of governance rules that detect certain conditions in the data, and take action to either correct an error or enforce a requirement.

Typically, these values slowly evolve as the governance programme expands its remit.

The physical data descriptions and business attributes are linked to the governance metadata via classification definitions. A classification definition is part of a classification scheme. Each classification scheme divides the data resources into course-grained groups according to a particular characteristic. So, for example, there may be classification schemes for confidentiality, integrity and retention. Here is an example classification scheme for confidentiality from an information governance definition. Confidentiality is used to classify the impact of disclosing information to unauthorised individuals.

- **Unclassified** – is information that is available to all and in the public domain probably. Open data is an example of unclassified data.
- **Internal use** – held and maintained within the boundaries of the organisation (note this doesn't mean the data has to be physically on-premises). This information is used to drive the operations of the organisation. It is used extensively within the business, can be shared with other organisations and has little impact if outside parties access the content.
- **Confidential** – based on a need-to-know model, these will be specific named users or possibly roles within an organisation. If data is lost or shared outside the group it could have limited impact on the organisation's brand, operations or finances.

  - **Business confidential** – differentiates the business from its competitors in some way and provides competitive advantage.
  - **Partner confidential** – relates to a partner organisation who expects the data is kept under control to the same level as its own business confidential classification.
  - **Personal information** – often known as PII (personally identifiable information). Could be employee or customer data for example and if breached may cause impact to that individual and by extension the company who has been expected to safeguard their data.
  - **Sensitive** – only for those who have need-to-know access. Can be very damaging if seen beyond this group.
  - **Sensitive personal** – again, information is about an individual. But here if the data is breached it can cause very long-lasting harm to that individual – data around a person's sexuality or health may be cases here.
  - **Sensitive financial** – financial information about the company such as predictions of future investments or performance are examples here.
  - **Sensitive operational** – the processes a company employs to do its business, which may differentiate them from the competition and be highly valuable or could be information around practices that are less than satisfactory around (say) employee rights and protection and be damaging if exposed.

- **Restricted** – the most sensitive of all. Data is restricted to a very small group of trusted people in the business. Disclosure of such information could be illegal and result in employees having lengthy jail sentences. Sources and all copies of data need to be accounted for and destroyed when no longer needed. There are three subtypes:
  - **Restricted financial** – details of the financial health of the organisation.
  - **Restricted operational** – details of the operational strategy, approaches and health of the organisation.
  - **Trade secret** – core ideas and intellectual property that underpin the business.

There is always a default classification that is assumed for data resources that are not explicitly classified. In this example, it is called **_Unclassified_**.

Classifications are either linked to the physical data definitions or the business attributes. The governance programme is built around them. Policies document the goals of the governance programme. These may be principles, regulatory obligations, standards or requirements delegated from other jurisdictions or governance domains (Peltier, 2016).

The way that policies are implemented is documented in governance rules (Jacob et al., 2017). These are documented in terms of the classifications – defining how data of a particular classification is to be managed in a particular circumstance.

A governance programme is only effective if:

1 It can be automated
2 It can be measured and validated

The automated actions are either functions called governance actions that can be deployed into the processing engines that process data, or workflows that coordinate the work of people and the processing engines.

Metrics that define the measurements to capture and the targets to achieve define how the governance programme is to be assessed. The measurement data may come directly from the governance actions and processes (e.g. how many times does an exception process execute) or data from other systems that reflect the goals defined in the policies (such as the number of customer complaints or the cost of correcting errors).

In general, the governance metadata is slowly changing. There are four main groups of activity:

- Establishing the core principles of the governance programme – led by the chief data officer (CDO) and their team, working with specialists on specific areas of compliance (such as legal teams and records management teams). They create the core policies, rules, metrics and classifications for the governance programme and create the initial breakdown of subject areas.
- Defining a subject area – for each subject area, the subject area owner works with subject matter experts and the CDO team to create definitions of the business objects, business attributes and the specialist governance rules, policies and classifications needed for the subject area. Classifications are also associated with the business objects and business attributes where the classification is always true for that type of data.
- Classifying data sources – owners of data sources are responsible for assigning the classifications to their data. This can be done directly by associating the classifications with the physical data descriptions, or via the semantic mapping of the physical data descriptions to the business attributes to pick up the classifications set up by the subject area owner.
- Monitoring a specific aspect of compliance – auditors and specialists in particular areas of compliance need to be able to review policies and rules associated with their area of expertise or responsibility and the level of exemptions and compliance that are being achieved. From this they may make changes to the rules of metrics, or take other actions to either broaden the scope of the governance rules, or tackle non-compliance, or investigate specific exemptions.

In addition to the governance metadata, the CDO team, subject area owners, data source owners, auditors and compliance specialists use the self-service capability of the platform to create the reports to monitor and measure compliance of the resources they are responsible for.

4.3.4   Combining metadata

All the metadata types can be linked to enable self-service users and the governance team. By doing this it provides a complete view of data both for data access and for governance. Figure 4.2 provides a simple example of all this metadata to illustrate how it can all be viewed to bring physical data definitions, business attributes and governance metadata together.

At the base of Figure 4.2 is an example of the data that is being described. Above it is some of the technical metadata from the physical data descriptions that is labelled 'structural metadata'. Structural metadata describes the way the data is organised (Hai et al., 2016). The mechanism for determining the structural metadata depends on the location of the data. For example:

- If the data is located in a database, then the structural metadata is the database schema and it can be extracted through a call to the database.

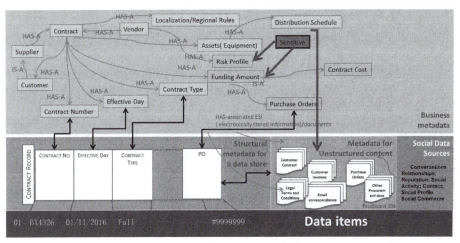

Figure 4.2   Example of a fragment of metadata describing contract data

- If the data is stored in a self-describing format such as XML or JSON format, the structural metadata can be extracted directly from the data.
- If the data is stored as a graph, the structural metadata describes the types of nodes, edges and any rules used to constrain the structure of the graph.
- If the data is in a well-defined format, such as a spreadsheet, then the structural metadata can be derived from the layout of the data.

The more planning that has gone into the definition of the schema or field descriptions for the data, the better the automatic extracted structural metadata can be. Some data has no structural information associated with it, and the mapping of a structure needs to be done through tooling to create the structural metadata. For example, Apache Hive supports the creation and mapping of relational structural metadata on arbitrary files (Bisoyi et al., 2017).

The structural metadata is important to explain how the data fields should be interpreted by technology. The business metadata provides the human view of how data should be interpreted and managed:

- The business attributes shown in Figure 4.2 are things like contract, vendor, supplier and customer. They are linked using phrases such as 'has a' and 'is a' relationships. They are the business objects for data held by the company in question and they link to the fields in the structural metadata.
- Contract number for example is part of the structural metadata. These are directly tied to the systems in use by the business. They are linked to the business objects and there could be several systems holding that data or similar that is linked back to the business object. They could also be referred to with different naming conventions – for example, the customer object may be linked to systems with structural metadata that refers to the customer as 'person', 'client', 'citizen', 'user' and so on (these are referred to as synonyms). Thus, the business metadata translates the technical implementation of the data store into a form that is more recognisable to the business.
- Finally, 'risk profile' and 'funding amount' are labelled 'sensitive'. The value 'sensitive' is a classification from the governance domain that indicates that this data and any underneath it must be treated as sensitive data and managed accordingly.

4.3.5   Information virtualisation metadata

This form of metadata describes the models that are used (logical and physical) to describe the data. 'Schema read' models were the de facto approach until around ten years ago, with modelling being a key requirement before relational databases were developed. They dictated the structure and physical deployment of the database. The rise of NoSQL or sche-maless databases has led to 'schema write' solutions where the database can have additional data elements added to it with little or no up-front modelling. This is useful when speed of change is necessary but does require the application developer to have an intimate knowl-edge of the database they are using to ensure data integrity is maintained appropriately.

4.3.6   Collaborative metadata

This form of metadata improves the ability of metadata to show a business user what type of data is available for their use.

● Collaboration metadata – enables the consumers of data sources to add notes and feedback on the quality and accuracy of both the metadata description and the data content itself. This enables the business to identify who has accessed what data, whether they felt it useful and any tags they may wish to apply. From these new groups that use the data in differing areas of the business, it may be possible to identify useful new communities created around that data.

4.3.7   Developing a metadata strategy

We have described a wide variety of metadata and sources for that metadata, so how do we make sense of all this? We know that we need to consider a solution that can encompass all forms of metadata, cloud-based and on site (legacy), that is composed of many forms and changing rapidly with the advent of external unstructured sources.

The proposal here is based around no vendor being able to come up with an all-encompassing solution and/or continue to build adaptors/connectors (APIs) that can consume all the forms of metadata produced by other vendors' tools. Open standards are required AND a highly flexible scalable solution, that can hold local repositories of meta-data where needed but can call other repositories easily when users need to extend their trawl for information to areas beyond their immediate systems.

This approach lends itself to a solution that is community driven, that is open source, such that everyone can adhere to community-driven adopted standards, using a very flexible engine to store metadata. Luckily, such an approach exists and is being driven from an Apache incubator project known as Atlas. (The Apache Software Foundation, or ASF, develops and manages more than 350 open source projects covering many technologies. The Atlas project resides within this framework.)

The following section describes the key components of the open source project that is Atlas.[3]

The elements of Figure 4.3 are described as follows. The core of the architecture is based on Titan, a graph database engine, that is a highly flexible NoSQL store. It enables relation-ships between different metadata elements to be described and where necessary easily extended as required. More on graph databases can be found in Appendix 2.

The core layer consists of:

● The type system: this forms the core of the architecture and is a model that allows users to define the metadata objects they manage. A 'Type' defines how a particular metadata object will be stored and accessed. It's a definition of all the things that make up the metadata object, and whether it's a superset for other types. So, for

---

3 For further information, see http://atlas.apache.org/Architecture.html

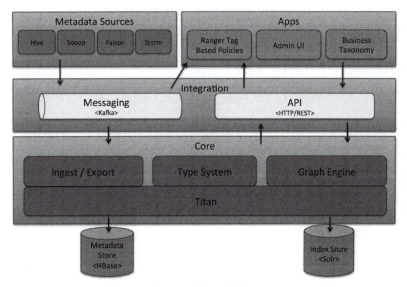

Figure 4.3   Apache Atlas Architecture – diagram of Apache (open source project)
Source: Copyright © Apache Foundation. Reproduced with permission.

example, a standard type already defined in Atlas is for a hive table (supported by Apache Hadoop) and it can consist of items such as name of the table the owner of the table, the create time, the columns in the hive table and so on. The entities of the type system are the actual entries, so in this case the name of the hive table could be 'customer', the owner of the table could be 'Fred' and so on.

The type defined can be seen as a guiding template for the information needed to define a metadata item:

- Ingest/Export: enables changes to metadata definitions to be consumed and changes made to be raised as events to allow other users of the metadata alerts as and when changes take place, enabling the business to react across the enterprise if a change is planned for.
- Graph engine: the way in which metadata is exposed and consumed by users and other systems is via a graph engine. Graph models are described elsewhere in this book (Appendix 2). It is used here to show the links between types and entities. The graph engine is also used to build indices within the graph to enable searches to be made more easily as scanning the entire graph to find entities or types would be extremely inefficient.
- Titan: Atlas uses the Titan open source graph databases as the way to instantiate the graph model. Titan can be thought of as the library in Atlas that enables anyone to identify where and what a metadata object is. The data is physically stored in Hbase for the metadata objects and Solr for the indices mentioned above. The integration layer consists of the API layer which uses a simple set of REST API calls that allows metadata types and entities to be written, read and updated, and the messaging layer that is based on Kafka (once again, open source software). Kafka is used to more loosely couple applications to the Atlas repository, for example, requests can be sent as a 'fire and forget' style which means the calling application can simply make a request and then move on to do other work and when a response is available be alerted to that and consume it at the most appropriate time.
- The metadata sources layer enables Atlas to support integration with many sources of metadata out of the box. Atlas supports some core open source data sources such as Hive and Sqoop but other more traditional sources (SQL Server, DB2, etc.) will be added over time. In fact, any source will be capable of being added if the vendor who owns the source or open community supporting the source is willing to write adap-

tors to integrate with the APIs and Kafka mentioned above. This is a critical point: the solution is not closed to anyone or wrapped with any proprietary code or licensing to prevent others from accessing the Titan metadata store. This forms the core of building an OPEN metadata store that enables metadata across the business and beyond to be pulled together and used as a single source of reference information about information assets. This means other metadata models can be ingested in real time or in batch mode in some cases and the metadata in Atlas shared with other metadata repositories if need be. This overcomes one of the huge stumbling blocks around maintaining and managing a consistent view of metadata within any organisation.

- The application layer consists of a variety of tools for driving governance within the enterprise, in particular the Admin UI which is web-based and allows the data steward to identify metadata, track changes to metadata and create new annotations to the metadata to clarify its purpose. Policies defined for the metadata can be added using the Apache Ranger tooling that enables a comprehensive security model to be built to support how the metadata can be accessed and used.
- A business metadata layer can be built that sits over the technical metadata defined and created in Atlas. An interface is available in Atlas that allows a simple business metadata hierarchy to be created and associates this with the various entities Atlas manages. This forms a powerful link from the business understanding of things to the technical definition of those 'things'.

The Apache Atlas incubator project holds great promise to bring an end to disparate sets of incomplete, non-standard metadata repositories that cannot be easily integrated. With a model as described above the opportunity arises to build a metadata framework that is complete, ubiquitous and easily consumed by all those that need to, whether they are machines or end users.

4.3.8 Bringing it all together

All the metadata formats and classification may leave the reader feeling a bit bewildered. The use of a simple graph model, as shown in Figure 4.4, demonstrates how the differing metadata types are related to one another at a macro level which can act as a useful 'sounding board' for discussion. Note that this work is not sacrosanct and is open to discussion, criticism and feedback. However, it is the authors' best guess on how metadata should be developed going forward and the reasoning behind that thinking.

This chapter has described the differing forms of metadata required to build a comprehensive 'library' around your data assets. Without metadata it is very difficult to enable governance and any form of self-service analytics that uses the metadata to expose data to a user who is entitled to access. Finally, metadata in a hybrid cloud become even more critical to control your assets when distributed over dedicated, private and public cloud instances.

4.4 Conclusion

The rise in data has simply exacerbated our ability to truly understand what we are storing in ever greater volumes and granularity. Metadata is the approach that describes our data, whether it be in motion or at rest. Without it data has no real meaningful context, and without context it is hard to draw conclusions from observing or analysing that data.

The challenge of good metadata management and governance of the data based around the metadata is one of the overriding challenges to information architects now, and for the medium term. New techniques that employ tooling, such as graph engines, will slowly start to emerge and help the situation, but these systems themselves will grow and need to be managed with rigour for them to remain useful over time.

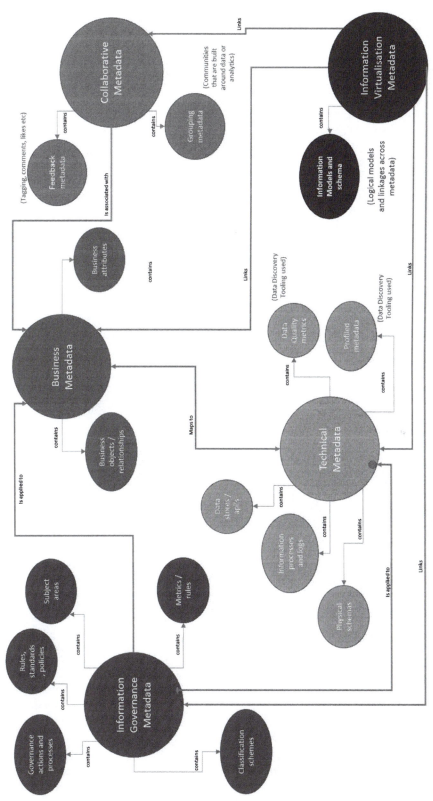

Figure 4.4   Simple graph model showing metadata types and linkage

This chapter has looked at different styles of metadata and how they relate to each other to form a comprehensive view of all data assets that a company uses, albeit from internal or external sources. It has also touched upon some open source tooling (Apache Atlas) that may be the best approach to dealing with the problem of data classification with metadata for the future.

 Study area

To test your understanding of the chapter please attempt to answer these questions, either by debating them in the class with colleagues or by writing them down to help formulate your answers.

Questions:

1 Can you describe the various forms of metadata?
2 Where might metadata be derived from?
3 Can you suggest some issues with gathering metadata – what can be automated? Think about the different database systems, terms used to define data, processes that data is subjected to and the consistency between them all.
4 How challenging is it to use the metadata practically to drive access to applications and systems? Think about how governance/access/security are applied and what role metadata can play.
5 Can metadata go stale? If so, what are the practical requirements to maintain up-to-date metadata and history of change?

Further reading:

- U.S. Geological Survey metadata
  - U.S. Department of the Interior. (2017). *Why do we need metadata*? [Online.] https://www2.usgs.gov/datamanagement/describe/metadata.php
- Data management for data stewards
  - Chatfield, T. and Selbach, R. (2011). *Data management for data stewards*. Data Management Training Workshop. Bureau of Land Management (BLM), Cooperative Institute for Climate and Satellites, North Carolina, North Carolina State University and NOAA's National Centers for Environmental Information.
- Metadata
  - Pomerantz, J. (2015). *Metadata*. Cambridge, MA: MIT Press.
- Metadata for digital collections – A how-to-do-it manual
  - Miller, S.J. (2011). *Metadata for digital collections: A how-to-do-it manual*. New York: Neal-Schuman Publishers.

References

Bisoyi, S.S., Mishra, P. and Mishra, S.N. (2017). Relational query optimization technique using space efficient file formats of Hadoop for the big data warehouse system. *Indian Journal of Science and Technology*, 8(1), pp. 2–3.

Davison, S., Coles, B., Doiel, R.S., Keswick, T. and Morrell, T.E. (2017). Building an open platform across diverse content and technologies. In: *Open Repositories 2017*, June 27–30, Brisbane, Australia.

Dong, R., Su, F., Yang, S., Xu, L., Cheng, X. and Chen, W. (2016). Design and application on metadata management for information supply chain. In *2016: 16th International Symposium on Communications and Information Technologies (ISCIT)*, (pp. 393–396). IEEE.

Greenberg, J. and Klas, W. (2016). Metadata for semantic and social applications. Paper presented at DC-2008: *Proceedings of the 8th International Conference on Dublin Core and Metadata Applications.* 22–26 September 2008, University of Göttingen, Germany.

Hai, R., Geisler, S. and Quix, C. (2016). Constance: An intelligent data lake system. In: *Proceedings of the 2016 International Conference on Management of Data* (pp. 2097–2100). ACM.

Haynes, D. (2004). *Metadata for Information Management and Retrieval* (Vol. 1). London: Facet Publishing.

Jacob, N.M., Yusuf, M. and Mbinya, C.M. (2017). Role of metadata in county governance performance: A case of county governments in Kenya. *International Journal of Management Science & Technology Information,* 24, pp. 35–40.

Kolaitis, P.G. (2005). Schema mappings, data exchange, and metadata management. In: *Proceedings of the Twenty-Fourth ACM SIGMOD-SIGACT-SIGART Symposium on Principles of Database Systems* (pp. 61–75). ACM.

Pal, J.K. (2016). Resolving the confusion over metadata-creation in digital archives. *Annals of Library and Information Studies (ALIS),* 63(2), pp.110–116.

Park, J.R., & Tosaka, Y. (2010) Metadata creation practices in digital repositories and collections: Schemata, selection criteria, and interoperability. Information Technology and Libraries, 293, pp.104–113.

Pei, Z., Chen, J., Jiang, M., Jiang, J., Wang, Q., Song, Y. and Zhao, M. (2017). Researchment of metadata-driven based informatization strategy of parameter' life cycle management. In: *2017 2nd Asia-Pacific Conference on Intelligent Robot Systems (ACIRS),* (pp. 109–113). IEEE.

Pillay, S., Sumin, A., Burnside, P.L. and Bank Of America Corporation. (2016). Build deployment automation for information technology management. U.S. Patent 9,323,513.

Rasouli, M.R., Trienekens, J.J., Kusters, R.J. and Grefen, P.W. (2016). Information governance requirements in dynamic business networking. *Industrial Management & Data Systems,* 116(7), pp. 1356–1379.

Renners, L., Rossow, T. and Steuerwald, R. (2016). Integrated visualization of network security metadata from heterogeneous data sources. In: *Graphical Models for Security: Second International Workshop, GraMSec 2015, Verona, Italy, July 13, 2015, Revised Selected Papers* (Vol. 9390, p. 18). New York and London: Springer.

Thomas R. Peltier. 2001. Information Security Policies, Procedures, and Standards: Guidelines for Effective Information Security Management. CRC Press, Inc., Boca Raton, FL, USA.

Ueda, M., Takata, N., Morishita, Y. and Nakajima, S. (2016). Utilizing various user moods for automatic recipe-metadata generation. In: *International MultiConference of Engineers and Computer Scientists* (pp. 115–129). Singapore: Springer.

Vaduva, A. and Dittrich, K.R. (2001). Metadata management for data warehousing: between vision and reality. In: *2001 International Symposium on Database Engineering and Applications* (pp. 129–135). IEEE.

Veneberg, R.K.M., Iacob, M.E., van Sinderen, M.J. and Bodenstaff, L. (2016). Relating business intelligence and enterprise architecture – A method for combining operational data with architectural metadata. *International Journal of Cooperative Information Systems,* 25(02), p. 1650007.

Verbitskiy, Y. and Yeoh, W. (2016). An end-user metadata model on object and element levels for business intelligence users. *International Journal of Business Intelligence Research* (IJBIR), 7(2), pp. 50–58.

Verma, C., Hart, M., Bhatkar, S., Parker-Wood, A. and Dey, S. (2016). Improving scalability of personalized recommendation systems for enterprise knowledge workers. *IEEE Access,* 4, pp. 204–215.

Zhu, W.D., Alon, T., Arkus, G., Duran, R., Haber, M., Liebke, R., Morreale Jr, F., Roth, I. and Sumano, A. (2011). *Metadata Management with IBM InfoSphere Information Server.* IBM Redbooks.

GOVERNANCE: THE HARDEST PART?

5.1 Introduction

Since the days of the Enterprise Data Warehouse (EDW), corporations have been struggling with the governance of data (Rahman, 2016). Ensuring data is trusted, secure, of the right quality, understood, correctly owned and managed, and disposed of in an acceptable manner has always been challenging. In the past, the vast majority of data was under the direct control of the company using that data. It was also generally limited to structured data surrounding Lines of Business (LoBs) such as HR, Finance, Supply Chain and so forth.

The rise of big data has created additional problems for governance in organisations (Bowen et al., 2017). The primary issue is that large amounts of cloud-based data are not controllable by organisations that wish to use it. For example, consider a company that wishes to use weather data, crime stats, pollution data, demographic data and bus routes. All this data can add value to some internal process or insight into what your customer is doing or desires. However, all this data is owned and published by third parties who may have differing standards for all the governance-related areas we have mentioned so far. It's worth noting that the cost of big data and information-related activities continues to grow. Estimates for data analytics spending is as high as approx. $50 billion by 2019 and with analytics up to $190 billion(!), so being able to govern and control such programmes is certainly important (Olavsrud, 2015, 2016).

At the moment, information governance retains its complexity and is extended to all forms of data within the umbrella of the company using it. A way must be found to understand how to manage all this data and ensure it is having a positive role to play rather than being simply data stored on disk (or some medium) with no value and indeed a cost associated with retaining it for little useful purpose. This chapter goes on to explore what data governance is and how organisations are tackling the big issues.

5.2 What is information governance?

Information governance sits alongside other areas of governance and control, namely:

- Corporate governance – how an entire company is managed and controlled, covering all its stakeholders from shareholders to management, customers, suppliers and so forth.
- IT governance – managing infrastructure and software, rather than the information that resides on these platforms.
- Risk management – identifying and minimising or eliminating risk is a part of any organisation's goal. Often, financial risk is a key concern, but retention of key staff, the relationship with competitors and suppliers, and the internal ability of the organisation to meet the strategy planned for all need to be considered (Peppard and Ward, 2016).

- Information governance – is about the control of the information passing through the organisation. It relies on being able to extract meaningful value from all the data within the organisation while ensuring the risk of sharing, distributing and transforming that data does not impact the business during its operations (Soma et al., 2016). Without information governance the entire process of information discovery and analysis will be sub optimal. External regulatory and compliance requirements are often key drivers for information governance. One key point to note here is that being able to effectively govern data and information means understanding what you have, where it is in the organisation, who owns it and at what stage in its life it resides there. This is aided by having a metadata strategy that deals with your data:

  o Effectively – metadata is used to enable those who need to understand and access it the means to do so in as simple as possible a manner.
  o Efficiently – the capture and maintenance of metadata is automated as much as possible.
  o Economically – metadata is only held when it is needed. Data of low value with no regulatory or compliance issues should be either disposed of or held in the cheapest possible manner for ad hoc use only.

The journey to become an organisation that effectively leverages all its information and the practices to achieve information management maturity and efficiencies requires connecting the people, processes and information within an organisation. The need to share information in a controlled, managed manner is vital to an organisation.

5.3 Issues that may exist in a business with poor governance

Here are some potential issues that may exist in an organisation that exhibits signs of poor information governance:

- Inability to access information quickly enough – a sign of issues with poor governance is the inability to react to changing demand. This can take multiple forms – from infrastructure issues to size of solution (scaling up OR down – a fundamental reason where people have shifted some workloads to the cloud), through to access to new data sets in a timely manner.
- Inability to recognise individual customers across platforms to produce a consolidated profile and understand and act on appropriate up-sell/cross-sell opportunities; as well as an inability to determine profitability, understand and manage risk exposure. This can be summarised as managing your master data with intense focus!
- No common framework to address integration/communication needs across organisation boundaries.
- Lack of understanding of financial exposures.
- Profitability not meaningful, clearly defined or understood – especially across differing business units.
- Information strategy and data management initiatives not linked to business priorities and needs. Results in initiatives that are not effective only serve one area of the business, possibly to the detriment of others – large organisations often suffer from this problem.
- Inconsistent measurement/data definition – a data quality problem.
- Too many reports/too little meaning – proliferation of similar reports all developed to differing standards, confusing as reports are circulated or move upwards through the organisation. There is a lack of a 'single version of the truth' supporting consolidated external and internal reporting.

- Many stand-alone, uncoordinated or redundant data silos – when working on the cloud with multiple teams building out multiple (possibly overlapping solutions) it can be even harder to understand which data is valid, which data is still being used or should be deleted. This has real, financial impact if those data sets grow in size and numbers over time and are all on (say) a public or private cloud, as continual billing will be in place for the resources used. Good governance is essential to control this 'spread'.
- Confusion from lack of common language around needs, solutions and approaches.
- Lack of confidence in realising benefits from business-technology investments.
- Inability to recognise and manage cross-initiative dependencies.
- Not effective leverage skills and resources across analytic initiatives, skills are siloed within departments, good governance and collaboration around understanding who is using what data can help to break down these barriers and create a more 'data driven' organisation.
- No centre of competency to execute/support information governance – especially challenging when dealing with hybrid cloud models where part/all of a solution may be managed by a third party.

5.4   Who is involved in information governance?

People are a key component to a successful information governance programme. They make decisions about the way information is classified, handled and used. Many organisations are concerned about information governance and are appointing Chief Data Officers (CDOs) to lead their information governance programme (Zhang et al., 2017). The CDO is responsible for setting up and running the information governance programme and is accountable for its results. CDOs are typically executives operating close to the board. They work with other business leaders to understand what type of information their teams use and its associated requirements. These requirements are then reflected in the policies, rules and classifications of the information governance programme – and the subsequent use of technology and procedures to implement them. The CDO seeks to establish a number of new roles in the organisation, which are typically given to existing staff.

- **Information owners** – an individual or a team is identified as the owner for each collection of information. This owner is accountable for the correct classification of the information and ensuring that all uses for that information comply with this classification. Information owners are at all levels in the organisation. Individuals are owners for their personal files. A manager may be the owner of team-level information. However, when it comes to the owner of business critical information, such as the customer master data system, then this is typically a senior manager or executive who delegates their ownership responsibilities to people in their organisation.
- **Information curators** – maintain the descriptive information (metadata) about an information collection to make it easier for others to find and reuse the information. An information owner may delegate the responsibility for correctly classifying an information collection to an information curator, however, the owner still has the accountability. Auditing processes verify that the curators (and owners) are classifying their information correctly since this is key to correct information governance actions.
- **Information stewards** – this role has the primary task of correcting errors in information. The information quality processes in the information governance programme typically detect these errors and provide notifications that are fed into a triage process that identifies which errors should be fixed by the information steward. The information stewards' work is heavily audited whenever they are working with information that controls or records the activity of the business since this is an opportunity to commit fraud.

In addition, we also have those who will exploit the information being managed by several roles within any organisation:

- **LOB data analyst** – this role has developed out of that once known as a 'Business Intelligence' (BI) practitioner. It calls for LOB personnel who are comfortable with a range of tooling that allows them to easily build reports and run queries from a variety of back-end engines. The key thing here is that the users have no knowledge (or need to know) what those engines are. The information is abstracted away by a 'virtual' layer that allows users to select information based on common terms they are already familiar with without needing to understand the intricacies of what goes on in the background. LOB data analysts use this virtual layer to spend their time analysing data for the business to exploit covering the 'here and now' or simple predictive analytics, for example, trends in sales, forecast of out of stocks in retail or reports to identify financial trends around mortgage holdings within a bank. So, they are able to look at large chunks of data and understand trends, and then communicate those trends to the company.
- **Data scientist** – a relatively new role that has grown from traditional statisticians, mathematicians and operational research analysts. These people use slices of the data from across the organisation (and external to the organisation) to look for new insights around how the company should move forward in the markets it operates or any new gaps the analysis might find. The data they use can be anything from traditional, legacy data sources to unstructured external data sources such as tweets, weather data, social media and sensor-based information. They understand mining and modelling techniques such as correlations, associations, clustering, regression and data mining. They use open source technologies such as R, Hadoop, Apache Spark, alongside Python and/or Scala to achieve their goals. They are deeply versed in creating and deploying large-scale, data-driven systems. The data scientist experiments with all these rich and diverse data sets to build models that can unlock new insights into how things operate and can be used in new applications to drive the organisation forward in some way (increase sales, reduce costs, offer new services/information to citizens etc.). They share their models with the application developer who deploys the new application using the model.
- **Application developer** – translates software requirements into workable programming code and maintains and develops programmes for use in business. Generally, application developers will specialise in a particular area, such as mobile phone applications, accounting software, Office suites or graphics software, and will have in-depth knowledge of at least one computer language, such as Java, or C++. Applications, or 'apps', can be written for a particular system, such as Windows or Android, or across numerous platforms, including computers and mobile devices. Over the years, application developers have had to rapidly adapt from building large monolithic applications that stood within the firewall of a company to using application programming interfaces (APIs), microservices and cloud-based approaches to deploying their solutions.[1] Their skills are constantly being tested as new ways of developing code are brought to the market, especially the open source movement. Job titles and specific duties may vary between organisations, but the role usually involves writing specifications and designing, building, testing, implementing and (sometimes) supporting applications, where this is much more likely to happen with microservice style models. They often work as part of a team with other IT professionals, such as software engineers and systems analysts, and write programs according to their specifications.

---

1. http://microservices.io/patterns/microservices.html

- **Data engineer** – these people (as their name suggests) are the ones who manage the work associated with moving the data assets around the company. Their role is a critical one – if data is not available at the right time, in the right format, for the right people, then the above roles cannot complete their tasks satisfactorily. The data engineer designs and develops code/scripts alongside building a 'supply chain' of data that passes through the organisation that uses structured and unstructured data from multiple sources. They actively engage in requirement workshops to understand the data needs of the business. They then use their skills to model the end state for any data (where applicable) and build the data pipelines to move and manage data around the organisation. They will almost certainly have had exposure to Relational Database Management Systems (RDBMSs) as well as the newer NoSQL databases (e.g. column-driven or key-value pairs) and content management and record management solutions. In today's world they will almost certainly have experience of Hadoop as a landing area for data and as an analytics platform and understand the implications of developing different data sets across multiple environments, that is on-premises (dedicated), public and private cloud.

5.5 What actually needs to be governed: dimensions for information governance

Information governance can be broken down into the nine key dimensions shown in Figure 5.1.

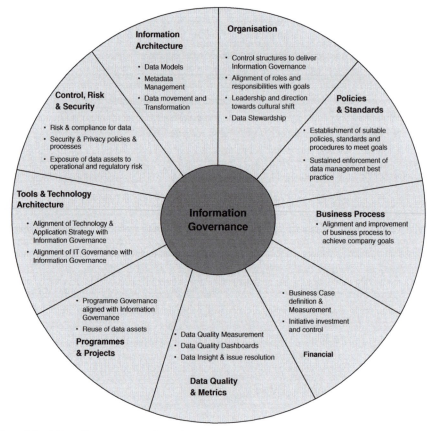

Figure 5.1   Information governance dimensions

We'll consider how each topic is impacted by the rise of cloud-based platforms and the complexities it raises when managing the legacy with the new data sets constantly being consumed by businesses today.

5.5.1   Organisation

Organisation provides alignment of the information governance requirements with business and technology strategies, and enables cultural movement towards improving data management and quality. It provides the foundations for data stewardship and the roles and responsibilities we have regarding the use of data.

5.5.1.1   *Types of issue addressed*

- There are 'boundary' issues across business areas; data is sometimes overwritten and this sometimes causes failure in operational processes.
- Lack of trust across business areas because one business unit does not use the same terms (business glossary) as another, leading to confusion in reporting and management of data which in turn leads to suboptimal decisions being made.
- There is no common forum for resolving data issues, so each business unit goes and creates its own data copies and structures to meet their specific business area objectives. Data quality often gets worse over time.

5.5.1.2   *Objectives of organisation in information governance*

- Establish a common information governance forum for all business areas where data issues are discussed and acted upon in a way that creates, not destroys, business value (Lombardi et al., 2016).
- Establish data stewardship and define the roles and responsibilities needed for better information governance.
- Establish organisation structures in business areas that will cooperate and act upon information governance and stewardship objectives, for example, change management, process owners, data owners.
- Enable mechanisms to incorporate cultural shift towards better information governance and identify the roadmap to achieve its delivery.

A better information governance organisation allows us to:

- Implement a model of data stewardship for our core data assets, where the roles and responsibilities of business and technologies areas are clearly understood and correctly acted upon (Wilkinson et al., 2016).
- Have a forum where the impact of data change is understood by all data stakeholders across the enterprise.
- Become more mature in the way the organisation operates, building a much more data-centric approach, improving data quality over time and becoming a better company for employees to work within and customers to do business with.

Several different models can be built to support governance. These are described below, but essentially any company undertaking a governance programme needs to understand how it wishes to control the influx of new ideas regarding data usage, the management of the data to be used and the responsibilities and accountabilities attributed to the key roles chosen to take the business forward.

How much control is retained centrally, versus a more distributed model, must be understood and the most appropriate model for any company put in place. It is possible to have

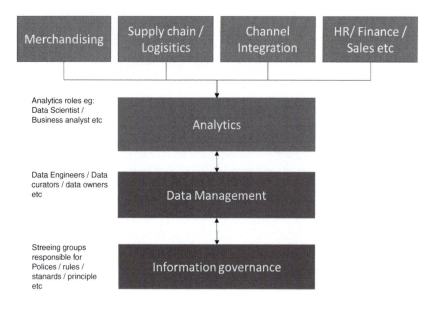

Figure 5.2   Centralised governance model

more than one model functioning across an organisation at geo or functional level – but all the differing structures must work in harmony to achieve the global initiatives that are required to move the company's information strategy forward. There are three fundamental models that could be adopted. These are described below.

- Centralised (Classic)
  This model centralises all key governance functions and data/information.

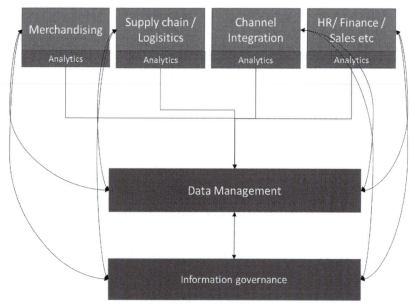

Figure 5.3   Hybrid governance model

○ Pros – highly efficient in resource quantity and process.
○ Cons – BUT possibly not as invested in the business, not really embedded in the organisation. There may be variability in responsiveness for each business unit due to pooled
resources and prioritisation.

● Hybrid

With the Hybrid model (Figure 5.3) we still centralise all the key governance functions –
primary governance and project management functions. Data and info management
remain centralised BUT analytics teams are close to business so become more responsive,
however, some central learnings may 'slip the net' if analytics teams do not coordinate well
with data management and information governance groups.

● Federated

Each business area is now supported by its own local teams, as shown in Figure 5.4. This
allows for rapid decision making BUT global standards that are required for important
operations may be missed and learnings across groups may be lost.

5.5.2   Policies and standards

Policies and standards support the formal adoption and enforcement of information
governance best practice in a company (Borgman et al., 2016). They provide the framework
for ongoing improvement of data management, enabling business operations to make data
quality and cultural improvement part of their DNA.

5.5.2.1   *Types of issue addressed*

● There are gaps in our data policies, rules and standards that allow the business to deploy
data sets in non-standardised ways, causing data issues that destroy business value.
● The way that the business implements policies, rules and standards is divergent to the
business data needs of the company.
● The inconsistent way that policies, rules and standards are implemented makes it harder
and more expensive for the company to meet regulatory and compliance requirements.

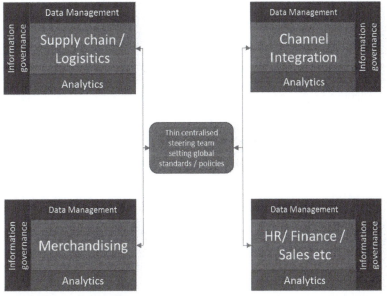

Figure 5.4   Federated governance model

5.5.2.2 *Objectives of policies and standards in information governance*

- To establish a consistent and structured policies and standards management framework for information governance that speaks to the business objectives (Cronemberger et al., 2017).
- To use agreed and consistent policies and standards to drive through best practice for data throughout business areas.
- To identify and address gaps in the organisation where policies and standards are either missing or applied incorrectly, that are destroying the business value of that data.
- To establish a process for ongoing improvement that incorporates the experience of implementing policies and standards back into best practice regimes.

Information governance policies and standards enable us to:

- Implement a model of data-related best practice throughout the business in a consistent and measurable manner.
- Understand where and why accepted data policies and standards are not being followed and invoke the authority to either enforce compliance or refine the policies and standards.
- Make business data improvement 'business as usual' and enable the business to learn to be a better, more customer-centric organisation.

5.5.3   Business process

Governance of business processes enables business areas to effectively manage and control the impact of data change. Risk to business operations and services resulting from data improvement projects can be better and more consistently managed.

5.5.3.1 *Types of issue addressed*

- Need to implement a data improvement project but find it difficult to really understand the risk of change.
- Changes to a business definition core rule are agreed but the business doesn't understand where and how the rule/definition is used across the business areas.
- The business finds it difficult to determine the cost change to business data across several areas.
- Regulatory and compliance change has been received and there is a need to quickly understand who is affected, how they are affected and which business operations are impacted.

5.5.3.2 *Objectives of business process in information governance*

- To establish a consistent framework for managing the impact of change across business processes.
- To apply a consistent set of processes to manage business data change within and across business areas.
- To create the correct framework for engagement between business areas and information governance data stewards.
- To measure the business benefits of data change across business processes and review it against the investment plan.

Business process management within the information governance framework enables us to:

- Understand and manage the way that data change is implemented in the business areas and the true impact to the business operations processes.
- Assess the cost and effort of data change prior to implementing any change, reducing the risk of business failures.
- Respond to regulatory and compliance requests in a faster and less effort-intensive manner, making for a more agile organisation that has its risks under control.

5.5.4   Financial

The financial component of information governance allows us to define the business case for data initiatives and the results of their implementation against the business case. It makes those initiating data change programmes become more accountable for cost and results to their business leaders.

5.5.4.1   *Types of issues addressed*

- Want to implement a data improvement project but need to understand how to present it to the Steering Committee so that funding is achieved and its value is clear.
- Want to use a consistent way of understanding funding and investment proposals for data programmes.
- Want to understand and measure the business value of data improvement programmes against the funding they received and the benefits promised.

5.5.4.2   *Objectives of financial process in information governance*

- To establish a framework for measuring and reporting the costs and benefits expected for a data change programme against the actuals delivered.
- To establish and agree the data change and investment model that data changes will be measured against.
- To define roles, responsibilities and mechanisms needed for the information governance framework to measure the value of implementing data change programmes.

The financial component within the information governance framework enables us to:

- Define a clear business case for data change initiatives and measure the delivery of benefits against the investment they received.
- Allow transparency and accountability of the investment decisions made and enables senior management to understand where more funding is (or isn't) appropriate.
- Enable the business to become more mature in the ways it invests and manages data change programmes.

5.5.5   Data quality/data life cycle management and metrics

Data quality and data life cycle governance enables data initiatives to be deployed with sustained, long-term benefits rather than simply short-term gains. It enables the business to collectively understand what is meant by 'good' data and therefore accurately measure how data programmes are improving data quality (Vaziri et al., 2017). Having good data also means having relevant timely data easily accessible and older data either archived in an appropriate manner or disposed of correctly.

5.5.5.1   *Types of issue addressed*

- There is recognition that the business must improve data quality but how can this desire be delivered and measured to ensure that it is being delivered consistently?
- Don't trust data from reports/dashboards/analytics – in general, the business cannot rely on the definitions and quality of data that are being passed to it.
- Projects are encountering data issues due to poor data in systems. How can risk be mitigated around programmes and projects and help to reduce programme cost?
- How to monitor, control and improve data quality for key customer data items (master data) and target business operation processes when it's not known which ones are broken.
- Removal of old/stale/non-valued data in a 'defensive' manner – that is being able to describe why the data was disposed of to support the utility or value of that data AND ensure regulatory obligations are met, such as the Federal Rules of Civil Procedure (FRCP), which were enacted as long ago as 2006.

5.5.5.2   *Objectives of data quality/data life cycle and metrics in information governance*

- To establish and agree across business areas a consistent framework for data quality by defining common criteria for measurement of data quality.
- To define the technology processes that demonstrate the impact of data improvement initiatives on the underlying data quality in systems.
- To identify where data quality issues exist within key data and engage with business process information governance to understand where and how business processes cause data issues.
- Maintain most appropriate data in enterprise without enduring the burden of cost of maintaining non-relevant data.

Data quality governance enables us to:

- Define a clear foundation for understanding what is meant by 'good' or 'bad' data quality; it allows us to have a common grammar for understanding and discussing data quality.
- Allows us to understand where data is 'broken' and together with business process governance, allows us to understand which process causes data quality issues.
- Enables us to be more strategic in the way we address data issues, addressing the root causes rather than just the effects.
- Keeps data growth controlled in an auditable manner.

5.5.6   Programmes and projects

Information governance across programmes and projects allows data initiatives to be deployed at a lower cost and lower risk. Data and process assets are reused wherever possible and methods, practices, processes and tools are applied consistently and effectively throughout the information and project life cycle.

5.5.6.1   *Types of issue addressed*

- Similar projects in other areas are known to have been completed in the past but it's impossible to identify the inventory of data assets that were produced, let alone know if they are reusable.

- Late to identify that data issues exist in source systems and databases and other repositories.
- The cost of programmes is too high; there is a need to understand what must be new spend and what can be reused.

5.5.6.2 *Objectives of information governance for programmes and projects*

- To establish an inventory of data-related methods, processes, tools and code that can be reapplied to other projects.
- To establish a common approach to define and deliver data programmes projects that can reduce the risk and project cost for the business.
- To identify common best practices for programmes and projects and assess how these are being adopted and adapted. Create a forum for tangible and intangible improvement for data-centric programmes.

Programme and project governance enables us to:

- Understand and reuse assets such as methods, processes and code in other related data initiatives, reducing the overall cost of our programme and project deliveries.
- Provides a common foundation and forum for a better managed information life cycle, with more control and measurable value points.
- Improve the level of maturity regarding how it manages its information assets within an organisation.

5.5.7 Tools and technology architecture

This dimension could be seen as a little controversial – why does it appear in the information governance dimensions at all? Well, technology governance ensures that the right people in the technology organisation have a structured forum to ensure technology delivery meets business needs. So it is important that the information governance functions must align with technology and application strategy and understand the impacts upon information governance and vice versa. The governance boards that manage these areas MUST align to allow a joined-up, holistic technology and information landscape that supports business objectives.

5.5.7.1 *Types of issue addressed*

- Does the existing technology governance we have in place speak to the company's business strategy and how can we constantly improve?
- Can we confirm that information governance, application strategy and technology strategy frameworks are aligned with business objectives through a common forum?
- Are all the key stakeholder areas involved and aligned so that they benefit from technology improvement?

5.5.7.2 *Objectives of technology governance*

- To review any ongoing improvement of the technology organisation, methods, tools and processes to deliver true business value.
- To establish a common forum to ensure full alignment of data strategy, application strategy and technology strategy with the business strategy and roadmap.

- To identify common best practices for technology governance and assess these against their usage in practice.

Technology governance enables us to:

- Understand how best to deliver business value through alignment of technology, data and application strategies and best practice.
- Provide a common foundation and forum for the governance bodies for technology, data and applications to improve the way value is delivered to business areas.

5.5.8　Control, risk and security

Information governance requires that policies, processes and technologies are in place to manage the control, security and risk associated with data management. This requires the preservation of the integrity, confidentiality and availability of data. This includes ensuring that not only the data itself is considered but also the processes are in place to make sure individuals only access the data that they are authorised to do so. This generally takes three layers of consideration:

- The network and infrastructure are hardened against attack from outside parties using approaches such as firewalls, secure mechanisms for moving data around the enterprise and so forth.
- Authentication and authorisation are managed rigorously with file permissions, access control lists, password control and authentication models such as Lightweight Directory Access Protocol (LDAP) are adhered to.
- Content protection through anonymisation and masking (obfuscation) of data, only allowing valid data to be viewed by those who are authorised to do so.

The control, security, risk and compliance framework must establish that regulatory and compliance requirements are fully met for data management in these areas.

5.5.8.1　*Types of issue addressed*

- Can we ensure and attest that all our data improvement initiatives are compliant with regulatory needs, for example, Sarbanes-Oxley Act[2], Basel III[3], BCBS 239[4] (are all banking requirements) and EU General Data Protection Regulation (GDPR)?[5]
- Where are our critical areas of risk for data and how are we managing them?
- How are our audit findings being addressed through the broader information governance and management programme?
- Which control, security, risk policies and standards are impacted by the new information governance initiatives? How will these change?

5.5.8.2　*Objectives of technology governance*

- To review existing policies, processes and technologies in place for control, security and risk and identify how these are to be changed.

2 http://www.soxlaw.com/
3 http://www.basel-iii-accord.com/
4 http://www.bis.org/publ/bcbs189.pdf, http://www.bis.org/publ/bcbs188.pdf
5http://www.itgovernance.co.uk/data-protection-dpa-and-eu-data-protection-regulation.aspx

- To establish a clear methodology for managing changes to the existing control and risk environment and assess the business impact of change.
- To identify an ongoing process for measuring the impact on control, security and risk as a result of data improvement initiatives and information governance.

Better information governance implications for control, security and risk are:

- Ensuring that any regulatory and compliance landscape is not damaged by data improvement programmes.
- Current policies and processes for data management may change; there is always a need to understand the impact and risk mitigate where necessary.
- Give an opportunity for reviewing and addressing outstanding audit actions and move towards a more mature organisation with fewer audit actions in the future.

5.5.9 Information architecture

Governance of information architecture enables business information to be utilised consistently within and across business areas. It drives the definition of business hierarchies/glossary and definitions to be more standardised so that the numbers across any analytics, whether simple reporting or complex models, mean the same thing in one part of the business as they do in another (Musiani et al., 2017).

5.5.9.1 *Types of issue addressed*

- Don't have a common definition of 'active customer', for example, it varies across business functions causing confusion when marketing, selling and simply understanding the customer wants and needs.
- Can't easily reuse similar work other projects have completed because their data structures differ.
- Spend too much time reconciling the myriad ways in which analytics can be delivered across the enterprise because the numbers mean different things.
- It is harder to plan rationalisation programmes and to incorporate new data from mergers and acquisitions because there is no common view of what the data should represent.

5.5.9.2 *Objectives of information architecture governance*

- To establish a common business glossary of data meaning and business data rules.
- To gain agreement across business areas and functions for use of common business glossary and implement its use.
- To establish common business data models, standards and reporting hierarchies.
- To establish a programme for reducing the cost of data management to business and measure its implementation against plan

Better information architecture governance allows us to:

- Increase the level of reuse of data assets and therefore reduce cost.
- Reduce the complexity of the information landscape and spend more time on improving business operations and less time reconciling the data and debating the figures.

5.6   Hybrid cloud solutions and impact on information governance

Data can be found, processed and managed on the cloud without investing in any local hardware. Large organisations with mature on-premises computing infrastructures are looking to Hadoop platforms to help them benefit from the vast array of structured and unstructured data from cloud-based sources. Organisations have feet in both cloud and on-premises worlds (Frost, 2017). In fact, one could easily argue that we already live in a 'hybrid' world.

A simple example of how hybrid cloud solutions simply 'leak' into organisations (and then need good information governance) could go something like this: a chief marketing officer (CMO) has a campaign based on previous sales history and likely propensity to buy a new product line based on those sales. All this data can be extracted from EPOS systems to get the historical data sets required and create some statistical models based on clustering data into likely product 'regions' or 'styles'. The IT department often has this data available or it can be made available.

As soon as the new product line is launched they want to identify customer sentiment to see if things are moving as hoped. For this they need external (Facebook, Twitter, blogs, news feeds etc.) data, and pull from these unstructured data sets key terms to describe and understand sentiment. This data is NOT under the control of the IT department and brings new challenges regarding security, quality, availability and so forth. (Note: for simplicity in this use case we haven't included the company's own web channels as this is under their control and can be managed as such.)

Much of this aspect of work is done by the departments themselves (IT are often too busy keeping the core systems running). As the data they require is in the cloud the marketing department may not feel they have to wait for the IT department to design and build a solution because they can get to work straight away and have a departmental solution ready in a short period of time – often using open source tooling.

However, once the IT department is aware of this work, they immediately concern themselves with issues like who actually owns the data being used, non-functional requirements such as availability, performance and any weaknesses in security. IT are concerned with these issues at one end of the spectrum and the business is concerned with speed and flexibility at the opposite end. Here is where information governance really comes into its own. The business has swiftly moved into a 'hybrid' mode of working with data coming from internal and external sources with differing levels of security, quality, availability and more characteristics.

It now becomes critical that ALL the information is subject to similar rules/policies/procedures/standards. Otherwise, information used in the business lacks any fidelity or level of trustworthiness in its use in decision making. Using the information governance dimensions that we outlined earlier we can consider and review:

- A clear definition of what the data actually means – the data models we create and use should act as 'maps' for any data sets being brought into the business and the rules/policies/standards associated with this data should be clearly articulated once and adhered to throughout the business. This includes security classifications to ensure information is shared appropriately and seen only by those authorised to do so.
- The organisation should have clear agreement on who owns the data and how it should be maintained and monitored to handle data quality. Stewards, curators and owners of data should be defined.

- Programmes and projects are all made aware as and when any new data sets are brought into the company's strategic set of data assets to ensure maximum reuse and consistency of use is applied.
- Data is brought into the company's data assets once and used many times to limit financial costs associated with gathering new data.
- If new tools and technologies are used by departments to gather data in any way – it can be assessed by the IT department and brought under central control if useful to other areas of the business.
- Core data assets have processes wrapped around them that manage the data over its useful life and is disposed of appropriately when its value is small or zero.

To achieve much of this there are two key elements required: firstly, an organisation capable of working in a flexible, dynamic manner to continually review and cope with the demands of new information being ingested into the company's 'vault' of data assets. We have talked about organisation models earlier in this chapter and some structures that might be useful to set up.

The second element is having some form of 'library' that can manage all the data assets within the company's 'vault'. The library must be able to classify, catalogue and allow easy retrieval of all manner of aspects associated with the data under review (its meaning within the business, its security level, structure, where it sources from, what processes have been applied to it, who owns it, who curates/manages it, where it's held within various systems and so on) as well as assist in actually retrieving the data itself. This is metadata and Chapter 4 delves into the details of how to manage metadata.

Information governance and metadata are tightly linked, and except for the smallest of organisations who may be able to handle their data in a manual way, metadata is crucial to an organisation's ability to fully understand its data assets.

5.7   Information governance and regulatory concerns

In today's world many organisations find themselves holding citizen-/customer-/patient-related data and there is a growing realisation within the individuals whose data is held and governments that this data is highly valuable and useful to those organisations and outside forces who may wish to use such data for their own purposes. Having this data held in multiple large repositories within a relatively small set of organisations (government bodies/hospitals/banks/insurers/retailers/social media sites etc.) makes it the target for these outside forces (Janssen and Van Der Voort, 2016).

Governments have recognised this and have been rapidly implementing all manner of regulatory and compliance requirements on these bodies to ensure personal data is held securely and in the most appropriate manner. One of the most recent (and we'll use this as an example here) is the General Data Protection Regulation (GDPR) which is a regulation coming out of the European Union which intends to strengthen data protection for individuals residing within the borders of the European Union. GDPR came into enforcement in May 2018 and replaced the Data Protection directive which was initially created in 1995. The GDPR will be applicable to any organisation that works within the EU market OR processes personal data that belongs to EU data subjects.

The guidelines are broad and in general cover processes that consist of any operation performed on personal data, automated or not, where personal data is defined as any data that directly or indirectly identifies an EU data subject, whether that data is based on them being a customer, employee or patient.

Key GDPR duties and obligations can be broken down into five areas:

- Rights of EU data subjects: the GDPR definitely seeks to enhance the rights of data subjects in the EU. For example, it has clearly described and clarified data subjects' ability to request access to and erasure of their information. Organisations will need to provide easier access to personal data, with clear and easily understandable information on processing. Making this information available gives data subjects insight into how their information is used, and the rights to withdraw that usage or reinstate that usage as they see fit.
- Accountability of compliance: organisations should be able to demonstrate compliance with the GDPR principles relating to personal data if requested to do so. GDPR has still to fully define what is expected here – but a good guess would be some form of reporting (at prescribed periods or on demand) to show compliance around things like use of data, processes data subjected to, lineage of data and security around the data at a minimum.
- Lawfulness and consent: processing of personal data will be lawful only if one of six factors the GDPR lists is in play (e.g. if it is necessary for the performance of a contract or if it is required for another regulatory compliance reason or legal hold). Consent is also one of these factors, and has strict requirements, including the fact that it can be withdrawn at any time (at which point an organisation would need to rely on one of the other factors to lawfully retain the data should it wish or need to do so).
- Security of personal data: organisations will have to report data breaches to regulatory authorities within 72 hours. If it is a serious breach, then all individuals whose data may have been compromised must be contacted. All data must have appropriate classification and procedures around it to ensure an appropriate level of security to the risk that it carries. Organisations will have an obligation to take security measures as part of the day-to-day running of the business, and it is still possible to be in breach if proactive steps are not taken.
- Data protection by design and by default: those who own and manage data must implement technical and organisational measures to demonstrate compliance with GDPR core principles. Data privacy for individuals should be the default action and should be designed into all organisational and technology processes.

Clearly, information governance and metadata management have a huge role to play here in ensuring that organisations have the necessary controls and information in place to allow all relevant data to be easily identified and shown to be managed in the correct way. Only through a strong information governance framework and well classified and controlled metadata can there be sufficient control for any reasonably sized organisation to effectively create, understand, report on and dispose of data securely. This must be done to a level that will satisfy any individual requesting their data assets held by a company or an auditor of such data.

Figure 5.5 describes how these five core areas could be managed through a framework that relies on good metadata and governance.

It's worth pointing out that failure to comply with the regulations could result in fines for non-compliance that can go up to €20 million OR 4% of total annual worldwide turnover for the parent company of any company involved, so this is a very real and serious undertaking.

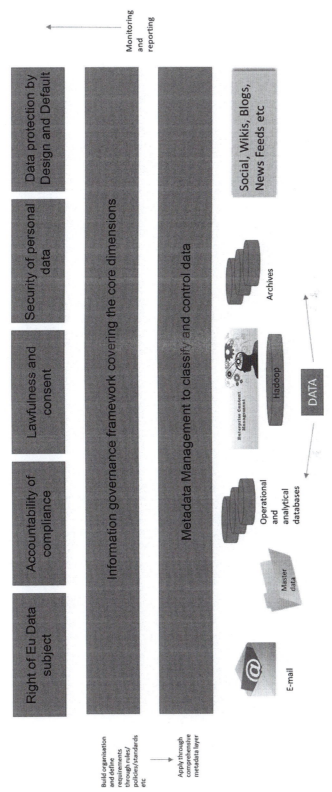

Figure 5.5 Information governance framework for GDPR

5.8 Conclusion

Governance in all its forms is a complex set of tasks and should be pervasive throughout an organisation. It enables both better business outcomes and the management of risk associated with dealing with data in non-compliant or regulatory ways. Differing models can be adopted for driving governance that covers a tightly controlled central set of functions through to a much more distributed model where governance is the role of each function and a central team acts only as the 'cop' to ensure policies are adhered to. By having a framework that describes where potential pitfalls can arise, a company can, at the very least, identify the areas they wish to focus on the most and make sure they are controlled appropriately.

The ever more stringent rules and regulations surrounding industries regarding personal data is making governance a central pillar for those organisations. Healthcare and banking are two examples of organisations which have come under increasing pressure from regulators over the last ten years and new rulings from large multi-national bodies, such as GDPR from the EU, will only focus more on this topic.

 Study area

To test your understanding of the chapter please attempt to answer these questions, either by debating them in the class with colleagues or by writing them down to help formulate your answers.

Questions:

1 What are the nine dimensions that support information governance – which one(s) do you feel are critical?
2 Describe some of the roles of users who manage data or use data.
3 Can you think of ways to balance the needs of businesses around speed to market and that of IT to maintain data safely and securely, enabling both parties to be satisfied? This may be referred to as the 'two-speed' problem – businesses want fast – IT can only go slow(er).
4 Information governance and metadata are closely intertwined in the management of information systems – describe how the differing roles work together to provide a comprehensive organisational model to support a business (think about the roles described above, any gaps, what metadata is needed and how it is derived).
5 Consider all the different ways in which data can be stored and how this impacts the governance of that data (think about where data could reside for live data, backup data, archive data, data on site, in the cloud and so on).

Further reading:

- What is EU General Data Protection Regulation (GDPR)?
  - EU (European Union). (2018). *The EU General Data Protection Regulation*, http://www.eugdpr.org/
- Governing the smart city: A review of the literature on smart urban governance
  - Meijer, A. and Bolívar, M.P.R. (2016). Governing the smart city: A review of the literature on smart urban governance. *International Review of Administrative Sciences*, 82(2): 392–408.
- Effectiveness of the Sarbanes Oxley Act on Corporate Governance: Evidence from Executive Turnover
  - Kim, Y. Han (Andy), Effectiveness of the Sarbanes Oxley Act on Corporate Governance: Evidence from Executive Turnover (May 9, 2016). Journal of Applied Business Research, Forthcoming. Available at SSRN: https://ssrn.com/abstract=2777553

References

Ballard, C., Compert, C., Jesionowski, T., Milman, I., Plants, B., Rosen, B. and Smith, H. (2014). *Information Governance Principles and Practices for a Big Data Landscape*. IBM Redbooks.

Borgman, H., Heier, H., Bahli, B. and Boekamp, T. (2016). Dotting the I and crossing (out) the T in IT governance: New challenges for information governance. In: *2016 49th Hawaii International Conference on System Sciences (HICSS)* (pp. 4901–4909). IEEE.

Bowen, K.J., Cradock-Henry, N.A., Koch, F., Patterson, J., Häyhä, T., Vogt, J. and Barbi, F. (2017). Implementing the 'sustainable development goals': Towards addressing three key governance challenges – collective action, trade-offs, and accountability. *Current Opinion in Environmental Sustainability*, 26, pp. 90–96.

Cronemberger, F., Sayogo, D.S. and Gil-Garcia, J.R. (2017). Assessing the role of executive involvement and information needs as socio-technical determinants of governance in IIS success. In: *Proceedings of the 50th Hawaii International Conference on System Sciences*.

Frost, J., CRM, F.A.I. (2017). ECM's move to the cloud: Good news for business, IG Pros. *Information Management*, 51(4), p. 22.

Janssen, M. and Van Der Voort, H. (2016). Adaptive governance: Towards a stable, accountable and responsive government. *Government Information Quarterly*, 33(1), pp. 1–5.

Lomas, E.J. (2016). Information governance: Models for delivery. Paper presented at CILIP Conference, 12–13 July, Brighton, UK.

Lombardi, R., Del Giudice, M., Caputo, A., Evangelista, F. and Russo, G. (2016). Governance and assessment insights in information technology: The Val IT model. *Journal of the Knowledge Economy*, 7(1), pp. 292–308.

M. Coyne, Emily & G. Coyne, Joshua & Walker, Kenton. (2018). Big Data information governance by accountants. International Journal of Accounting & Information Management. 26. 00-00. 10.1108/IJAIM-01-2017-0006.

MacLennan, A. (2014). *Information Governance and Assurance: Reducing Risk, Promoting Policy*. Facet Publishing.

Musiani, F., Cogburn, D.L., DeNardis, L. and Levinson, N.S. (eds) (2016). *The Turn to Infrastructure in Internet Governance*. Springer.

Olavsrud, Thor. (2015). IDC says big data spending to hit $48.6 billion in 2019. [Online.] http://www.cio.com/article/3004512/big-data/idc-predicts-big-data-spending-to-reach-48-6-billion-in-2019.html, last accessed 25 January 2018.

Olavsrud, Thor. (2016). Big data and analytics spending to hit $187 billion. [Online.] http://www.cio.com/article/3074238/analytics/big-data-and-analytics-spending-to-hit-187-billion.html#tk.drr_mlt, last accessed 25 January 2018.

Peppard, J. and Ward, J. (2016). *The Strategic Management of Information Systems: Building a Digital Strategy*. John Wiley & Sons.

Rahman, N. (2016). Enterprise data warehouse governance best practices. *International Journal of Knowledge-Based Organizations* (IJKBO), 6(2), pp. 21–37.

Soma, K., Termeer, C.J. and Opdam, P. (2016). Informational governance: A systematic literature review of governance for sustainability in the information age. *Environmental Science & Policy*, 56, pp. 89–99.

Tallon, P.P., Ramirez, R.V. and Short, J.E. (2013). The information artifact in IT governance: Toward a theory of information governance. *Journal of Management Information Systems*, 30(3), pp. 141–178.

Vaziri, R., Mohsenzadeh, M. and Habibi, J. (2017). Measuring data quality with weighted metrics. *Total Quality Management & Business Excellence*, pp. 1–13.

Wilkinson, M.D., Dumontier, M., Aalbersberg, I.J., Appleton, G., Axton, M., Baak, A., Blomberg, N., Boiten, J.W., da Silva Santos, L.B., Bourne, P.E. and Bouwman, J. (2016). The FAIR Guiding Principles for scientific data management and stewardship. *Scientific Data*, 3, p. 160018.

Zhang, H., Lee, Y., Wang, R. and Huang, W. (2017). Chief data officer appointment and origin: A theoretical perspective. *Advances in Management Information Systems Research (General Track)*, AIS Electronic Library.

Part III

PRACTICAL APPLICATION ISSUES

CHAPTERS

6

UTILISING THE PROMISE OF OPEN DATA

6.1   Introduction

We first need to define exactly what we mean by the term 'open'. For this book, we consider four aspects: open source, open standards, open data and open architectures. For a deeper breakdown of these areas please see Appendix 3. This chapter concerns itself with how we could apply open standards to open data to better understand the data locked up in varying formats in large open data repositories that governments, non-governmental organisations and others create (e.g. Land Registry offices, National Statistics, local councils and charities).

For open data to deliver on its potential, these organisations should adopt well-defined, popular standards for the definition and delivery of open data to end users. In addition, developers, businesses and citizens, as well as the government, should be able to augment open data to enable a richer view of the data itself and relationships between different data. A tagging approach is proposed to describe open data, with a small, default vocabulary defined by government, which is then significantly extended and enhanced through end user contributions, which are peer verified analogous to the 'folksonomies' found in tools like Wikipedia. In combination, these capabilities provide a solid basis for the development of new value applications as well as the use of analytics tools to determine new linkages across multiple open data sets.

Note: our examples come from UK government but should be applicable in other regions/industrial or commercial sectors.

6.2   Using open data

The rise in government use of open data in the UK has been swift and wide ranging.[1] It's now possible using data.gov.uk to identify a wide range of data sets that *could be* used to help solve a variety of problems for citizens and businesses throughout the UK. Open data and the resulting transparency it brings has become a powerful force in starting to help drive public policy (Bertot et al., 2014). Open data offers opportunities to benefit the public sector, citizens, businesses and the UK as a whole, and the availability of open data (security considerations permitting) is only set to grow.

However, there are still challenges to overcome in getting open data used as a pervasive tool to design new applications that drive value creation (Magalhaes et al., 2017). This value

---

1 Open data is the idea that certain data should be freely available to everyone to use and republish as they wish, without restrictions from copyright, patents or other mechanisms of control. The goals of the open data movement are similar to those of other 'open' movements such as open source, open hardware, open content, and open access. The term 'open data' itself is relatively recent, gaining popularity with the rise of the internet and World Wide Web and, especially, with the launch of open-data government initiatives such as Data.gov and Data.gov.uk.

creation can transcend organisational boundaries and national borders – for example, using anonymised and aggregated open data sets from the UK National Health Service can be of great value to other countries and businesses.

6.2.1   Current issues with open data

Although open data is now seen as widespread and freely available from government sources,[2] it is still difficult to consume because:

- Different formats and standards exist for published data.
- Differing periods of latency to submit information exist as do publication frequencies.
- Data quality can still be suspect (e.g. missing or invalid data).
- Data sets which should be available across different localities can be missing over time.
- It is difficult to find whether particular open data sets exist, and even when located, it is difficult to understand the context of the data.
- Data changes over time and it's not always easy to understand these changes. This makes it very difficult to develop applications which require data to remain consistent and valid over time.

6.2.1.1   *The key elements of an effective open data solution*

To address these issues and bring open data to life to deliver the promised benefits of open data, an effective open data solution must support three key capabilities. In combination, these capabilities enable a diverse range of consumers to easily access, read, understand and analyse open data (Bogers et al., 2017). It is the effective analysis of open data which creates new value through the discovery of linkages between open data sets.

6.2.2   Data standardisation

Open data sets should be identified using a simple, widely available and universally accepted naming scheme. In reality, this means that the WWW scheme of uniform resource locators (URLs) should be used to locate open data sets. URLs provide excellent integration with a diverse range of users, organisations, tools and systems.

The data within an open data set should be available to users in a single, standard form, which is both machine and human readable. Within an open data set, individual data elements should be described using name-value pairs. Open data elements should support a full range of alphabetic, numeric and other simple data types, along with the ability to group individual data elements into more complex structures such as lists and objects, which enables a fuller representation of real-world entities.

The most widely adopted standard to enable this should be the JSON data standard (http://json.org/) to describe its content. JSON has been specifically designed to be a light-weight interchange format and has been widely adopted across the World Wide Web.

6.2.3   Data access and data change notification

Access to open data is provided via APIs, as these provide a standard mechanism which allows programmatic access to open data. APIs are used to query open data sets, as well as deliver open data which may change in real time.

---

2 https://www.gov.uk/government/consultations/making-open-data-real

APIs should use the REST protocol for data requests, and this is the vast majority of the access that consumers will make. The REST protocol uses HTTP and is therefore ubiquitous. It also has an easily understood naming convention (URLs) which can be used to provide a global namespace for open data which is integrated with the World Wide Web.

There are also open data sets which change in real time (effectively streaming data) and these open data sets should be provided via an open messaging protocol, again based upon HTTP, which supports asynchronous delivery (such as the MQTT protocol (mqtt.org)). This messaging protocol is fully internet enabled, and used by a diverse range of systems such as Facebook Messenger, again supporting the importance of ubiquity of access.

6.2.4   Metadata tagging

Alongside the source data in an open data set there should be metadata which allows consumers to understand its specific meaning. Metadata can be applied at all levels within an open data set; from individual data elements to an entire data set. Moreover, metadata tagging should provide information about the source of the open data to help data consumers understand who has created the data, effectively identifying the data provenance. Metadata can therefore be used to understand precisely the data within a particular open data set, as well as understand the similarities and differences across diverse data sets.

Metadata tags are provided both by the original curators of an open data set, as well as its users. This second approach is often called a 'folksonomy' (Pandya and Virparia, 2017). In a folksonomy, users apply public tags to open data sets to aid them in the search and analysis of data items. Typically, this will give rise to a classification based on usage and frequencies, in contrast a typical taxonomy is only specified by the owners of open data sets. This practice of collaborative tagging uses the wisdom of the crowd to augment the formal tagging structure provided by default.

Given the ubiquity of social media, metadata should use both hashtags and usernames (#hashtag, @username) for describing what the data is and who created it (Lorentzen and Nolin, 2017). These metadata tagging mechanisms are simple, pervasive and well under-stood by all.

The use of a separate metadata store for government-defined and end user-defined tags provides enormous flexibility when using a collection of open data sets. This separation of metadata allows a system to be built with a small initial set of tags to describe critical aspects of the data, which can have more information added later as new ideas emerge. For example, initially tags might describe data elements using synonyms to help link data sets. Later, additional tags could be added which allow data consumers to express a quality preference for data via a 'like' metadata tag.

Later in this chapter, we'll see how analytics processing can use the metadata tags to identify new links between data and data sets. We'll also see how metadata tags can identify which groups are interested in which data and begin to promote collaboration across its use.

Figure 6.1 shows the proposed logical architecture for creating open data sets which enables insight through analytics to create new value by linking together formerly disparate data. The following sections describe the elements of Figure 6.1.

6.2.4.1   Existing data sources

These are the source systems from which data is created. We don't propose any changes to these systems. They are used, however, to create the JSON data sets which capture open data.

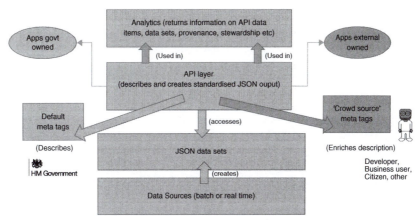

Note: The data sources can be used to extract data in a variety of formats if so wished BUT it is essential that it is exposed in a JSON format for end user consumption whether that is consumed in batch or real time.

Figure 6.1   A proposed logical architecture to support open data

6.2.4.2   JSON data sets

These are the standardised open data sets which are described in the JSON interchange format. These data sets are named according to a URL which includes data.gov.uk, the owning department, and the name of the data set. These data sets contain the same information contained in current data.gov.uk data sets, whether that's a CSV file, a spreadsheet or other format, but formatted in JSON. Each field also has a name, which will serve as a reference point for metadata, whether government or user defined.

6.2.4.3   Default metadata tags

These metadata tags are defined by the government or controlling body and kept to a relatively small list based on a controlled vocabulary (Koivisto and Choi, 2016). The metadata tags use the same URL naming convention as the JSON data set and are also described in JSON. The name-value entries in this metadata data set link the metadata tags to the open data set names and field references. The use of JSON schema can be used here to maintain structure around the metadata elements within the metadata, ensuring that a set of properties for each metadata element can be well defined. The metadata becomes the 'key' to unlocking the value of the data it refers to. Exploit the analytics to create new communities through the use of social media to grow an effective open data ecosystem by connecting users and consumers of common interest data.

Example of JSON schema for simple metadata tagging:

```
"$schema": "http://json-schema.org/draft-04/schema#",
 "title": "Dataset1",
 "type": "array",
 "items": {
  "title": "DataElement1",
  "type": "object",
  "properties": {
          "tags": { "type": "array", "AltName": {"type": "string"},
                              "datasource": {"type": "string"},
                              "like": {"type": "number"},
    }
  }
}
```

The schema above can be used to describe the structure of the metadata file(s) used internally and externally to describe a data set. As can be seen from above they are easy to describe and human readable but allow control to be defined around how metadata should be structured. This is critical if we are to use the metadata tagging to its fullest potential.

6.2.4.4 'Crowdsourced' metadata tags

These metadata tags are 'crowdsourced' from data users, such as developers, business users and citizens, possibly drawing on lessons learned from initiatives such as the DBpedia.[3] The structure of this JSON file is similar to the default metatags, and differs in the origin of the tagging information.

6.2.4.5 API layer

This layer provides standardised access to the JSON data sets, including metadata. Using a clearly defined URL, users are able to easily access open data sets, and their associated metadata. They use the HTTP REST protocol for the more usual static data requests, or a lightweight messaging protocol for open data which is updated in a more real-time manner. Users always use the HTTP REST protocol accessing metadata whether static or real time.

The API layer also provides access control, flow control, monitoring and metering of data to enable the fair allocation of resources to users. This is particularly helpful when managing different competing demands, such as a large organisation who may wish to frequently retrieve large amounts of data compared to individual citizens.

6.2.4.6 Applications

These can be owned by government or owned by external agencies, but follow the same mechanism to access open data. Specifically, these applications always use the API to access open data; they do not have access to the JSON data files, including their metadata.

6.2.4.7 A worked example

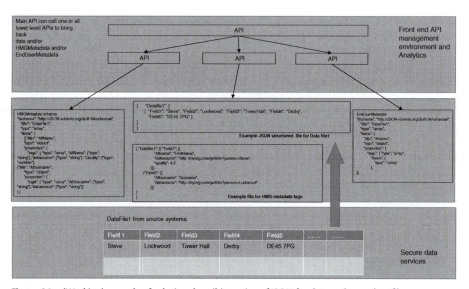

Figure 6.2 'Working' example of solution describing using of JSON for data and metadata files

---

3 http://dbpedia.org/about

The simple example shown in Figure 6.2 describes a single file, with a single row within it. The fields are named (arbitrarily) Field1, Field2 … to Field X. Each field can be defined using the JSON schema on the left-hand side of Figure 6.2; we've called it HMG (Her Majesty's Gov. – just to show how it could be a government open data file). This describes each field in turn within the schema with alternate labelling for the field and/or additional data regarding its provenance and quality. Note that the original name for the field could also be placed in here simply by adding a new element to the array within the item titled Altname called (say) OriginalName with appropriate structure defined, meaning all metadata that HMG wish to define that is associated with Field1 can be stored in a single location.

In addition, the JSON schema on the right-hand side of the diagram allows end users (developers, citizens, even employees with organisations making use of the data set) to further tag the data to enrich its context and meaning still further. The structure of the JSON schema has been left 'open ended' at this moment as it needs to be discussed and defined as to what should be held in there, and of course, can be changed as learnings are made. Further 'alternate names' for fields, rating tags, usernames of those who add new metadata, comments and so forth could all be added here.

We now are in a position to make use of this data to look for new terms and insights within the data. Simple queries of the JSON data sets could identify all terms for a data item, identify the quality for the data from HMG and check how it's rated by end users and so on.

This idea can be further extended by considering two data files that have been tagged in such a manner and using a graph style structure that shows how the metatags can be used to connect seemingly disparate data sets. We can see in Figure 6.3 how the combination of the two sets of metadata from HMG and end users can be combined in a graph-style structure (vertices and edges) to identify potential new linkages across what, at first sight, would appear to be unrelated data files. The linkages can be identified at the data file level (Person to Person relationship) or at the data item level (ChristianName to ChristianName relationship) or both (find me files that are tagged as 'persons' with fields that are tagged as ChristianName).

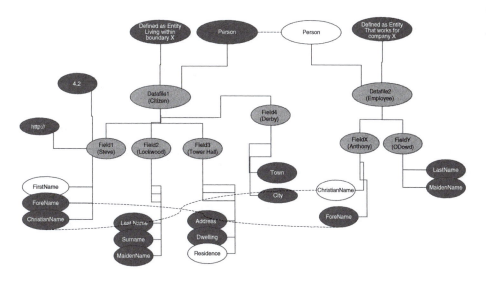

This approach divorces the data from its context
Light grey = Fieldnames,
Dark grey = Metadata (Controlling Org. generated),
White = Metadata (End user generated)
We can identify linkages in the graph using the metadata (dotted lines)

Figure 6.3   Using metatagging across two data files

6.2.5 The benefits of analytics: discovering new linkages in open data

Effective analytics is the goal of open data, whereby users derive meaningful insights from data both within and across open data sets. Analysis of a single data set is definitely interesting, and this is enabled in the architecture by standard data formats and standard data access via APIs. The power of analytics becomes more significant, however, when different open data sets are linked together (Payne et al., 2017). This cross-linking is enabled using the metadata tags provided by government and users. Metadata tags are used to identify linkages across different data sets using different aspects of the data represented by the tagging process. Moreover, the addition of new tags to an existing data set allows potentially new analyses to be performed when new metadata provides the 'missing link' between data sets which were once considered disjoint.

There are two phases to the effective analysis of linked data, involving the creation, then analysis, of linked data structures. The detailed representation of these data structures is not covered in this book, but there are many options available. The first phase is for analytics tools to build the linked data structures which effectively model the linkages between open data sets using the metadata tag. The second phase is for analytics tools to process these linked data structures to derive new insight. There are a variety of analytics tools available to model and process these data linkages, varying from traditional technologies, which join common terms across disjoint data sets, all the way to graph technologies. Graph technologies are particularly interesting for this form of analytics, because their data structure enables semantic queries which extend across multiple related entities to derive new insights. The availability of open data and associated metadata now enables the very effective creation of these graph structures.

End user applications which exploit open data use many of the same techniques as analytics tools or may just use the output results from analytics tools. The focus of applications is to take the insight from open data to create new value applications. These applications might range from near real-time mobile technologies to more report oriented, less frequently accessed, applications. An example of a real-time application might be a mobile traveller application which combines relatively static mapping data with more dynamic information from public transport systems with live data to assist with journey planning.

Metadata tagging also enables greater insight into the production and usage of open data. Firstly, where open data sets have similar or overlapping metadata, it's likely to be an indication that data sets are similar to each other. This introduces the possibility to connect data producers of these similar data to enable synergies. Secondly, because of the use of controlled APIs for data access, open data usage patterns are better understood. This introduces the possibility of connecting users with similar data interests, whether in a particular data set, or related data sets that others have found interesting. Combining all these techniques together, it's easy to see which users and data sets are key to an open data ecosystem; these 'sentinel' entities are effectively local centres in an open data marketplace.

6.3 Other issues

1 It must be stressed that this solution is only as good as the number of organisations that would elect to adopt this approach. If only a small set of departments goes forward with this idea the opportunity to link data and gain greater insights into

what is useful and what is not is lost. The greater the take-up the more widespread and richer the metadata becomes to exploit. Although there is effort in building the metadata, the benefits are potentially great, enabling a whole new range of applications to be built that may not have been considered previously because it has simply been too difficult to identify, manipulate and retain confidence in the data sets needed.

2   The physical architecture – who has to own and maintain the database that holds the metadata, who hosts the databases(s) and what are the costs of maintaining this additional set of functions. This could be a hybrid model with certain data remaining in-house and only available at some charge, some hosted on the cloud at lowest cost the market will bear by third parties or any combination in between.

3   Who deals with API management – this function has potentially great worth as it will offer (through analytics) the chance to identify patterns of usage of APIs and understand how the public, business and other third parties are consuming the data. This opens up the possibility of developing a marketplace for data (if so wished) or simply opening ever more relevant data sets based on consumption of resource.

4   Is a chief data office and small team required to govern this solution? Should the government build a small group that oversees the solution and ensures it's not being abused in any way? This could be in policing the external metatagging taking place, the quality of the data being published, looking at where charges for certain data sets to certain consumers would be appropriate and so forth.

5   Who will update the external tagging of data – what is the incentive for other parties beyond government to do this? (Building eminence and being seen as an expert in this field may be sufficient to drive uptake – see signalling theory (Connelly et al., 2011)).

6.4   Conclusion

For the effective processing of open data, it's important for open data systems to adopt an approach to managing metadata in a consistent manner. This chapter outlines one approach that could work if take-up was sufficient. Without such a metamodel the prom-ise of open data being brought into easily consumable analytic solutions remains a great challenge. There are a number of key conclusions that should be acted upon by anyone wishing to adopt this or a similar approach:

● An open data architecture should be built on key standards for open data formats, access to open data via APIs, and extensible metadata to describe these open data sets.

● These standards should be built on standards that are already widespread, namely JSON and REST APIs accessed through use of standard URL naming conventions.

● A suite of analytics can be built on this well-architected open data which provides new linkages between disparate open data sets, new insights from the analysis of these data linkages and identifying communities of interest around those who share the same data through tags they have added (crowdsourced).

● The issues discussed around open metadata in Chapter 4 and using a metadata repos-itory such as Apache Atlas are related topics. Atlas itself is graph based so the tagging approach described in this chapter lends itself to such a model.

Study area

To test your understanding of the chapter please attempt to answer these questions, either by debating them in the class with colleagues or by writing them down to help formulate your answers.

Questions:

1 What are the stumbling blocks to effectively using open data – is it really open?
2 What other approaches could you think of beyond the one described in this chapter?
3 What key thing would you adopt to improve open data sets if you could (Hint: think about structure of data, different sources of data, different people using the data)?
4 What privacy concerns are associated with open data?
5 How would you decide whether to make a data set open or not?
6 There is a cost associated with publishing and consuming open data – who should pay?
7 How could the publication of open data be encouraged to benefit everyone?

Further reading:

- Project Open Data
  - US Government. (2017). Open Data Policy – *Managing information as an asset.* https://project-open-data.cio.gov/
- What is open data?
  - The Open Data Institute (2017). https://theodi.org/what-is-open-data
- Open data and the knowledge society
  - Wessels, B., Finn, R., Wadhwa, K. and Sveinsdottir, T. (2017). *Open data and the knowledge society.* Amsterdam: Amsterdam university Press.
- Open data – Getting started guide
  - Open Data. (2017). [Website.] https://centerforgov.gitbooks.io/open-data-getting-started/content/

References

Bertot, J.C., Gorham, U., Jaeger, P.T., Sarin, L.C. and Choi, H. (2014). Big data, open government and e-government: Issues, policies and recommendations. *Information Polity*, 19(1, 2), pp. 5–16.

Bogers, M., Zobel, A.K., Afuah, A., Almirall, E., Brunswicker, S., Dahlander, L., Frederiksen, L., Gawer, A., Gruber, M., Haefliger, S. and Hagedoorn, J. (2017). The open innovation research landscape: Established perspectives and emerging themes across different levels of analysis. *Industry and Innovation*, 24(1), pp. 8–40.

Connelly, B.L., Certo, S.T., Ireland, R.D. and Reutzel, C.R. (2011). Signaling theory: A review and assessment. *Journal of Management*, 37(1), pp. 39–67.

Davies, T.G. and Bawa, Z.A. (2012). The promises and perils of open government data (OGD). *The Journal of Community Informatics*, 8(2), pp. 1–4.

Dietrich, D., Gray, J., McNamara, T., Poikola, A., Pollock, P., Tait, J. and Zijlstra, T. (2009). *Open Data Handbook*. [Online.] http://opendatahandbook.org. Accessed on 30th August 2018.

Grand, A., Wilkinson, C., Bultitude, K. and Winfield, A.F. (2016). Mapping the hinterland: Data issues in open science. *Public Understanding of Science*, 25(1), pp. 88–103.

Gurstein, M.B. (2011). Open data: Empowering the empowered or effective data use for everyone? *First Monday*, 16(2), pp. 1–5.

Janssen, M., Charalabidis, Y. and Zuiderwijk, A. (2012). Benefits, adoption barriers and myths of open data and open government. *Information Systems Management*, 29(4), pp. 258–268.

Kucera, J. and Chlapek, D. (2014). Benefits and risks of open government data. *Journal of Systems Integration*, 5(1), p. 30.

Lorentzen, D.G. and Nolin, J. (2017). Approaching completeness: Capturing a hashtagged Twitter conversation and its follow-on conversation. *Social Science Computer Review*, 35(2), pp. 277–286.

Magalhaes, Gustavo & Roseira, Catarina. (2017). Open government data and the private sector: An empirical view on business models and value creation. Government Information Quarterly. 10.1016/j.giq.2017.08.004.

Pandya, S.D. and Virparia, P.V. (2017). Folksonomy-based information retrieval by generating tag cloud for electronic resources management industries and suggestive mechanism for tagging using data mining techniques. In: *Web Usage Mining Techniques and Applications Across Industries* (pp. 80–91). Hershey, PA: IGI Global.

Reichman, O.J., Jones, M.B. and Schildhauer, M.P. (2011). Challenges and opportunities of open data in ecology. *Science*, 331(6018), pp. 703–705.

7

ETHICS

7.1 Introduction

We are living in a period of unprecedented change. Throughout human history there have been periods of intense creativity and innovation. Periods that have transformed society and shaped culture. Periods that have delivered new technologies, new economies and new uncertainties. Joseph Chamberlain said in the late nineteenth century 'I think that you will all agree that we are living in the most interesting times. I never remember myself a time in which our history was so full, in which day by day brought us new objects of interest, and, let me say new objects for anxiety.'

During the first industrial revolution of the late eighteenth and early nineteenth centuries we saw a transition from hand production methods to machines, new iron production processes, chemical manufacturing, and use of factory systems powered by water and steam. It was without doubt a period of great transformation in which greater productivity was achieved, new wealth created and social transition took place with the emergence of the new middle classes. The industrialization of society also came with great impact on people. Poor working and living conditions in overcrowded cities resulted in worsening public health and decreased life expectancy for many. There was exploitation of child labour to meet market demands, enslaving whole families in poverty and irreversible environmental change through urbanization. All factors which resulted in policy change by government and new standards for society.

Following the information and digital revolution in which evolving technologies have created new networks and environments in which to operate, we now live in a society ever more interconnected and interoperable. A kingdom of convenience in which information is sourced on demand, and social networks allow for collaborative delivery and engagement across continents and time zones. A society under ever more surveillance. Fuelled by data the continuum has shifted and made us ever closer, ever more interdependent and ever more independent. Commoditisation of data has driven digital economies across the globe and big data analytics has spawned a fourth industrial revolution. The ability to control our home central heating remotely through smart plugs and thermostats, catch up on our favourite TV series when we want and where we want, monitor our children's academic progress while finishing that report for work and simultaneously ensuring that a healthcare provider is on hand to visit and take care of elderly parents is becoming the new productivity. Ever time-constrained we live in a world of convenience. We have an app for almost everything, smart devices to improve our lives and intelligent technologies to enable freedom. Access to information services and digitised technologies is the new entitlement for society, the new wealth fuelled by free-flowing data. On reflection and giving consideration to societal history one wonders: at what cost?

In the wake of today's rapid evolution of data-fuelled technology, the borders between the physical and virtual worlds are being opened as we augment our biological existence. Data, personal data included, can have many positive uses and outcomes, but there are many risks in a data-driven business model. Research from Gartner Inc. predicts that, by 2018, 50 per cent of business ethics violations will occur due to improper use of big data. Indeed, there are already many cases of questionably unethical data analytics practices resulting in unwarranted surveillance and privacy violation. There's no doubt data is an asset but it also presents risks. The collection and storage of large quantities of personal data is a risk to individual privacy and breach of privacy is a risk to an organisation's reputation.

Very little is understood about the ethical implications underpinning the Big Data phenomenon, from social media data to open data. With the potential goldmine of valuable insights from social media data (see, for example, EMOTIVE, discussed in Chapter 2), there has been an increasing realisation that ethical issues are not always dealt with in appropriate and meaningful ways. Up until 2017 there has been little attention dedicated to ethical implications of big data analytics applied to social media data sets. This of course is not just a recent issue as social media has been around for a number of years. Back in 2006, a Harvard-based research group gathered the profiles of 1,700 college-based Facebook users. They wanted to determine how their interests and friendships changed over time (Lewis et al., 2008). The anonymous data was released to the world, enabling researchers to reuse the data set to look for further research findings. However, other researchers quickly discovered it was possible to de-anonymise parts of the data set, which compromised the privacy of the students. None of the students were aware their data has been collected (Zimmer, 2008). Of course, this research made headlines for all the wrong reasons and raised difficult issues for scholars. Can so-called 'public' data on social media sites be used for research or by organisations? Do researchers/organisations have to request permission to use the data? Privacy campaigners see this as a key battleground where better privacy protections are needed.

In this chapter, we examine ethical expectations and perceptions of users in relation to the increasing adoption and use of analytical systems over social media user-generated data sets. We also look at the changing privacy and ethical landscape for organisations and the impact it will have upon them and the wider society.

7.2   Who is using your data?

As society's knowledge of big data is becoming broader, the ethics surrounding big data analytics, and the way in which organisations obtain and use consumers' data from social streams, such as Twitter, Instagram, Snapchat and Facebook, is becoming increasingly questionable. Boyd and Crawford (2012) state that with the emergence of big data, little is understood about the ethical implications. For example, is it ethical for researchers to justify their actions of consumption and analysis of data, simply because the data is accessible? Any data on human subjects inevitably raises privacy issues, and the real risks of abuse of such data and its analysis are difficult to quantify (Boyd and Crawford, 2012).

In 2011, the American discount retailer Target developed an algorithm capable of finding customers who were about to become pregnant and even approximate their due date. The company could then market these customers directly for baby and pregnancy products. The programme was so successful that sale of products for pregnant women increased by 30%. While this sounds great there was, however, a problem, an overtly inhumane creepy problem. The algorithm was so successful, so accurate, that one day an angry parent stormed into a Target store to complain about the marketing of pregnancy products to their 16-year-old daughter. Their complaint was that the company wanted her to get pregnant! What the parent didn't know was that she already was. The magnitude of this event was not felt by everyone, but it raised the question of data ethics – questions regarding the trade-off between commercial interests and the rights and freedoms of the individual in a digital marketplace. To have known precisely what the algorithm had concluded in a physical environment would have required access to the most private thoughts of the individual, constant surveillance and observation to a level that makes an Orwellian novel seem almost trivial. Ironically, Target's story resulted in a major security leak, the loss of 70 million customer records, a sizeable economic loss for the company from which it is still recovering.

In February 2015, a story about Samsung's Smart TV went viral. Journalists investigating the company's privacy policy discovered that all conversations in the room where the TV was located were being recorded and processed by the company as part of the speech to text conversation service. The conversations were then digitally delivered to a subcontractor and processed into text form. Confusion over whether there were options for opt in or opt out of the service fuelled a story that Samsung spies on its customers. Samsung responded 'we take privacy very seriously'. A year later a further news story broke that Samsung televisions had been hacked by the UK and US security services primarily to listen in on conversations of suspected terrorists. However, the indiscriminate nature of their action has prompted many concerns from both global governments and citizens.

Richards and King (2014) discussed how society is currently experiencing a Big Data revolution. Existing privacy protections that were once used to protect an individual's personal information are no longer substantial. With the use of modern-day technology and data analytics, the collection of personal data by not only organisations, but also the government is ever increasing. Richards and King's (ibid.) study claims that it is similar to the industrial revolution, in the sense that society has been left radically changed since the evolution of big data analytics. It is transforming society and the way in which data is being captured, processed and analysed, through the ever-emerging scope of practical uses, with a range of databases and social streams being mined to gain insights and predictions on human behaviour (Richards and King, 2014). Whether this is morally correct or seen as ethical seems to not be questioned by many researchers. In the eyes of businesses, mining and analysing data enable them to provide a better service by predicting shopping behaviour, for example, which in turn can tailor marketing towards each individual. Therefore, organisations may believe that by providing this better quality service, the infringement upon personal information is justified, particularly if the personal data is willingly provided through organisational databases. However, individuals provide this information unaware of the fact that the information will be stored and analysed in ways which they may not have considered before providing it.

Owing to big data analytics becoming such a growing trend, there is an increasing awareness in the value of the collection of personal data, as well as the risks (Smith et al., 2012). Not only are organisations becoming increasingly aware of how they can harness these techniques to better themselves, but consumers are becoming aware of the effect that it has on them, and how their personal information is being manipulated. According to Smith et al. (2012), consumers often voluntarily upload personal details to a company's website, however, this does not necessarily mean that at the time of input they understand that their information will be recorded and stored for use by the organisation for the foreseeable future.

Kenny et al. (2012) discuss how data analytics enables organisations to collect consumers' data, and through the use of data analytics tools, customer engagement initiatives can be improved. Organisations can view user click-paths, drop-off points and even e-commerce reporting such as product views, purchases and so on. This enables organisations to easily interpret the data and see what generates the most sales and traffic through their websites (Kenny et al., 2012). Although this is an effective method, ethical concerns are raised in this research, due to the reasoning that customers may have unknowingly divulged this information.

In 2016, a blog by Nunez on Gizmodo claimed that Facebook's Newsfeed had been manipulated by a small team of editors to inject news topics on peoples' walls of 'black-listed' possibly 'propaganda' material. Facebook's Newsfeed algorithm determines what you see on your wall and what you don't see. It is supposed to calculate items of interest based on analytics of your internet history, likes, dislikes and interests. It is then adjusted by a team of researchers who advise that they take account of thousands of factors. Nevertheless, Gizmodo claim that this conduct was biased against right-wing conservative news items. Whether this is true or not, it highlighted that Facebook's systems were in no way neutral and that news items presented to Facebook users were not necessarily a presentation of accumulated user-generated content and interest in current events. It was in fact a combination of algorithms and human intervention without the application of transparent policies or decision making. It was allegedly the instrument of a new trend – 'Fake News'. Just like the propaganda machines of previous industrialised conflicts – be they through military action or cold – activists will feed off the media machines of the day, manipulate the trusted social environments and utilise the evolved technology to serve their respective ideological and economic interests. The integrity of social media is in decline, with newsfeeds manipulated just like the brand presentation of individuals' perfect 'Facebook lives'. One wonders how long communities of activists and avatars can continue to remain viable.

The digital business model of raw harvesting and use of personal data for the benefit of shareholders or political organisations is under threat. Incidents of capitalised surveillance by government and corporate entities, lack of transparency, manipulation of social media neutrality and the continuing, ever increasing mishandling of consumer's personal information have resulted in an environment of growing mistrust. All this raises issues around informed consent, the permanency of their data within an organisation and the extent to which consumers are aware of how their information is being used. Zwitter (2014) argues however, that there are three categories of big data stakeholders: Big Data collectors, Big Data utilisers and Big Data generators. Big Data generators are often quite small 'units' individuals or devices say, but the collectors are rapidly reducing to a small set of 'super' players (e.g. Google, Amazon, Microsoft, IBM).

Therefore, it must be considered that it could be the consumers, the 'big data generators', who are contributing to the threats of organisations' use of the data, as they are the ones who are providing the firms with the personal information. Agreeing with this, Hanneman and Riddle (2005) state that between the three, power is inherently relational in the sense of a network definition of power. However, Zwitter (2014) argues that despite providing the information, individuals do not consider being the subject of research, and do not necessarily believe that their information will be retained and analysed. Recent research by Cognizant highlights that 50% of consumers are willing to pay a premium to transact with companies they trust. The reverse is equally true, with 57% stating they would stop doing business with a company they believe has broken their trust by using their personal data irresponsibly, with just over a third (37%) willing to take legal action against the company. Consumer confidence is low, corporate reputations at stake. Some may say we are living in the most interesting times; what is apparent is that we are in the midst of a trust revolution.

'Big Data is mistakenly framed as morally neutral or having benefits that outweigh any costs', according to Martin (2015). His study presents the fact that there are many ethical issues arising from the negative externality of surveillance caused by persistent tracking of society, and that in the future there may be destructive demand for consumer information (Martin, 2015). Agreeing with this, Helbing (2015) states that undermining society's privacy cannot work well; in the long run, society will begin to question trust, and this will eventually undermine trust in the government. This could lead to an inefficient society, as there is the necessity for a combination of both control and trust. We may be beginning to see this effect in people's trust of political figures around the globe based on their (perceived?) lack of trust in the information that surrounds these individuals and groups.

Ideas of privacy in big data analytics and social media analytics are largely complex, leading to a variety of ethical issues in this field. Despite there being a range of studies covering ethics in big data and social media analytics in business, research is yet to explore individuals' awareness regarding the analysis of their data from social streams by organisations and whether there is a variance between demographics regarding the ethical concerns. Recent research around proposed codes of ethics is discussed in the following sections, followed by a review of some of the major ethical dilemmas in social media analytics, which among other issues include informed consent, privacy and data ownership.

7.3   Code of ethics

Pierce and Henry (1996) have categorised ethical decisions related to computer technology into three primary influences, namely:

i   the individual's own personal code,
ii   any formal code of ethical conduct that exists in the workplace,
iii   exposure to formal codes of ethics.

Nowadays it is becoming more common for analytics companies, most academic institutions and research-based departments and organisations to have some form of formalised ethics review. This is often conducted by an ethics board, widely known as Institutional Review Boards (IRBs), Research Ethics Boards (REBs) or Independent Ethics Boards (IEBs), which are tasked with assessing the morality and ethical implications of a piece of analysis and research by weighing its risks to benefits and ultimately assuring and protecting the rights and welfare of the subjects under study. Moreno et al. (2013) point out that social media data specifically raises new challenges for IRB boards as there is little-to-no guidance regarding how an ethics board should review studies involving social media. In their review of ethics and practicality of even simple uses of social media in the social work domain, Rumbawa et al. (2016) highlight that not enough research and guidelines have been established to make a clear stance on the ethicality of social media use and analytics. A number of researchers recently attempted to address this issue. Shilton and Sayles (2016) interviewed 20 social media data scientists to elicit opinions regarding three main ethical principles that have traditionally been of importance, originally put forward in the influential Belmont Report (DHHS, 1979): respect for persons, beneficence and justice. These core principles were related to the social media context (Shilton and Sayles, 2016, pp. 1–2) as follows:

- Respect for persons – most widely interpreted as a mandate to obtain informed consent when collecting private data. If interpreted broadly the authors (ibid.) suggest that much of public social media data documents work processes and practices that may have required informed consent for data collection in other settings. Although the logistics of informed consent for big data is considered to be a significant challenge.
- Beneficence – generally understood in the context of 'do no harm' and an assessment of risks and benefits, encouraging researchers to think through possible negative consequences of their work. A major social media-related issue here is often understood to be the difficulty of guaranteeing individual or group/community level anonymity, where effects of the work may result in harm to an individual or a community.

- Justice – widely understood to address the fair and equal distribution of costs and benefits to potential research participants. This relates broadly to the selection of research subjects. For instance, the main issue with social media is that online participants are largely self-selecting and tend to be more affluent and educated than the general population. It is also not always clear whether participants from vulnerable populations (e.g. children) are included.
- Related to addressing the issues highlighted above, the work by Chessell (2014) from IBM, proposes an ethical awareness framework specific to big data and analytics. The framework is centred around nine primary facets that any analytics effort should consider (ibid., p. 1);

1 Context – For what purpose was the data originally surrendered and how far removed from the original context is its new use?
2 Consent and Choice – Is there a choice, with what alternatives, and possibility to opt out?
3 Reasonable – Is the use of data reasonable?
4 Substantiated – Is the analysed data appropriate, authoritative, complete and timely?
5 Owned – Who owns the resulting insight? What are the responsibilities and obligations related to it?
6 Fair – How equitable are the results and is everyone properly compensated?
7 Considered – What are the consequences of data collection and the analytics?
8 Access – Does the data subject have access to their data?
9 Accountable – Can results be checked by the interested parties and unintended consequences detected and corrected?

A somewhat more concise set of guidelines was put forward by the Digital Analytics Association (DAA), which is an association that brings together analytics experts, and proposes an ethical code of conduct that members must subscribe to. This is based around five principal tenets (DAA, 2016):

1 Privacy – Hold consumer data in highest regard and to do everything possible to keep personally identifiable information safe, secure and private.
2 Transparency – Encourage full disclosure of consumer data collection and analytics practices.
3 Consumer Control – Opt out of data collection/tracking (although this does not account for opting out of analytics processes – i.e. specifying what analytics I am willing to allow and which ones must not be conducted).
4 Education – Educate and define all parties involved (e.g. employer, clients, etc.) as to what practices may be considered invasive and risky.
5 Accountability – Act as a steward of customer data.

A number of companies have also developed their own codes of ethics, including Terradata, a major big data analytics company (Terradata, 2016). Willis et al. (2013) have employed and provide 'The Potter Box' as an application model for big data that analytics stakeholders could use as an ethical compass. 'The Potter Box' (a model originally designed by Ralph B. Potter, Jr in the 1960s) deals with first identifying the facts, then the values, before setting two binary opposites as borders, and then finally making decisions that are devoid of 'personal motivations'. Willis et al. (ibid.), however, acknowledge that applying this ethical model is relative, and that there are no fixed universal principles available. This is more broadly echoed by the Association of Internet Researchers' ethics working committee (Markham and Buchanan (2012)), who contributed significantly to the ethics discussion and published two reports in 2002 and 2012 with the intention to provide guidance on ethics for internet-related research activities. Their most recent report by Markham and Buchanan (2012) consulted with over 20 experts and ethicists in the field, including social media experts. Some of the key ethical principles brought forward in their report can be summarised as follows:

- Since 'harm' is defined contextually, ethical principles are more likely to be understood inductively rather than applied universally; when considering ethical questions, practical judgement attentive to the specific context is key.
- The obligation to protect the community/individual/person is greater the more vulnerable a community/individual/person is likely to be.
- As all digital information at some point involves individual people, consideration of principles related to research on human subjects may be necessary even if it is not immediately apparent how and where individuals are involved in the analysed data.
- Rights of subjects (e.g. social media users) must be considered carefully and in different contexts the rights of subjects may outweigh the benefits of research/analytics applications.

A reference guide recognising the various broader internet-based research questions is provided within Markham and Buchanan (2012, pp. 17–18) and may be of some use to researchers when considering data analysis of internet-based sources, where the guide specifically considers:

i the type of information that might be collected,
ii major types of interaction (contexts),
iii key ethical questions that ought to be raised and considered (ibid.).

Chessell (2014) points out that as perceptions around ethics of big data analytics are becoming established, these will in time guide regulation and legislation, and hence the choices we make as practitioners and researchers will ultimately determine the level of legislation imposed around the technology and our subsequent ability to pioneer in this emerging area.

7.3.1 Ethical issues

The most recent report in the United Kingdom (UK) is by the British Information Commissioner's Office (ICO) entitled 'Big Data and Data Protection'. The ICO is an independent regulatory office that enforces and deals with a number of privacy and data-related laws, regulations and guidelines in the UK. Their report (ICO, 2014) discusses the emerging significance of big data in several fields such as management, marketing, national security, et cetera, and considers what data protection issues may arise from harnessing such big data in various ways. In their report, they list the data protection requirements. Among these requirements, for example, it is a necessity to ensure that the processing of personal data is 'fair', especially when big data is being used 'to make decisions affecting individuals' (ibid., p. 3). The report explains that there are numerous examples of big data analytics that are involved in the processing of personal data. For example, information can be collected from social media or loyalty cards, and the report stresses the importance of organisations complying with the UK Data Protection Act (DPA) guidelines. The report mentions that while some organisations are developing approaches that cater to an ethical context of gathering and harnessing big data, there are still some issues surrounding the claim that data protection principles are not suitable for big data. While the report acknowledges that there is some flexibility within the DPA, it stresses that the public ultimately has a right to privacy.

7.3.2 Privacy and informed consent in analytics

Van den Hoven (2008) explains that in spite of privacy being a vague concept that is difficult to define, most privacy scholars agree that it is important. He goes on to elaborate that the public debate regarding privacy in the twenty-first century has three positions. The first is that there is so much personal information available about people that there is no need to be concerned with privacy. The other is that 'Western Democracies' cannot afford individual privacy because the 'common good' is simply a bigger concern. The third stance is that there are many reasons for individual privacy and that hence it should be protected. Van den Hoven (2008) argues that there is a difference between governmental and non-governmental agencies' reasons to collect personal data. Governmental parties may need the data to serve its citizens better. While the same logic could also apply to commercial parties, Van den Hoven (2008) asserts that there could be a bigger risk of data exploitation – they may not be bothered at all with the interests of the data subjects.

Richards and King's (2014) research highlights the ethical dilemma of what they describe as the 'Big Data Revolution' that they believe is influencing several types of human activities, such as dating, shopping and voting, to name a few. They stress the necessity of setting regulations now before the current practices become the default norm, hence difficult to change. They argue that big data has embowered institutions and now requires the development of the field of big data ethics. Their view is the data being gathered in vast quantities generates analytics, hence new data. They call for the recognition of privacy as a rule, although they do acknowledge that the concept of privacy is changing. Keeping information secret is not the rule of privacy, as Richards and King (2014) view it, but rather managing the flow of information in ethical ways. They also recognise that shared information could still be confidential – which can be extended to secondary use of big data. The researchers also point out that big data companies must be transparent in order for governments to make informed decisions; they argue that transparency can prevent the exploitation of big data.

Similar to Richards and King's views on big data and new data, Sax (2016) explains that analysing big data leads to the creation of new data. He claims that the conduct of big data companies revolves around the concept of 'finders keepers', in that 'those who find something that is not held by anybody, are, as they found it, the legitimate owners of that which they have discovered' (ibid., p. 5). He adopts Kirzner's (1978) theories to justify the use of new data: as long as the original personal data was ethically and legally obtained, the data miner should be free to exploit the data. He claims that the original data subjects, because of their obliviousness to the new data that their own personal data generated, do not actually own this data, hence the big data company is the owner of this data, because through its analysis (often of personal data) new data was generated. However, Boyd and Crawford (2012) explain that there is a difference between being in public, such as sitting in a park, and being public such as actively seeking attention. They argue that most social media users are unaware that their data is being collected and used, and importantly they might not give their consent if they would be given that option.

7.3.3 Fair selection of users

In their white paper on business ethics and big data, the Institute of Business Ethics (IBE, 2016) discuss the importance of veracity in big data analytics (see Chapter 1 for veracity of data). Specifically the authors highlight the following contrast: 'traditional statistical methodologies rely on samples that are chosen to be representative of the whole population being analysed, whereas the new big data sets, might not be statistically accurate and could produce flawed results' (ibid., p. 6). Boyd and Crawford (2012) point out that while Twitter is a platform that can present a sample within a certain context that offers a convenient method to conduct statistical analysis, Twitter users do not represent the vast majority of a population, and that some users own multiple Twitter accounts – making Twitter data, in their opinion, not a representative sample. Subsequently some groups or individuals might accidentally be accorded more visibility and hence be favoured or discriminated against (IBE, 2016). Nunan and Di Domenico (2013) also express their concern that users as young as 15 years old and even younger (Krotoski, 2013) are often using social media, using smartphones to access different social media platforms nearly everywhere they go, leaving behind rich data for potential analytics. Further issues are introduced with data collection algorithms that are limited by platform specific APIs and internal data sampling lacking transparency, which tend to introduce a number of systematic biases into social media data collection practices (Boyd and Crawford, 2012).

Given the real ethical risks of abuse of social media data and insights derived from analytics, it is important to understand not only the moral dilemmas faced by analytics users and researchers, but also the general awareness around the analytics methods used. Since these techniques are employed for analysis of social media users themselves, these users are effectively the 'potential' participants (often without their knowledge) of such studies and analytics.

7.4 The trust economy

Ethical issues have always been a consideration for businesses. We have seen throughout history how the rights of workers evolved during the first industrial revolution and how the importance of environmental protection has more recently transformed business strategies. Now, in the digital age, getting data ethics right has greater importance than ever before.

Huge and persistent concerns exist in regard to consumer confidence and trust. The 2008 financial crash caused many consumers to lose trust in weakened financial institutions. Trust in government is gradually evaporating following allegations of surveillance; and in the wake of the Volkswagen (VW) emissions scandal, customer trust in the automotive industry is at its lowest level, with just 36% of consumers indicating trust in the industry. The impact for VW was not only a reputational crisis but a financial one too. Following revelations that VW had misrepresented emissions measured and reported for its diesel-powered vehicles the company stock lost 20% of its value and it has had to significantly reduce its investment plans.

Trust is the foundation of our relationships in a digital society and the treatment of privacy is the balance established between companies and people. While in a recent survey 90% of consumers have concerns about privacy, hacking, loss of control, intrusion, piracy and scamming, only a few of those surveyed abandon the internet as a result. Consumers don't differentiate between privacy and protection, for them it is all about trust. Trust is a pact, an agreement, a fundamental understanding between consumer and business. In the digital economy trust is profit – the business model for many internet companies who rely on collaboration and sharing in a marketplace where consumers trade data for convenience. Thought leader Rachel Botsman, who coined the concept of 'collaborative consumption', speaks of 'reputation capital', that is, the value of reputation in the collaborative sharing economy. She uses examples of the peer-to-peer marketplace that matches personal demand and supply where reputation and trust are the currency. In one example, a landlord on Airbnb purchased a cat to avoid getting a negative review from a guest who had seen a mouse running across the floor of the apartment he was renting. As Airbnb's slogan says, '2 million listings, 60 million guests. 191+ countries. Trust is what makes it work' – trust between complete strangers, brought together through new technologies; trust based on the development of personal relationships rather than empty transactions.

For consumers, trust is about expectations. Hasselbach and Tranberg (2016) more precisely define it as about something or someone living up to your expectations. Your expectations as a consumer in digital space, in turn, are defined by various factors. It could be everything from the design of a website that creates certain associations to personal experiences or things you've heard through the grapevine. Trust can be achieved through different types of seals and certifications, where independent third parties ensure what a company does can be trusted. Companies that earn the highest trust are those that clearly define how they will use the information they collect, give consumers full control of their personal data and offer fair value in return. The shift in control is not only being driven by economic factors based upon customer expectations, global privacy standards and regulations are changing too. The most comprehensive of these, the European Union's General Data Protection Regulation 2016 (commonly known as GDPR or 'the Regulation'), establishes a number of requirements for companies which process European residents' personal data. Created to protect the rights and freedoms of individuals while enhancing confidence in the digital economy the Regulation sets out requirements for companies to exercise greater accountability over their collection and processing of personal data. It provides greater control for individuals through enhanced rights and use of consent for the certain processing, including profiling, and sizeable enforcement regime, of up to 4% global turnover, for Supervisory Authorities to levy on business entities and organisations who are non-compliant. The Regulation is seen as a control shift not just for the empowerment of individuals but also for businesses. For many organisations, at first glance, the GDPR is a further compliance burden in already challenging times. Its complexity and inclusion of the principles of proportionality, demonstrable accountability and consumer control mean that businesses can no longer rely on assuming a defender position. To truly implement the spirit of the Regulation requires proactivity. It requires a maturing of risk frameworks, greater understanding of the risk–reward nexus between data monetization and privacy infringement, and a development of the link between personal relationship, reputational enhancement, consumer expectations and corporate ethics. It is changing the corporate discussion from one of defender position and burden of compliance to that of an opportunity to refocus on what is important to the business: to generate business value in a marketplace based upon trust.

7.5 The future – thriving in the new landscape

There is a trend towards developing ethical approaches to the use of personal data. Several commentators have advocated the need for an ethical approach that goes beyond compliance with legal requirements. Robin Wilton, Technical Outreach Director at the Internet Society, recently commented: 'The only next step for business is to move from a liability and compliance mentality to a more ethical approach, where people are doing things because it's in accordance with their values: I'm not doing this to tick a box; I'm doing this because I think it's right' (Hasselbalch and Tranberg, 2016).

The Information Accountability Foundation has been working on a Big Data Ethics Initiative, which proposes as set of ethical values for assessing big data initiatives summarised as:

- Organisations should define the benefits of the analytics
- They should not incur the risks of big data analytics if the benefits could be achieved by less risky means

- The insights should be sustainable
- The processing should respect the interests of stakeholders
- The outcomes of the processing should be fair to individuals and avoid discriminatory impacts

Some companies are implementing such values or indeed developing their own sets of ethical principles. Essentially ground rules for establishing how the organisation will use personal data, they typically stress the importance of transparency and fairness. An example of this is Aimia who manage loyalty programmes such as Nectar. Aimia have developed as set of data values known as TACT (Transparency, Added Value, Control and Trust).

> **Transparency** means telling customers what data is being collected, how it is being collected and how it is being used. **Added** value means making customers aware they will receive rewards for their participation. **Control** is about giving customers control over the data they provide and enabling them to share it and to opt out. **Trust** means giving customers confidence that the data will only be used in ways that you say you will use it and only share it with partners you have identified.

Aimia's approach not only highlights the need for ethical principles to ensure reputation; it also highlights that in publishing them they are marketing their brand for trust. They are advertising to consumers that we respect your rights and you test us on them.

Other companies are also taking a proactive response to ongoing global standards and rights to build customer's digital trust.

In the case of LEGO, they have over 50 million children playing in their online universes. When a child logs onto services which require parental consent, they use a LEGO ID. Initially the company considered using social media connect buttons because many children were already on social media. However, they chose not to as they were unable to gain assurance from such platforms as to what type of data would be reaped from its sites. LEGO says it has a corporate responsibility as to how subcontractors and partners use data of its customers, just like the company is accountable for its physical suppliers' environmental and social behaviour. As a result there are no third-party cookies on LEGO websites aimed at children under the age of 13 years.

Another example is GPS hardware company TomTom. They promise to delete all data that would make it possible to identify you or your device from the location data they received within 24 hours after your device is powered off. In fact, they even state in their privacy policy that they do not know where the user has been and are unable to tell anyone else or recreate the data, even if forced to. Many companies have for some time embedded Privacy by Design solutions into their data processing and management systems. Under GDPR Privacy by Design will in fact become a legal requirement. Privacy by Design is the idea that the default setting of the service is private and that it's designed and developed with privacy as a point of departure, not an afterthought. In big data analytics the concept of Privacy by Design is often associated with anonymisation or techniques to pseudonymise personal data. One such technique is differential privacy which involves injecting noise into the answers of data set queries in order to retain anonymity at an individual level. The case of Pokemon GO, launched in July 2016, is a classic example of where privacy and ethics are an afterthought. Children are the primary users of the game, in which you catch Pokemons in the real world through your smartphone's camera using virtual reality technology. However, Pokemon GO did not consider users' privacy. A cocktail of incidents in which children were harmed and sharp criticism from privacy experts on the level of inbuilt tracking led to data protection supervisory authorities and politicians to demand answers regarding the company's use of the data.

To many the concept of Privacy by Design is about business philosophy and culture. In early 2017, Jane Horvath, Senior Director of Privacy at Apple, described the company's approach to privacy and data ethics: 'Data Ethics is for Apple to understand what is right and what is "wrong" seen with the customers' eyes. Privacy is strategically and intentionally part of the product design. All product teams have a privacy expert as a member, who is involved from the very beginning of all processes.' Apple believes that their technology should give individuals control over the way their data is collected, used and shared.

There is, without doubt, an emerging market of privacy tech. We are seeing products being developed as a direct response to consumer demand and concerns over surveillance and data breaches. These products are being developed to complement user friendliness with privacy controls and respect for consumers – products that are shaping the market and further building the concept of data ethics into consumable benefits. For example, DuckDuckGo is a search engine whose slogan is 'switch to the search engine that doesn't track you'. Founded in 2006 as an alternative to Google, its brand is built on privacy and ethics. Another example is Wire, an encrypted video chat service created by former Skype investors as a user-friendly and privacy-focused alternative. To date, investments in data ethical business continue to rise. Privitar, a big data analytics service who describe their product as 'privacy-preserving data mining', recently received $1 million in start-up capital. According to its own description, Privitar is designed to collect information while simultaneously maintaining individuals' privacy. They clearly identify privacy as a competitive parameter. Other examples of venture capital investment include CognitiveLogic, another big data analytics service, focused on addressing privacy implications of correlating data and analysis in the health service, and Brave, a browser that blocks invasive adverts and monitoring, founded by Brendan Eich, former director of Mozilla. Brave recently received $205 million in venture capital in order to make it faster, more private and easier to use. Finally, there is Digi.me. A British-based platform that enables users to assemble their financial and health data and set their own sharing parameters or even sell the data to other companies. Digi.me is becoming increasingly popular with investors. Part of the personal store trend, Digi.me makes clear promises about privacy and ethics to consumers about how their data is processed and gives them direct control over its use. The company recently received a significant investment to build out the platform. All of these companies are building services to disrupt the market, all of them well financed with investor backing, all of them loved and trusted by users, all of them with privacy and ethics as their competitive advantage. The future is clearly changing because of some leading lights seeing the dangers ahead and wanting to create a more ethical and sustainable environment in which to operate.

7.6   Conclusion

Privacy is a fundamental human right written into international convention and widely recognized in law. In its physical context the right to a private home life in which individuals own and control the keys to entry are accepted and upheld. In the digital context the interconnectivity of technology and the intrusive mining of data have led to a lack of transparency about the use of personal data, and lack of control of its use which have eroded consumer confidence and trust. Both trust and collaboration are fundamental to the principles of a successful digital marketplace. If privacy is the right and expectation, data ethics must be the facilitator. More and more organisations are coming to market with privacy and ethics embedded in their culture and demonstrable in their product service offerings – their ethical values embedded in delivering business value.

In the wake of today's rapid evolution of data-fuelled technology the borders between the physical and virtual worlds are being opened as we augment our biological existence. Data, personal data included, can have many positive uses and outcomes, but there are many risks in a data-driven business model. Data scientists have for some time broken big data into five dimensions: volume, variety, velocity value and veracity. However, maybe it is time for a fifth dimension: viability. The fifth dimension would demonstrate that the processing of data is ethically viable (and could be linked to value). With the introduction of GDPR, the ethical landscape seems to be changing, but there are still many challenges ahead if we are to make the most of this digital revolution.

 Study area

To test your understanding of the chapter please attempt to answer these questions, either by debating them in the class with colleagues or by writing them down to help formulate your answers.

Questions:

1 What is GDPR and what are the implications for:
    o Business and the wider society?
    o Impact on the organisation's bottom line?
2 What is TACT?
3 What did LEGO do that showed they had their customers' interests in mind?
4 Which search engine does not track your search queries?
5 Can devices in your home record what you are doing?
6 What are the three key capabilities that an effective open data solution must support?

Further reading:

● How might GDPR change in the future and why might GDPR not work on a global scale – the trouble with European data protection law
    o Koops, B.J. (2014). The trouble with European data protection law. *International Data Privacy Law*, 4(4): 250–261.
● Ethical organisation – When organizations are too good: Applying Aristotle's doctrine of the mean to the corporate ethical virtues model
    o Kaptein, M. (2017). When organizations are too good: Applying Aristotle's doctrine of the mean to the corporate ethical virtues model. *Business Ethics: A European Review*, 26(3): 300–311.
● A new perspective on privacy
    o Taylor, L., Floridi, L. and van der Sloot, B. (2017). Introduction: A new perspective on privacy. In: *Group Privacy* (pp. 1–12). Cham: Springer International Publishing.

References

Botsman, R. (2012). The currency of the new economy is trust. TEDtalk video, September 2012. https://www.ted.com/talks/rachel_botsman_the_currency_of_the_new_economy_is_trust, last accessed 28 June 2018.

Bowker, G.C. (2005). *Memory Practices in the Sciences*. Cambridge, MA: MIT Press.

Boyd D. and Crawford K. (2012). Critical questions for big data: Provocations for a cultural, technological, and scholarly phenomenon. *Information, Communication & Society*, 15(5), pp. 662–679.

Chessell M. (2014). Ethics for big data and analytics. IBM Whitepaper. Available at: http://www.ibmbigdatahub.com/whitepaper/ethics-big-data-and-analytics, last accessed 8 September 2016.

DAA (Digital Analytics Association). (2016). *The Web Analyst's Code of Ethics*. Available at: https://www.digitalanalyticsassociation.org/codeofethics, last accessed 28 June 2018.

DHHS (Department of Health and Human Services) (1979). Protection of human subjects: Notice of Report for Public Comment, Federal Register, United States Department of Health and Human Services, *Federal Register*, 44(76), pp. 23191–23197, Available at: https://web.archive.org/web/20111017133845/http://www.hhs.gov/ohrp/archive/documents/ 19790418.pdf, last accessed 13 August 2016.

Hanneman, R. and Riddle, M. (2016). Introduction to social network methods. Chapter 10: Centrality and power. http://www.faculty.ucr.edu/-hanneman/nettext/ C10-Centrality.html, 2005.

Hasselbach, G. and Tranberg, P. (2016). *Data Ethics: The New Competitive Advantage*. Copenhagen: Publishare.

Helbing, D. (2015). Societal, economic, ethical and legal challenges of the digital revolution: From big data to deep learning, artificial intelligence, and manipulative technologies. *Social Science Research Network* [online]. Available at: http://ssrn.com/abstract=2594352, last accessed 2 March 2017.

Horvarth, Jane (2017). Contribution in: CPDP 2017: *Ethics, Observational Platforms, Mathematics and Fundamental Rights*, January 2017 (video). Available at: https://www.youtube.com/watch?v=SaGCwFJ8sLg, Accessed on 3th August 2018

IBE (Institute of Business Ethics) (2016). Business ethics briefing: Business ethics and big data, 52(6), pp. 1–8, Available at: https://www.ibe.org.uk/userassets/briefings/b52_bigdata.pdf, last accessed 7 September 2016.

ICO (Information Commissioner's Office) (2014). Big data and data protection, Available at: https://ico.org.uk/media/for-organisations/documents/1541/big-data-and-data-protection.pdf, last accessed 8 August 2016.

Kenny, R., Pierce, J., & Pye, G. (2012). Ethical considerations and guidelines in web analytics and digital marketing: A retail case study. In: *AICE 2012: Proceedings of the 6th Australian Institute of Computer Ethics Conference 2012* (pp. 5–12). Melbourne: Australian Institute of Computer Ethics.

Kirzner,I. M. (1978). Entrepreneurship, entitlement and economic justice. In: J. Paul (ed.), *Reading Nozick* (pp. 383–401), Totowa, NJ: Rowman & Littlefield.

Krotoski, A. (2013). *Untangling the Web: What the Internet is Doing to You*. London: Faber and Faber.

Kranzberg, M. (1986). Technology and history: Kranzberg's laws. *Technology and Culture*, 27(3), pp. 544–560.

Lewis, K., Kaufman, J., Gonzalez, M., Wimmer, A., & Christakis, N. (2008). Tastes, ties, and time: A new social network dataset using Facebook.com. *Social Networks*, 30(4), pp. 330–342.

Markham, A. and Buchanan, E. (2012). Ethical decision-making and Internet research recommendations from the AoIR Ethics Working Committee (version 2.0). Available at http://aoir.org/reports/ethics2.pdf, last accessed 28 June 2018.

Martin, E.K. (2015). Ethical issues in the big data industry. *MIS Quarterly Executive*, 14(2), 67–85.

Moreno, M.A., Goniu, N., Moreno, P.S. and Diekema, D. (2013). Ethics of social media research: Common concerns and practical considerations. *Journal of Cyberpsychology, Behavior, and Social Networking,* 16(9), pp. 708–713.

Nunan, D., and Di Domenico, M. (2013). Market research and the ethics of big data. *International Journal of Market Research,* 55(4), 505. doi: 10.2501/IJMR-2013-015

Nunez, M. (2016). Facebook's trending news is a total mess, *Gizmodo.co.uk,* August 2016.

Pierce, M.A. and Henry, J.W. (1996). Computer ethics: The role of personal, informal, and formal codes. *Journal of Business Ethics,* 15(4), pp. 425–437.

Richards, N.M. and King, J. H. (2014). Big data ethics. *Wake Forest Law Review,* 49, p. 393.

Rumbawa, N., Evans, S., Hein, J., Bocalan, S., Reis, R. and Little, S. (2016). The ethics and practicality of using social media platforms in social work clinical practice: A systemic review. [Online.] Available at: http://csusm-dspace.calstate.edu/handle/10211.3/170307, last accessed 9 September 2016.

Sax M. (2016). Big data: Finders keepers, losers weepers? *Ethics and Information Technology,* 18(1), pp. 25–31.

Shilton K. and Sayles S. (2016). 'We aren't all going to be on the same page about ethics': Ethical practices and challenges in research on digital and social media. In: *The 49th Hawaii International Conference on System Sciences (HICSS) 2016,* HICCS, Hawaii, USA.

Smith, M., Szongott, C., Henne, B. and Von Voigt, G. (2012). Big data privacy issues in public social media. In: *Digital Ecosystems Technologies (DEST), 2012 6th IEEE International Conference* (pp. 1–6). IEEE Campione d'Italia, Italy, June 2012.

Terradata (2016). Code of Conduct. [Online.] Available at: http://www.teradata.co.uk/code-of-conduct/?LangType=2057&LangSelect=true, last accessed 7 September 2016.

Van Den Hoven, J., & Weckert, J. (eds.). (2008). *Information Technology and Moral Philosophy.* New York: Cambridge University Press.

Willis III, J.E., Campbell, J. and Pistilli, M. (2013). Ethics, big data, and analytics: A model for application [Online]. Available at: http://apo.org.au/resource/ethics-big-data-and-analytics-model-application, last accessed 17 September 2016.

Zimmer, M. (2008). 'More on the "Anonymity" of the Facebook dataset It's Harvard College', *MichaelZimmer.org blog* [Online]. Available at: http://www.michaelzimmer.org/2008/10/03/more-on-the-anonymity-of-the-facebook-dataset-its-harvard-college/, last accessed 1 April 2017.

Zwitter A. (2014) Big data ethics. *Big Data & Society,* 1(2), p. 2053951714559253. https://doi.org/10.1177/2053951714559253.

Part IV

FUTURE DIRECTIONS

CHAPTERS

WHAT LIES AHEAD

8.1 Introduction

Trying to make predictions as to what might happen over the next 20 years can be difficult, but, ironically, with all the data we have, shouldn't this task be much easier?

Let's first look at some of the trends we expect to continue with reasonable confidence and from that we can extrapolate some more focused insights:

1 Data volumes will continue to grow and we can't see an end to this expansion in the foreseeable future, as more unstructured and sensor-based data is brought online.
2 Data will gravitate towards the cloud for reasons of cost, implementation times and ease of access to data for analytics.
3 We will need new approaches to analyse these quantities of data.
4 Security and personal data must be better addressed in cloud-based solutions and must consider regional requirements such as GDPR.
5 A hybrid cloud environment will be needed to meet that which business will demand.
6 Predictive/Prescriptive and cognitive solutions will become much more mainstream and automated to help businesses make decisions in an optimal manner and humans interact with tooling in a more natural way.
7 Skills and talent to build out these next-generation solutions may be a bottleneck.
8 Small companies will be able to enter the market more easily with cloud-based solutions so expect companies that solely rely on generating analytics for others to spring up.

From these trends let's look at some of the things one of the companies who lead in these spaces expect to happen. IBM tries to predict five things that will happen in the next five years, and does this cyclically. The three that stand out for 2017/18 and align with our thoughts are: determining indicators of mental health and wellbeing (through natural language processing); smart sensors (analysing big data from sensors); personalised medical treatment through using your DNA (cognitive computing and the need for quantum computing and/ or neuromorphic computing). All of these predictions involve the techniques that have been detailed within the book, however, for these predictions to come true, the techniques and methods will have to be further refined and used in various combinations.

- IBM believes in the next five years that systems will analyse what we say and write to determine our mental health and physical wellbeing. By looking for patterns in our speech and writing, which can be analysed by new cognitive systems, this will provide tell-tale signs of early-stage developmental disorders, mental illness and degenerative neurological diseases that can help doctors and patients better predict, monitor and track these conditions (IBM, 2017). In this chapter we will look at the potential link between information overload and mental health, and the developments we might see over the next five years.

- With the development of smarter, cheaper sensors, IBM forecasts that they are most likely to be used to detect environmental pollution. They claim that new, affordable sensing technologies deployed near natural gas extraction wells, around storage facilities and along distribution pipelines will enable the industry to pinpoint invisible leaks in real time. Most pollutants are invisible to the human eye, until their effects make them impossible to ignore. Methane, for example, is the primary component of natural gas, commonly considered a clean energy source. But if methane leaks into the air before being used, it can warm the Earth's atmosphere. Methane is estimated to be the second largest contributor to global warming after carbon dioxide (CO_2) (IBM, 2017).
- Full DNA sequencing is on its way to becoming a routine procedure (IBM, 2017). In 2014, the New York Genome Center and IBM started a collaboration to accelerate the race to personalised, life-saving treatment for brain cancer patients. IBM announced, in 2015, another collaboration with more than a dozen leading cancer institutes to accelerate the ability of clinicians to use Watson to identify and personalise treatment options for patients. Recently, IBM and Quest Diagnostics announced a new service that helps advance precision medicine by combining cognitive computing with genomic tumour sequencing (IBM, 2017). For these types of systems to improve we will also need better processing power. Quantum computers are exciting because they can solve types of problems that take conventional computers a long time to do or even can't do at present. In this chapter we will look at the introduction of quantum computing and the impact it will have on society.
- Neuromorphic chips will transform the way cognitive and AI-type analysis is undertaken, allowing processing to be done much closer to the point at where the data is created, rather than having to deal with the expense of moving data from source to some large data centre. This will be embedded in devices such as mobile phones to help automate decision-making for consumers or in drones to identify defects in cell towers for telcos or maybe recognising seismic patterns for the oil industry.

Clearly, there are some very exciting times ahead for the digital revolution that could be akin to the Industrial Revolution. However, as with the Industrial Revolution, there are some areas that will need great consideration and this chapter will outline the road ahead and the potential negative societal impact these systems might have on the world.

8.2 Understanding the link between mental health and big data

In the next few years we will have to address the volume of data and information we generate (Abbasi et al., 2016). Failing to do so could have a severe impact upon our mental health. In today's digital competitive environment, it is evident both professional and personal survival in modern society clearly depends on individuals' abilities to absorb increasing amounts of information. The amount of information created every two days is equivalent to that created from the dawn of civilisation until the year 2003 (Siegler, 2010), proving one of the fastest-growing quantities on this planet is the amount of information being produced (Jackson and Farzaneh, 2012).

There is a common perception that the younger generation, 'Digital Natives', have grown up engaging with modern technologies at a younger age and have greater under-standings of the concepts and are more adaptive (Teo, 2016). This results in fewer chances of information overload due to naturally developed skills and intuitions of interacting with information, since technologies are an integral part of their daily lives. The other common perception is that the older generation within the workplace struggles to maximise technology due to adapting later in life to modern technologies and suffers with information overload due to acquiring skills cognitively before effectively applying them towards their information responsibilities (Correa, 2016). The general feeling is that the older generation is more experienced, conscious and more attentive to detail, however, requires greater time to adapt to change.

However, are these simple common perceptions hiding something a little more sinister? Is there a link between information overload and mental health – in other words, how we process information interruptions? The number of 15- to 16-year-olds frequently feeling anxious or depressed has doubled over the last 30 years, increasing the need to determine the causes of poor mental health (Ciarrochi et al., 2016). There are many factors that affect mental health, but we believe one of them is how today's younger generation has an insatiable thirst to be connected to the digital world 24/7.

The younger generation are addicted to their mobile devices and are constantly attached to them awaiting the next message from the ever-increasing number of communication applications (Anshari et al., 2016). Therefore, the user is in a constant state of alertness, multi-tasking between information interruptions and rarely having the time to switch off from the demanding social world. From previous research, we know the impact this can have on employees within the workplace, but we are yet to study teenagers (Jackson et al., 2002). For example, multi-tasking email alongside other communication media, such as phone and face-to-face meetings, increases the risk of becoming stressed. Results from our research at the Loughborough Centre for Information Management showed that the majority of participants (92%) displayed an increased stress response, with many recording elevated blood pressure (23) and heart rate (14) readings, during email and phone use. With multi-functional smartphone devices like BlackBerrys and iPhones enabling workers to be accessible 24 hours a day, unlike ever before, it is likely that there will be an increase in stress levels (Marulanda-Carter, 2013). Another concerning aspect is that many employees do not realise that they are stressed. In Marulanda-Carter's study users perceived themselves not to be stressed when the physiological findings showed their bodies were under increased stress (Marulanda-Carter, 2013). This would indicate that employees might find it difficult to self-regulate their use of communication media to ensure they do not become overwhelmed by stress. This signifies that long-term, short, sharp increases such as this can lead to long-term chronic health conditions such as hypertension, thyroid disease, heart failure and coronary artery disease, as well as impacting upon mental health (Info Blood Pressure, 2008; Whiting and Williams, 2013).

So the key question is, does this information multi-tasking have a greater effect on teenagers as they are yet to develop the skillset to manage the volume of multi-tasking requests? Earlier indications show that the older generation is actually better equipped to deal with information multi-tasking, but how they gained that skillset is still to be determined. So, the proposition here is not that all social media is bad, as there is research that shows that interacting with social media can help reduce stressful situations and, for example, aid cancer patients' recovery. It is, however, to determine if there is any correlation between poor mental health and multi-tasking between information interruptions in the teenage population. If the link is shown it will radically change our digital landscape as we know it, and we are likely to see a heavy investment in both data and information brokers that will reduce the impact information overload is having. We will need very clever analytics to provide just-in-time data, information or knowledge and the system must link to our physiological and psychological state to determine when is the best time to interrupt the user to deliver the required data, information or knowledge.

8.3   Detecting emotions

The prospect of empathetic systems (i.e. computer systems that are able to recognise and adapt to a user's emotional state) has long excited many across a wide array of different disciplines (Picard and Klein, 2002). From security to healthcare, from interface design to driver safety, the ability to understand the emotional state of the user and adapt accordingly will have significant impact on all aspects of day-to-day life. Whereas the prospect of empathetic systems has long been a pipe dream, recent technological advancements, specifically in the domain of wearable sensors and visual imaging, have led to empathetic systems becoming a feasible proposition, although, as of yet, this dream is yet to become a reality. However, over the next five years it is likely to come to fruition.

Dating back to 350 BC, the question of what emotion is has been a hotbed of discussion over the past two and a half millennia, originating with the ancient Greek philosopher, Plato, who believed that the ability to experience and express emotions was a core element of our being; however, caution was given to its use within the decision-making process. Whereas emotion has a place within this process, Plato warned that it should not replace logic and reasoning when deciding on how to proceed. As time passed, Aristotle debated whether emotion should play a bigger part within the decision-making process in order to ensure the best course of action is followed.

More than two millennia later, the insights of these forefathers are still highly regarded and respected to this day. Many alternative insights have been provided during this time and even though some of these viewpoints have achieved acclaim, the fact that emotion is essentially a stateless entity results in a fair degree of uncertainty in the merits of each. It is for this reason why many different emotional theories still exist and the reason why the question 'what is emotion?' is still unresolved.

Whereas emotion as a concept is still debated, there is no argument about the relative merits of its study in the modern world. Emotions are intertwined in everything that humans think and do and are formed based on a wide range of different influences, including evolution, past experiences and personality. Due to the influence that emotions have in everyday life, it is important to understand and consider how they can be handled to best ensure the general wellbeing is met.

One area of life where emotion plays a major role is that in communication/interaction. Ever since Charles Darwin's theory of evolution, the link between emotions and how species interact with one another has been strong. Historically, emotional-based interaction traits were modelled around the need for a species to survive, but even though this concern has been rendered obsolete in modern times, these traits are still commonplace even to this day. The interaction between multiple people is completely tailored to the emotions being exhibited by all parties and therefore the result of the interaction can dramatically differ based on the emotional states present. So within this field what do we expect to see over the next five years?

8.3.1   How will emotions be used?

Within the next five years we will be able to accurately detect emotions from cameras using just pupil dilation recognition. This is where the size of your pupil will indicate the emotions you are currently feeling, for example, confusion, anger, sadness, happiness, disgust, fear, shame or surprise. At first glance the advantages of being able to do such a thing might not be clear, but let us explore a number of scenarios.

From an information-retrieval viewpoint web cameras on computers (that could determine pupil dilation) could be linked to internet searching sites like Google. When users type in a search query and are presented with the results, the camera could detect the emotions being invoked by the text being displayed on the screen. This information could then be used to create a more personalised search in the future and also give feedback to web masters about the impact their content has had and whether that aligns with their expectations. For example, the content of a website or the design of the website might cause confusion or surprise, which was not intentional. The feedback could then be used to improve the readability or design of the website.

The same approach discussed above could be linked to various applications like word processors or email applications. If a user sends an email to one or even multiple colleagues, the sender could get feedback on the emotions the email has invoked. If the email caused confusion, for example, and this was identified, it could lead to an early intervention to rectify the issue. Likewise, if an electronic document was circulated to employees within an organisation the system could gain feedback on how it has been received. Maybe certain sections of the document caused fear or confusion, and others happiness or anger; the intelligence gained from the system can aid in informing the document creator about the outcome of their work.

Outside of the office environment we could see this technology used in cars. A camera in the car could determine the emotions of the driver. Sharing this information with third parties along the driver's journey could lead to personalised marketing. If, for example, you were driving your car and your current emotion was happiness, electronic billboards would tap into your emotion by displaying an advert that would be received well by someone in a 'happy' state of mind, rather than someone who might be in an angry state of mind. If the emotions of the driver were linked to the satellite navigation system in the car, you could determine the happy or sad roads across the world. This of course could then be used by car manufacturers to determine if one car is better than another for driving along particular roads – so real-time feedback about the comfort of the car, taking into consideration road conditions and the driver's emotion. With the development of emotive sensors we will see a new industry emerge over the next five years that will have a massive impact on our daily lives.

8.4   Improving cancer care through social media

Those diagnosed with cancer often experience strong emotions such as sadness, distress, anxiety and fear (Hong et al, 2012). Emotional expression is extremely important for adjusting to and coping with cancer (Kennifer et al, 2009). Cancer survivors report the internet as the second most important source for cancer information and support after health professionals (Klemm et al., 2003; Peterson and Fretz, 2003). There is good evidence that online support lessens feelings of isolation and provides a forum to share emotional experiences, which can help those with cancer to cope, manage their cancer symptoms and increase their optimism and quality of life (Eysenbach, 2003; Hong et al., 2012; Klemm, 2003). For example, Maggie's Online Centre offers a supportive community for people to share their thoughts and experiences of cancer in an anonymous way and offers practical, emotional and social support online by Maggie's nurses who respond to users' statements and emotional expressions. Within the next five years we will see the application of techniques from computational linguistics in the analysis of cancer patients' emotions in online social networks (OSNs). From the analysis, information can be compiled and used to enhance the emotional health of the patient; this is crucial given the established link between a cancer patient's emotional health and their recuperation. To date, most psycho-oncology research uses non-internet-based data sources, such as randomised trials. The advantages of using 'open' internet-based data sources such as OSNs can be understood in terms of access, magnitude, timeliness and organic modes of emotional expression.

This work will be extremely important for understanding emotion and its potential to transform the recuperative life cycle of cancer patients, particularly in view of the ongoing reports of emotional distress during cancer treatment. For example, psycho-oncological research reports on interventions, such as telephone support, which enhances the expression of affect (Donnelly et al., 2000). While not all such research consequently reports on enhanced recovery, it is axiomatic in the literature that emotional distress depresses the immune system which in turn is detrimental to effective recuperation (Jencks, 1995; Barraclough, 1999). The enhancement of a cancer patient's emotional health is therefore an established adjunct to oncological treatment (e.g. Kennifer et al., 2009). Much of the psycho-oncology work draws on non-internet-based data sources to analyse patient emotion, such as randomised trials (Gokal et al., 2016). However, cancer survivors are increasingly turning to the internet – as a source of support it is second only to health professionals (Klemm, 2003; Petersen and Fretz, 2003; Kennifer et al., 2009). Internet-based OSNs involve users voluntarily posting updates about life activities (e.g. Zhao and Rosson, 2009), maintaining social relationships, gathering information, seeking help and expressing emotions (Sykora et al., 2013). But is this source of support actually helping cancer patients enhance their emotional health and associated recuperative capacity? Currently we lack an evaluation of this (Hong et al., 2012).

The future research in this area will address the question: does OSN use positively impact the emotional health of cancer patients? Through better understanding it will be possible to have a personalised OSN that will have a positive impact on that person's cancer treatment. Ultimately, by understanding the emotions throughout the cancer treatment it could be possible to determine if a treatment is actually working through using case-based reasoning and to provide feedback to pharmaceuticals about the emotional effects the treatment has on patients to aid them in future drug developments.

Of course, we also see several cognitive solutions that have focused on supporting specialists in oncology to identify the correct treatment for patients. IBM's Watson has had success in assisting specialists to identify new treatments based on a patient's medical history, ethnicity and other factors.

8.5 Quantum analytics

As we have discussed in this book, with ever-increasing complexity, and the increase in big data, social media, cloud- and mobile-based services present massive challenges and opportunities for government, organisations and society. Through the blended mix of Data Science and Decision Sciences we will see the research agenda focus on the development and application of rigorous methodologies and algorithms that can extract value from information contained within data to support both private and public sector decisions and policymakers in understanding, evaluating and improving the performance and choices of firms, organisations and individuals.

We will see computing-based solutions provided to scientists and businesses, to help them achieve objective decisions, within the paradigm of multiple constraints, given data on many relevant variables that are typified in being diversely correlated. There are real-world problems that need to be solved within the boundaries of specific constraints – such as those of real-time decision-making from large, multi-mode, unstructured data sets. In all instances, the solution to the problem will take the form of an algorithm to be run on an information processing machine with the data providing the input and the value of the output. The constraints of the physical implementation of each platform mean some problems are not practically solvable within the space of known classical algorithms – we will refer to this as the set of *hard problems* (which include, for example, Non-deterministic Polynomial-time (NP) and NP complete). Many of these hard problems also pose serious challenges to industry, for example, technical capability that could affect profit. A few examples where critical business spaces are limited by hard problems include: design for manufacturing process, predictive maintenance, autonomous decision making, scenario planning, medical diagnostics, social analytics and behaviour prediction, early warning systems for natural hazards, drug design and well-known optimisation problems such as the travelling salesman problem, PCB trace layout and cable routing (capacitated minimum spanning trees).

To do this a new form of computing needs to be developed. Quantum computing is one avenue that shows promise. A team of Google and NASA scientists showed how a quantum computer was 100 million times faster than a conventional computer. But moving quantum computing to an industrial scale is difficult.

At present, 'Researchers think that a device that can deliver on the promise of quantum computing is between five and twenty years away' (Government Office for Science, 2016); and that 'Within a decade we will probably have quantum computers with 50 to 100 qubits' (Government Office for Science, 2016). Quantum Data Science is becoming a reality, for example, the University of Technology Sydney has recently launched its Centre for Quantum Software and Information that 'is dedicated to the development of the software and information processing infrastructure required for future quantum technologies'. We will see researchers taking challenges facing industry and presenting a new approach to Decision Sciences and also 'in identifying not only where quantum technology can apply to existing markets but also the new markets and business opportunities that quantum technology might bring about' (Government Office for Science, 2016).

8.5.1 Quantum analytics development

There are likely to be many areas of quantum analytics development, but we have focused on what we believe to be the big three over the next five years, as shown by Figure 8.1. The areas that will benefit from quantum analytics will be developments in design for manufacturing (products/artefacts), predictive maintenance, autonomous decision making, computer-assisted diagnosis, recognising and learning complex financial fraud/cyber-threat plans, within massive data sets.

> **Quantum machine learning (QML):** is a newly emerging interdisciplinary research area, bridging the gap between theoretical developments in quantum physics and the applied research of machine learning and data science. The benefit will be to use the advantages of quantum information (e.g. states of a quantum system) to improve classical methods on a quantum computer, for example, developing efficient implementations of quantum-based clustering, classifiers, regression, optimisers and neural networks. These are fundamental algorithms and essential tools in machine learning for pattern recognition, prediction, classification and optimisation in Data and Decision Sciences. The advances of neural and deep learning algorithms in pattern recognition and feature learning demonstrate how computational speed and optimal representations may dramatically boost the robust capabilities of machines. At the same time, the increasing volume of data, from high resolution cameras, digital sensors, networks and the ubiquity of data sources, for example, robotic distributed applications and the Internet of Things, demands continuously more capable and

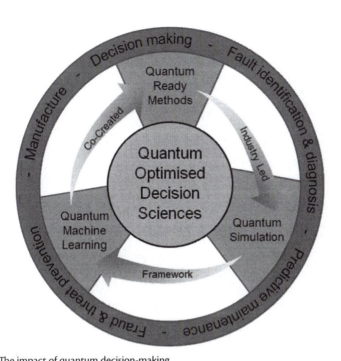

Figure 8.1   The impact of quantum decision-making

fast algorithms. Thus, using large-scale quantum mechanics and algorithms to reduce computational complexity, improve generalisation and to deal with incomplete, noisy and high-dimensional data will be key in future technology. We will see the development of learning patterns and transferable models with speed and improved generalisation performance (e.g. discriminative features adaptive to individual variety) from complex data which will enable technology to autonomously recognise unusual behaviours, unusual internet activities, unusual climate or geological conditions, failure in complex systems, etc. Prediction and autonomous decision systems with quantum technology will integrate closed-loop learning and interactive systems to monitor a large variety of systems, from networks to data, sensors and cyber-physical systems (Figure 8.1).

Quantum simulation: the zero-prototyping design paradigm, or 'right first time', is quickly becoming established in key areas of national importance, including the automotive and pharmaceutical industries. Within this paradigm, the parameter Design Space (which for automotive designs might include the requirement to meet various regulatory emission targets, as well as optimising maximum speed, weight, fuel economy, etc. (perhaps over a number of different vehicle types) must be explored through careful simulations. The present virtual Design of Experiments, far from being full-factorial, is limited for large systems to perhaps a few hundred design settings, with very few samples over the probability distributions of uncontrolled effects, so providing limited robustness analysis. Targeting such design optimisation at the exponential speed up of a quantum computer will both relieve the bounds on the design space dimension, and enable the use of more faithful subsystem models. Producing algorithms that optimally partition workload on the quantum computer, integrate into current workflow and satisfy the needs of a multi-centre, multi-national design team, provides a clear example of the project aim. For example, Markov Chain Monte Carlo (MCMC) methods, such as Metropolis-Hastings and

Gibbs Sampling algorithms, are most apt at inference in such high-dimensional situations characterised by disparate levels of correlation; this is of relevance across disciplines – from universe sciences to nano-metre scales, from economics to biology. However, in practical applications, the prolonged run times to convergence of such MCMC chains is a shortcoming, hindering inference over acceptable timescales. As part of the research, 'low hanging fruits' will be identified to provide an immediate solution. For example, algorithms which will be run on a quantum platform, such as MCMC algorithms, offer themselves readily for such upgrading. Another area that we have identified with project partners is in more direct modelling including solving fluid dynamics problems such as the Navier Stokes equations. In all areas the development of algorithms that are optimised for given quantum information processes (QIP) technology capability will be addressed.

Co-creation framework and methodology – Quantum ready: existing methods (e.g. build fast, fail fast; right first time) will have to be analysed to determine their fitness value in a quantum ready environment. It is likely existing methods must be adapted and novel ones created to fully support and take advantage of quantum approaches that will enable the extraction of value from information contained within data to support both private- and public-sector decisions and policymakers.

The development of quantum technologies will form a new platform of activity in quantum preparedness and readiness, for a wealth of worldwide industry. Spearheaded by industry focused problems, across a diverse spectrum of key industries, this development of the next five years will offer significant added value opportunities for the competitiveness of businesses, to solve real-world problems with the future processing capabilities of quantum technologies (i.e. in enhanced automated diagnostic capabilities and decision-making).

8.6   Neuromorphic chips

Many companies are reviewing architectures that are inspired by how the brain works, for example, IBM Research is investing deeply in the development of this new form of computing.

Traditional computers consume vast quantities of power in relation to the human brain (the human brain can process images, audio and text – in fact all five senses whilst consuming only very low amounts of power). This is due to the unique way the human brain has evolved over thousands of years to be able to receive such data and process it efficiently and most of the time automatically with no real effort by the person in charge of the brain!

New chips with a brain-inspired computer architecture powered by millions of neurons and synapses are being developed by a number of companies (Intel, IBM and others). The chips are really several specifically trained elements that are networked together to handle differing tasks like recognising colours, sounds, patterns.

An example of an emerging compute fabric is the IBM SyNAPSE neuromorphic chip. This chip enables sensory perception in mobile and IoT applications by implementing a low power scalable architecture. The version developed in 2016 is the IBM TrueNorth chip which contains 1 million neurons and 256 synapses implemented using 5.4 billion transistors and consuming only 73mW. TrueNorth achieves this by challenging several requirements that constrain traditional compute fabrics including exactness of data representation, synchronicity of events, error tolerance and energy/frequency optimisation. As part of a cognitive hardware and software ecosystem, this technology creates new possibilities of transformative applications and devices with sensory perception. These include applications in robotics, healthcare, public safety, environmental protection and many others.

8.7   AI – job reduction?

There are many dark forecasts of what the next wave of technology will do to likely job prospects, and one area of information management that continues to raise concern is how the use of big data and machine learning (and its sub set, deep learning) will carve out a whole new tranche of jobs currently done by middle managers. Without doubt the new breed of cognitive solutions that are trained (often with neural networks as a key component) enable computers to move into fields that haven't really been explored to date. Healthcare (diagnoses), Banking (financial advice), Retail (personal shopper assistants), Legal (virtual solicitor/barrister) and many more could pave the way for much more effective and faster decisions to be made. However, these models are only as good as the training and bias could be introduced if the data supplied (knowledge corpus) isn't sufficient or the experts used are too narrow in their training of the system. So, it's likely that the problem space will either be quite specific, or simple enough that it could be 'crowdsourced' for training purposes to make sure the trained system delivers reliable answers for the vast majority of problems it is asked to review.

This leaves a very long tail of problems where computers and humans can still use such models, but the humans involved will be using the machine's interpretation of the possible options as another input into their own judgement. This will help to answer the 'long tail' of questions where the answers are not clear-cut but require a computer to use vast amounts of data – probably unstructured (e.g. text, video) to build possible solutions that give an indication of how precise the computer thinks its solution is and the confidence it assigns to that solution.

This leads the authors to believe that humans will have cognitive/AI-style solutions that will augment our ability for the difficult problems (not clear-cut) but there will be a hollowing out for those simpler decision points around jobs. This isn't a new phenomenon – jobs have continually been replaced by other roles over the ages as technology has advanced, but it will let us consider what roles will be of value in this new world.

8.8   Conclusion

Without question the world ahead is going to become more analytical than ever before. There will be an increase of data every year by 40%, and according to BAE Systems Detica, it is more likely to be 54%, and some even estimate that there is going to be a 100% increase for the top companies (Manyika et al., 2011; Detica, 2017). Being involved in analytics has never been so interesting and very much in demand, as the amount of data is doubling every 18 months and industrial organisations store a large proportion of this data (Bughin et al., 2010). A good example of industry generating and storing data is that of Rolls-Royce, as they are collecting huge amounts of data from their turbines. A new Boeing 787 generates over half a terabyte of data during every flight which should be analysed in almost real time (Salimi and Salimi, 2017). As the world becomes more connected by the IoT, there will be a greater thirst to try to piece all of this information together like a gigantic jigsaw puzzle to get better insights to aid both business and society. With the transformative introduction of quantum and neuromorphic computing, it will not only speed up processing but eventually provide us with new ways of working that currently we cannot quite comprehend. Without a doubt these are the most exciting times to be involved in the analytics industry and to benefit from them as an end user (e.g. online personalised shopping). In these exciting times, we must shape the future, but we must also consider the impact our actions will have, and the ethical considerations should always be at the forefront of our ideas and plans.

 **Study area**

To test your understanding of the chapter please attempt to answer these questions, either by debating them in the class with colleagues or by writing them down to help formulate your answers.

Questions:

1 What analytics would you need to determine personalised online social networks (OSNs)?
2 What are your predictions for the next five years?
3 What are the ethical concerns around sensors that can determine human emotions?
4 What impact will quantum computing have on analytics?

Further reading:

Please use additional resources to further your understanding of the following:

- Affective computing and sentiment analysis
  ○ Cambria, E., Das, D., Bandyopadhyay, S. and Feraco, A. (2017). Affective computing and sentiment analysis. In: Cambria, E., Das, D., Bandyopadhyay, S. and Feraco, A. (eds), *A practical guide to sentiment analysis* (pp. 1–10). Cham: Springer International Publishing.
- Case-based reasoning
  ○ Richter, M.M. and Weber, R.O. (2016). *Case-based reasoning.* Berlin: Springer-Verlag Berlin.
- Semantic technologies like ontologies
  ○ Lee, K., Lee, J. and Kwan, M.P. (2017). Location-based service using ontology-based semantic queries: A study with a focus on indoor activities in a university context. *Computers, Environment and Urban Systems,* 62, 41–52.

References

Abbasi, A., Sarker, S. and Chiang, R.H. (2016). Big data research in information systems: Toward an inclusive research agenda. *Journal of the Association for Information Systems,* 17(2), pp. 1–32.

Anshari, M., Alas, Y., Hardaker, G., Jaidin, J.H., Smith, M. and Ahad, A.D. (2016). Smartphone habit and behavior in Brunei: Personalization, gender, and generation gap. *Computers in Human Behavior,* 64, pp. 719–727.

Barraclough, J. (1999). *Cancer and Emotion: A Practical Guide to Psycho-Oncology.* New York: John Wiley & Sons.

Bessen, J.E. (2016). How computer automation affects occupations: Technology, jobs, and skills. Boston University School of Law, Law and Economics Research Paper No. 15–49. doi: http://dx.doi.org/10.2139/ssrn.2690435

Bughin, J., Chui, M. and Manyika, J. (2010). Clouds, big data, and smart assets: Ten tech-enabled business trends to watch. *McKinsey Quarterly,* 56(1), pp. 75–86.

Ciarrochi, J., Parker, P., Sahdra, B., Marshall, S., Jackson, C., Gloster, A.T. and Heaven, P. (2016). The development of compulsive internet use and mental health: A four-year study of adolescence. *Developmental Psychology,* 52(2), p. 272.

Correa, T. (2016). Digital skills and social media use: How internet skills are related to different types of Facebook use among 'digital natives'. *Information, Communication & Society*, 19(8), pp. 1095–1107.

Detica, BAE Systems. (2017) The big data refinery: Distilling intelligence from Big Data. A BAE systems whitepaper.

Donnelly, J.M., Kornblith, A.B., Fleishman, S., Zuckerman, E., Raptis, G., Hudis, C.A., Hamilton, N., Payne, D., Massie, M.J., Norton, L. and Holland, J.C. (2000). A pilot study of interpersonal psychotherapy by telephone with cancer patients and their partners. *Psycho-Oncology*, 9(1), pp. 44–56.

Doyle-Lindrud, S. (2015). Watson will see you now: A supercomputer to help clinicians make informed treatment decisions. *Clinical Journal of Oncology Nursing*, 19(1), pp. 31–32.

Eysenbach G. (2003). The impact of the internet on cancer outcomes. *Cancer Journal Clinicians*, 53, pp. 356–371

Gokal, K., Wallis, D., Ahmed, S., Boiangiu, I., Kancherla, K. and Munir, F. (2016). Effects of a self-managed home-based walking intervention on psychosocial health outcomes for breast cancer patients receiving chemotherapy: A randomised controlled trial. *Supportive Care in Cancer*, 24(3), pp. 1139–1166.

Government Office for Science (2016). *Quantum Technologies: Blackett Review*, Government Office for Science Ref: GS/16/18.

Hong Y, Peña-Purcell NC, Ory MG. (2012). Outcomes of online support and resources for cancer survivors: A systematic literature review. *Patient Education and Counseling*, 86(3), pp. 288–296.

IBM (2017). 5 in 5 Predictions. http://research.ibm.com/5-in-5/mental-health/, last accessed 25 April 2017.

IBM Quantum Experience (2017). The future is quantum (website), http://www.research.ibm.com/quantum/

Info Blood Pressure. (2008). *Info Blood Pressure.com* (website), http://www.infobloodpressure.com/consequences-of-high-BP.html, last accessed 8 March 2016.

Jackson, T., Dawson, R. and Wilson, D. (2002). *Case Study: Evaluating the Effect of Email Interruptions within the Workplace*. EASE, https://dspace.lboro.ac.uk/2134/489, last accessed 28 June 2018.

Jackson, T., & Farzaneh, P. (2012). Theory based model of factors affecting information overload. *International Journal of Information Management*, 32, pp. 523–532.

Jencks, M. (1995). *A View from the Front Line*. London: Maggie's Caring Cancer Centre.

Kasabov, N., Scott, N.M., Tu, E., Marks, S., Sengupta, N., Capecci, E., Othman, M., Doborjeh, M.G., Murli, N., Hartono, R. and Espinosa-Ramos, J.I. (2016). Evolving spatio-temporal data machines based on the NeuCube neuromorphic framework: Design methodology and selected applications. *Neural Networks*, 78, pp. 1–14.

Kennifer, S., Alexander, S., Pollak, K., Jeffreys, A., Olsen, M., Rodriguez, K., Arnold, R. and Tulsky, J. (2009). Negative emotions in cancer care: Do oncologists' responses depend on severity and type of emotion? *Patient Education and Counseling*, 76, pp. 51–56.

Klemm, P., Bunnell, D., Cullen, M., Soneji, R., Gibbons, P. and Holecek, A. (2003). Online cancer support groups: A review of the research literature. *CIN: Computers, Informatics, Nursing*, 21(3), pp. 136–142.

Ladd, T.D., Jelezko, F., Laflamme, R., Nakamura, Y., Monroe, C. and O'Brien, J.L. (2010). Quantum computing. [Online.] arXiv preprint arXiv:1009.2267.

Linke, N.M., Maslov, D., Roetteler, M., Debnath, S., Figgatt, C., Landsman, K.A., Wright, K. and Monroe, C. (2017). Experimental comparison of two quantum computing architectures. In: *Proceedings of the National Academy of Sciences*, 201618020.

Malin, J.L. (2013). Envisioning Watson as a rapid-learning system for oncology. *Journal of Oncology Practice*, 9(3), pp. 155–157.

Marulanda-Carter, Laura. (2013). Email stress and its management in public sector organisations. PhD Thesis, Loughborough University. Available at: https://dspace.lboro.ac.uk/dspace-jspui/handle/2134/14196, last accessed 28 June 2018.

Medtronic. (2010). About Tachycardia (Fast Heartbeat). Available at: http://www.medtronic.co.uk/your-health/tachycardia/, last accessed 9 March 2016.

Pastur-Romay, L.A., Cedrón, F., Pazos, A. and Porto-Pazos, A.B. (2016). Deep artificial neural networks and neuromorphic chips for big data analysis: Pharmaceutical and bioinformatics applications. *International Journal of Molecular Sciences*, 17(8), p. 1313.

Pastur-Romay, L.A., Porto-Pazos, A. B., Cedrón, F. and Pazos, A. (2017). Parallel computing for brain simulation. *Current Topics in Medicinal Chemistry*, 17(14), pp. 1646–1668.

Peterson M, Fretz P. (2003). Patient use of the Internet for information in a lung cancer clinic. *Chest*, 12, pp. 452–457.

Picard, R.W. and Klein, J. (2002). Computers that recognise and respond to user emotion: Theoretical and practical implications. *Interacting with Computers*, 14(2), pp. 141–169.

Salimi, F. and Salimi, F. (2017). *A Systems Approach to Managing the Complexities of Process Industries*. Oxford: Elsevier.

Siegler, M. G. (2010). Eric Schmidt: Every two days we create as much information as we did up to 2003. [Online]. Available at: http://techcrunch.com/2010/08/04/schmidt-data/, last accessed 12 October 2015.

Sykora, Martin & Jackson, Thomas & Elayan, Suzanne. (2013). Emotive Ontology: Extracting Fine-Grained Emotions from Terse, Informal Messages. International Journal on Computer Science and Information Systems. 8. 106-118.

Teo, T. (2016). Do digital natives differ by computer self-efficacy and experience? An empirical study. *Interactive Learning Environments*, 24(7), pp. 1725–1739.

Trabesinger, A. (2017). Quantum computing: Towards reality. *Nature*, 543(7646), pp. S1–S1.

Whiting and Williams. (2013). Why people use social media: A uses and gratifications approach. *Qualitative Market Research: An International Journal*, 16(4), pp. 362–369. doi: http://dx.doi.org/10.1108/QMR-06-2013-0041

Zauderer, M.G., Gucalp, A., Epstein, A.S., Seidman, A.D., Caroline, A., Granovsky, S., Fu, J., Keesing, J., Lewis, S., Co, H. and Petri, J. (2014). Piloting IBM Watson Oncology within Marjorie Glass Zauderer, Ayca Gucalp, Andrew S. Epstein, Andrew David Seidman, Aryeh Caroline, Svetlana Granovsky, Julia Fu, Jeffrey Keesing, Scott Lewis, Heather Co, John Petri, Mark Megerian, Thomas Eggebraaten, Peter Bach, and Mark G. Kris Journal of Clinical Oncology 2014 32:15_suppl, e17653-e17653

Zhao, Dejin & Rosson, Mary Beth. (2009). How and Why People Twitter: The Role that Micro-blogging Plays in Informal Communication at Work. GROUP'09 - Proceedings of the 2009 ACM SIGCHI International Conference on Supporting Group Work. 10.1145/1531674.1531710.

APPENDIX 1: BIG DATA ANALYTICS PLATFORM – ADDITIONAL COMPONENTS

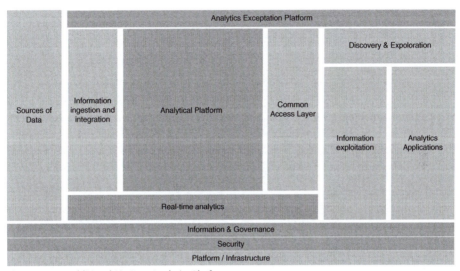

Figure A1.1   Additional Big Data Analytics Platform components

This appendix briefly outlines the other components that exist in the Big Data Analytics Platform described in Chapter 3. These are the light grey areas in Figure A1.1.

Sources of data

A big data system is expected to cope with the ingestion of data from many differing data sources that cover the spread of velocity, variety and volume characteristics such sources bring. The Big Data Analytics Platform must be capable of dealing with anything from traditional databases to complex real-time streams, as well as images, video, sound and everything that can be digitised.

Historically, data from on-premise solutions still forms an important core of an organisation's operations and the reference data and transactional data from these systems are still highly relevant, for example core customer data, financial transactions and so forth. In addition, some external third-party data such as marketing data makes up these forms of source data.

The last ten years have seen an explosion of new forms of data available which must all be catered for, from social media, to news feeds, to image and video, and a plethora of sensors that feed IoT-type solutions for manufacturing and consumer use.

Information integration and ingestion

This component manages the processes and environments that can capture, transform and move data to ensure quality data is prepared for storage in the analytic platform layer. This component is capable of processing the data whether it arrives in batch, near real time or real time. The output from this layer can also be used for real-time analytics or passed into other applications for use downstream. Some of the common functions found in this component are:

- ETL – Extract (from all the sources mentioned above), Transform (apply business rules to data to standardise and cleanse data) and Load (process data into the analytic platform layer or other targets).
- Change Data Capture – Where data needs to be moved in near real time, Change Data Capture (CDC) techniques can be applied that often read logs or techniques such as trigger, SQL or queue-based replication.

More recently, the need to capture unstructured information, such as documents or even video, and extract useful information from them, such as key entities, concepts and keywords, has become important. There are multiple approaches that generally use some form of annotator and are based on Unstructured Information Management Architecture (UIMA) approaches to solve these problems.

Common access layer

The Common Access Layer (CAL) is used to allow any potential user of the Analytics Platform access to that layer. It has a number of capabilities that allow data to be prepared in such a way as to be suitable for users, whether they be data scientists, business users or other actors who need access to the analytic platform (including other systems).

It can include:

- Data virtualisation – This builds a semantic layer to the data that allows end users access to the data in the analytic platform layer with little or no knowledge of the data that resides within. These techniques have been available with traditional database systems using techniques such as views, but have extended into other requirements such as Hadoop-based platforms over time.
- Data federation – Often seen as the 'poor relation', this can be a very useful technique when trying out new thinking. Federation allows multiple connections to different engines and the queries can be harmonised through a single interface. Can suffer from performance, the weakest link in the chain being the slowest system to respond, but caching techniques can help here.
- Self-service – Actually moves data from the analytic platform layer to a new data store to allow that new dataset to be manipulated as required. Often used for data scientists so they can experiment with new combinations of data to find new results.
- Open APIs – Enable a variety of actors (users and systems) to access the analytic platform layer as a series of calls to return (generally) well-controlled and constrained data sets to the calling systems. APIs make use of standards such as REST interfaces to ensure a standard and easily adopted approach is used.

Information exploitation

This component is used to derive useful insights from the analytical platform which in turn can be turned into actions by the business to improve some aspect of the business. There are a variety of tools available to help at this stage, ranging from SQL to OLAP queries, data mining, statistical models and novel visualisation approaches. We also add to this area the more recent advances in cognitive tooling and artificial intelligence to enable simpler human machine interfaces and approaches that are non-deterministic.

Here are some key areas in a little more detail:

- Core analytical techniques – These cover everything from simple reporting to more sophisticated analytics for both structured and unstructured data. These tools have been available in one form or another for many years; recent focus has been on ever more sophisticated visualisation of analytics to assist end users in spotting trends or anomalies more easily.
- Predictive analytics – These techniques cover areas such as statistical analysis, data mining, content analytics and unsupervised machine learning models. These tools and technologies allow users to take existing samples of data and 'see forward' with predictive models to help businesses gain a degree of understanding of what could be.
- Prescriptive analytics – Helps businesses to generate actionable insight and decide on what the next best action for an activity could be. These approaches use optimisation models to help automate decisions using the information available and taking known constraints into account.
- Cognitive analytics – The newest approach in this component has started to enable machines to understand, reason and learn from being trained in certain domain specific areas. It uses a variety of techniques that involve data mining, pattern recognitions and natural language processing to draw inferences from knowledge bases built to support the domain in which it is being applied. The key thing to recognise is that responses are based on probabilistic scores, generally a level of precision around an answer and the confidence that the answer is correct. This is very different from the analytics section we described in the first part of these bullet points.

Analytical applications

This component covers specific applications developed to make use of the analytical platform. Examples could be:

- Customer experience – Applications that make use of analytical insights to offer the customer a better experience, for example recommendation engines for online shopping or selecting the best financial product when dealing with a bank through one of its online channels.
- Fraud and anti-money laundering – By using all the available transactional data and combining this with data obtained from other sources (e.g. Companies House in the UK for Director details, newsfeeds for details on individuals, etc.), it becomes possible to identify anomalies in financial patterns and identify the key actors who took part in the transactions. Of course this is a very simple summary of a complex process that analytics can now help enormously.

The data created within these applications may be valuable to the analytic platform and can be fed back to extend the data sets that reside there.

Discovery and exploration

This component is very different to the previous two. While still making use of the data in the analytic platform, it is now used to create 'sand boxes' which end users can run a variety of tools against. The data sets tend to be very complex and the tooling is equally so to enable very fast analysis and hypothesis-building against the data. Users are encouraged to 'fail fast' and try many different things with their data while looking for new clues within the data to exploit. This allows those currently termed 'data scientists' (and we mentioned earlier in Chapter 3, these seem similar to what were called operational scientists in the past) to search across all the data at their disposal. Data Science is considered to be a new approach to making discoveries within data. It utilises a deep understanding of mathematics, statistics, visualisation and programming languages such as Python, Scala Java and 'R' to 'deep dive' into the data. It also enables any new findings and techniques to be shared and collaboration to be fostered among communities of data scientists to accelerate learning in new areas.

Platform/infrastructure

This covers a variety of platforms now available that range from traditional in-house platforms through to the cloud-based platforms available in today's world:

Traditional platforms – (The 'old' way of doing things.) We refer to these as the on-premises, bespoke deployed and build solutions that clutter company data centres around the world. Even with virtualisation, these data centres carry enormous cost – often capital expenditure – that businesses must refresh regularly as the demands of new software solutions and growth within the business dictate. If the business wishes to split or divest elements it is often a difficult process to carry out as hardware is physically held at particular locations and may require new hardware to be bought for new locations and solutions ported across.

- Cloud solutions – These are now becoming more ubiquitous as more and more companies are offloading the workloads that do not need to be kept on-premises (generally for security or compliance reasons). We can break these cloud-based solutions into public and private cloud solutions that take the form of:
  - Infrastructure as a Service (IaaS) – basically means rent hardware! IaaS is comprised of highly automated and scalable computer resources that are 'wrapped' with cloud storage and network capability which enables self-provisioning, metering and billing, and on-demand elasticity for these resources. These are all provisioned as a set of virtualised resources generally run on behalf of a customer by third-party providers and charged for on a usage basis.
  - Platform as a Service (PaaS) – sits over IaaS, providing a set of services upon which applications can be built. It allows customers to deploy core middleware such as databases, web servers and so on. The provider of such services is responsible for the maintenance of all the services it offers, while the end customer is responsible for the applications they build using these services. This offers a developer many advantages. For example, the platform can frequently change or upgrade operating system features as required and can help remote development teams collaborate on projects as the solution is all cloud-based.
  - Software as a Service (SaaS) – the final way to deploy a cloud-style platform is SaaS. This takes the level of abstraction of the service up a notch to the point where the

customer is renting a prebuilt solution for an area of the business. This is run from the cloud. As such it tends to be successful with customers who are either 'born on the cloud' or who can categorise the requirements around data as not being sensitive information where a data breach could be critical. There is a perception that data on the cloud is less secure than on a company's own site – however, this is beginning to change and the SaaS providers can demonstrate the security of their solutions to a great degree nowadays.

At this level companies don't have any upfront investment to make other than (maybe) migrating some data sets onto the new cloud solution. Most of the responsibilities to run and maintain the solution are now outsourced to the provider and the model is a 'pay as you go' one. The solution is accessed via the web through any device (browser, tablet, mobile phone, for example) and can be accessed globally at any time. This makes it very powerful for applications that always need to be on – the cloud provider caters for these requirements.

APPENDIX 2: GRAPH DATABASES

We added this appendix as a primer to understanding just a little about graph databases. The idea of graphs is so central to that of open metadata and in turn governance that it can't, in our opinion, be left out.

A hybrid cloud solution for analytics requires metadata to be stored in many locations and federated to build up a complete picture; ideally each metadata store would be underpinned by an instance of Apache Atlas holding core metadata and any extensions relevant to that set of data being managed. So let's explore what a graph database is a little detail.

A graph database is another example of technology created to fix a problem that relational databases simply weren't designed to handle. The modern graph database, pioneered by Neo4j inventor Emil Eifrem,[1] is a data storage and processing engine that makes the persistence and exploration of data and relationships more efficient.

Graphs behave similar to how people think – in specific relationships between discrete units of data. A way to understand graph databases is to imagine yourself in a room with a team of people. You're about to tackle a new project. What's the first thing you do? You start jotting down ideas on a whiteboard; within a few moments you find yourselves circling some concepts and connecting them with lines. You are modelling a graph.

Traditional database management systems store data in tabular form – rows and columns – but the information we deal with on a daily basis – including our knowledge of family members, co-workers and bank accounts – exists in relationships. Why shoehorn data into tables and rows if it only slows the work and complicates or restricts the analysis? By storing data relationships directly as a graph – made up of nodes or vertices, connected via relationships or edges to form a mesh of information – we reduce complexity and eliminate the extra work involved in transforming the data from the model to storage.

In graph theory, structures are composed of vertices and edges (nodes and connections). Graphs consist of an ordered pair, that is, a vertex (or node) and edge(s) or line(s). A graph is defined as a set of vertices and edges. Nodes can represent entities such as people, businesses, phones or just about anything you want to track. There is no limit to the number of nodes and edges a graph may have.

So what exactly makes graphs different? Here are some of the key differentiators to other database management systems:

- They are classed in the NoSQL category (note there are several differing db classes here: doc stores, column-driven, key-value pairs and the graph itself). Schema are very easily extended – just add a new edge and node (edges and nodes have properties that define them).
- Unlike other dbs which store data in rows, columns, or key value pairs, a graph db stores all its information in the nodes and edges previously mentioned.
- Adding information about the nodes and edges creates a **property graph** which represents the structure of data inside a graph database.
- Some other databases can implicitly represent a graph db (simple three columns in a relational database – triple – can be a starting point for example); but only a graph database explicitly represents a graph.

---

1 https://neo4j.com/blog/contributor/emil/

- All other databases need to rely on aspects such as self joins or some such helper to work, but graph databases can traverse from one object to the next because these objects are organised to have index-free adjacency.
- Graph dbs solve problems that other dbs simply take too long to do *or* just cannot do.

Graphs can be used to model many things – for example, networks of computer communications, social networks, routing problems and genomics; and of course it's critical to helping the 'Semantic Web' deliver on its promises. Various bodies have tried to identify differing classes of graph databases and one approach that seems to work for business is: social, intent, consumption, interest and mobile. The deployment of such solutions can lead to competitive advantage by allowing sophisticated queries to be built across huge graphs that may never have been attempted before.

Graphs rapidly grow in size and one of the main challenges to using graphs for many different things is the processing time required to work through all the permutations of data that relatively small graphs can produce. Ever heard of the Six Degrees of Kevin Bacon game?[2] That's a graph problem that shows how most actors can be linked in some way to the one actor – Kevin Bacon!

Querying graphs is all about traversing the edges of the graph. Graph queries answer problems such as, 'Find a path through the graph that starts at a particular node and ends at another node.' There could be several differing paths to get between the two nodes. In addition, we can use the edge information to learn from the connections along any particular path. This could be as easy as which route has the fewest number of edges (finding the shortest path) to something much more complicated like identifying nodes in the graph that are important as 'clusters' that link different parts of the graph together. Both nodes and edges can store additional properties such as key-value pairs. This is important because all of the data in your organisation is only important in how it relates to other data points. The value of the data rests in data relationships; graph databases let you get at that value more quickly and easily. Graph visualisation of data relationships leads to a fuller picture of what's happening, so that users have better insight.

The property graph is one view that has come from graph theory; each node of a graph can be labelled in some manner (a simple ID number could suffice) that is unique and each edge labelled likewise.

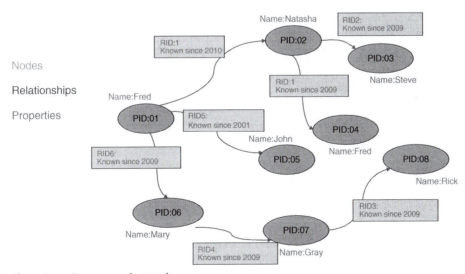

Figure A2.1   Property graph example

---

2 https://en.wikipedia.org/wiki/Six_Degrees_of_Kevin_Bacon

Note these are all unidirectional relationships which means that although Natasha has known Steve since 2009, Steve may not have known Natasha at all. Also we have two Freds as nodes, each with their unique IDs. Without more data we don't know if they are the same person or not.

Here are just two examples of typical patterns we can look for in graphs that can be important to understanding relationships within a graph; these are taken in the context of a 'social network' but could easily be considered as nodes on a computer network or connections drawn from call data records (CDRs) for a Telco company.

Between-ness centrality

This is a node in the graph that has a path that acts as a 'gateway' to other portions of the graph network; it is the node with the best path to connect all the network together. To link this to Chapter 6 in our metadata considerations, this could be an individual who is using data across two differing areas of the business and has identified some new ways that data can be used to assist the business. In Figure A2.2 the diagram to the left shows the concepts, and that to the right shows the individual in a network of people who acts as that 'gateway' is Nessa.

Degree centrality

The node with the most connections to other nodes. The diagram on the left in Figure A2.3 shows the concept and the diagram on the right that node in a set of relationships between people is Chris. These could be very important data items that straddle a lot of areas in the business, for example as reference and/or master data.

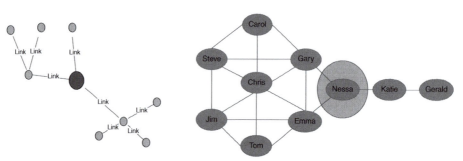

Figure A2.2 Between-ness centrality

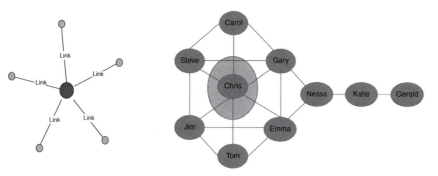

Figure A2.3 Degree centrality

APPENDIX 3: OPEN STANDARDS

Open standards

Open standards promote interoperability and information integration by using open, published specifications for APIs, protocols and data and file formats. This enables simplification of data sharing between different internal and external business systems, and is a critical first step to optimising location and company independent processes.

There are many definitions and a lot of confusion around what constitutes an 'open standard'. These range from published but proprietary interfaces to true standards body-supported and widely adopted open interfaces (such as XML and JSON). We can adopt the following as a meaningful gauge as to whether a standard is 'open' in the true sense of the word.

1. Does the standard enjoy broad adoption? Is there multiple vendor implementation of the standard, or is the standard 'tailored' by vendors to suit their own offerings and needs?
2. Does the standards governing body have public interfaces and solicit public input for future iterations of the standard? Apache Software Foundation is a strong proponent of such an approach.
3. Is the (emerging) standard on a path to long-term stewardship, perhaps through an official standards body or and effective open source community?

Open architecture

Open architectures are designed to allow the construction of solutions that are built of modular, loosely coupled services. Each service is independent of the others to ensure teams can isolate and distribute work to the most effective organisation within or even outside the business that is having the solution developed. Micro services and serverless computing work in this manner. They enable easier integration of activities into common workflows that increase collaboration within and among all teams. These approaches assist promoting agile development practices.

Open source software

Open source software promotes licensing standards and leverages community development and collaborative innovation. A lot of confusion also exists around the term open source. It is actually three things:

1. A licensing approach that prioritises the rights of users
2. A way of developing software
3. A community with open participation

The first component of open source – and the 'formal definition' – is the approach to licensing the software. Open source is not freeware, shareware or unlicensed – it's just licensed in a different way to traditional commercial software. In formal terms, open source means that the licence is one of about 60 licences authorised by the Open Source Initiative (OSI).

Open Source is also a development methodology which uses a community approach to developing software, based around peer review. Since the code is openly published, everyone can see whether it is good or bad code – and offer feedback on how to improve it. This then promotes a meritocracy of developers – you get to be a key player by writing good code.

Finally, open source is all about open community – not just for developers, but for users and partners as well. Projects such as Linux, Apache and Eclipse offer a level playing field where anyone can participate, based on merit. Community innovation is at the centre of open computing, and has been a core reason for its rapid growth and technological progress.

The community-driven approach to problem solving is not new – it's been at the centre of the 'academic method' in universities for many years. It's just a new approach for the modern software industry. The academic method essentially comprises someone inventing something new, publishing it (for example, through writing a paper), and then other researchers reviewing it, learning from it and building innovation on top of the original invention.

Previously, this community approach to innovation tended to be possible in the same physical location – where the community could get together to work on the solution. However, the advent of the internet and collaborative tools has enabled people to work jointly on solving problems even if they live thousands of miles apart and have never met.

By bringing together the best minds from across IT vendors, universities and individuals, common problems can be solved faster and more effectively.

Open data

Open data promotes the concept that certain information will be made freely available to everyone to use and republish as they wish, without any restrictions or control. As governments open up more and more data, this is likely to drive growth, ingenuity and innovation in the local economy. The UK Government's strategy – by department – is outlined on the Data.Gov.UK website. This has made many positive steps towards support of open data. However, certain government data sets – notably the Ordnance Survey maps of the British Isles – will not be made generally available for free, as they are funded by taxation and commercial licence revenues, which is seen by some as a limitation.

GLOSSARY

Apache Atlas: Metadata framework based on the Titan graph engine to enable efficient cataloguing of the data residing within a Hadoop environment and more. Provides the core requirements to enable good governance of the data within the Hadoop engine.

Apache Hadoop: An open source software framework that enables large data sets to be broken up into blocks, and distributed to multiple servers for storage and processing. By distributing the data sets across multiple servers, and the use of map-reduce and other constructs (see 'Map-reduce' below), large unstructured or structured data sets can be processed economically.

Apache Hive: Built over Apace Hadoop, Hive provides a SQL-like interface to allow data in various databases to be queried in a familiar manner to most analysts.

Apache Kafka: Takes the role of a traditional messaging system, in the form of a publish/subscribe model for event ingest and integration with other services. Data can be parallelised into topics which are created by producers, then consumers can take these messages and process them from the queue multiple times for different purposes.

Apache Lucene: An open source project that delivers a high performance and full-featured text search engine library which is written entirely using Java.

Apache Ranger: Security framework and tooling for the Apache Hadoop engine.

Apache Software Foundation (ASF): Develops and manages more than 350 open source projects covering many technologies. The Atlas project resides within this framework.

Apache Sqoop: A tool for managing bulk movement of data between Apache Hadoop and structured data stores.

Apache Solr: The open source platform for searches of data stored in HDFS in Hadoop. It uses the Apache Lucene Java search library at its core for full-text indexing and search.

APIs: Application Programming Interface is a collection of programming instructions and standards for accessing a web-based software application. Most companies use APIs today to enable developers to be able to use a company's software services to encourage use of the back-end that a company provides. Examples are Amazon or eBay, which allow developers to write their own front-end but embed services from those companies to access those features.

Bayes Naïve: A set of probabilistic classifiers (such as simple binary yes/no or a number of classes like massive, large, medium, small, tiny) that uses Bayes' theorem at its core.

Cloud computing: Uses remote servers hosted/managed over the internet by a third party to remove this work from an in-house data centre. Permits rapid deployment of solutions from infrastructure hosting to software as a service and enables a clear 'power by the hour' billing regime that moves from the Capex to Opex model, which saves unnecessary expenditure.

Cognitive computing: Generally follows a model that covers understanding, reasoning, and learning. It can cover aspects of machine learning, data mining, statistical model building, use of neural nets and other techniques to achieve its goals.

Column-driven: Refers to columnar databases rather than the more traditional row-designed databases: column-driven databases are often useful for analytic solutions where only certain fields in a row are needed for any results returned; by designing for columns rather than rows, much less data needs to be moved.

Content stores: Also known as content repositories, these can store a variety of content formats, enable read and write capabilities, access control and so on. Content repositories are the key source for collaboration, e-mail archiving, records management, case management and more.

Cyber-physical systems: The integration of the real world with the digital world to enhance some process. Examples could be autonomous vehicles, self-configuring work benches for human beings to build a far greater variety of things than in the past, tracking patients' health with sensors and so on.

Data analysis: Being able to process data sets to yield useful insights from that data – can be from simple reporting through to complex machine learning algorithms.

Data gravity: Describes how as data accumulates over time, it becomes larger and denser, or has a greater mass.

Data Lake: Fulfils a number of purposes: an analytics sand box for exploring data to gain insight; an enterprise-wide catalogue to find data across the enterprise and to link from business terms to technical metadata; an environment for enabling reuse of data transformations and queries; an environment where users can access vast amounts of raw data; and, finally, an environment for developing and proving an analytics model and then moving into production.

Data management: Covers the organising, securing and storage retrieval from any number of data storage systems and middleware.

Data marts: Fed from the data warehouse, these are subject area related (finance, supply, HR, procurement, etc.) and enable flexible reporting alongside the BI interface chosen; what-if analysis may also be included to allow users to model future probable scenarios. Data marts often use MOLAP- or ROLAP-style models to store and manage the data to be queried.

Data provenance: Refers to the process of tracing and recording the origins of data and its movement between databases.

DB2: IBM's flagship relational database.

Decision trees: A 'root and branch' diagram that describes all of the decision alternatives and their possible outcomes from the root. For example, when considering whether to offer a loan or not there could be several paths that describe the probability of the loan being repaid depending on age, income, location and so forth.

Deep natural language processing: Sometimes also referred to as Natural Language Understanding, it concerns itself with the understanding of speech or text to be able to more than simply extract verbs or nouns, but to understand the meaning and context of sentences. The purpose of this is to enable computer systems to take some form of action based on the intent of the input given to a system while understanding all the acronyms, synonyms, or even idioms used to form a question.

Disaster recovery: The capability to enable data to be recovered from a catastrophic failure of a data centre; copies of data are held on a remote off-site location. Metrics to define recoverability to a point in time are Recovery Time Objective (RTO) – how long the systems can be down – and Recovery Point Objective (RPO) – how much data can be lost when the system goes down. This means that if the RPO is, say, 10 minutes, there must be capability in place to be able to back up data within 10-minute increments to ensure no more than 10 minutes of data is unrecoverable.

Docker: A mechanism to encapsulate an application's needs and be shared with other docker containers across a single OS instance – generally seen as more efficient than a VM.

Enterprise Data Warehouse: The single source of truth for structured data across the enterprise; used for all strategic reporting across the entire business.

Federal Rules of Civil Procedure: The Federal Rules of Civil Procedure (FRCP) govern court procedure for civil cases (rather than criminal cases, which are governed by the Federal Rules of Criminal Procedure) in the US Federal District Courts.

Fuzzy Rule-Based System: Deals with problem sets that don't follow simple logical if-then programming models but adds probability into this construct – for example, traditional logic could state:

If has four wheels and engine, then vehicle is a car.

Fuzzy logic lets us state:

If has four wheels and engine, then vehicle is *probably* a car

This approach allows for uncertainty when dealing with our solutions and enables us to infer outcomes rather than explicitly state them.

Global Data Protection Regulations (GDPR): The EU General Data Protection Regulation (GDPR) replaces the Data Protection Directive 95/46/EC and was designed to harmonise data privacy laws across Europe, to protect and empower all EU citizens' data privacy and to reshape the way organisations across the region approach data privacy.

Graph engine/database: A graph database is essentially a collection of nodes and edges. Think of these as simply circles (nodes) connected by lines (edges) to other circles. Each node represents an entity (e.g. a person or business) and each edge represents a connection or relationship between two nodes.

Heterogeneous data: All forms of data, as opposed to homogeneous data (i.e. the same form).

Hybrid cloud: Simply the scenario where an enterprise has, or needs to have, public, private and on-premises deployments of their solutions; this 'hybrid' environment needs managing and integration enabled across key points to drive maximum business benefit.

Internet of Things (IoT): The connecting of physical devices, vehicles, buildings and other items (including people) using sensors, software and network connectivity to enable those devices to exchange information and ultimately share selected information at a central point.

JSON: JavaScript Object Notation is a lightweight data-interchange format that is easy for humans to read and write. At its simplest it is a collection of name/value pairs but the value part can be a record, array, named list and more.

Key-value pairs (KVP): A set of two linked data items: a key, which is a unique identifier for some item of data, and the value, which is either the data that is identified or a pointer to the location of that data. The data element can be many differing things: a string, a numerical value, an array and so forth. Often used within NoSQL databases.

Lexical Answer Type (LAT): When building solutions that allow complex questions to be asked of a corpus of data, the Lexical Answer Type is an important identifier as it identifies terms in the question that indicate what type of entity is being asked for. For example, 'Who is the prime minister of the UK?' It identifies a person (who) and prime minister (perhaps defined in an ontology as 'leader of Govt').

Lines of Business (LoBs): A discrete area of the business; could be a 'vertical' element such as supply chain (i.e. a discrete function within the business) or an area such as HR that is a 'horizontal' element and spans across the entire business.

LOB data analyst: An analyst who works within a specific function within the business – for example, HR, supply chain, finance, marketing and so forth.

Logic learning lachine (LLM): A machine learning method based on the generation of intelligible rules. In particular, it is an efficient mechanism for implementing Switching Neural Networks (see below).

Logistic regressions: Statistical analysis method used to predict a data value based on prior observations of a data set. Predicts a dependent data variable by analysing the relationship between existing independent variables.

Machine Learning (ML): An approach to software application development that allows applications to derive predicted outputs from a set of inputs without specific programming. Uses some form of training on a sample of typical data.

Map-reduce: Is at the core of Apache Hadoop; it allows for massive scaling across hundreds or even thousands of servers to query very large data sets; as it is normally disk-based it can be slow.

Metadata: Meta-data, or data about your data, provides data administrators and business users with descriptions of the data or informational objects that they can access. There are several forms of metadata, business (a description of the 'thing' being stored that is understood by the business) and technical metadata (a description of how the data is stored, based on the storage approach being used) being the best known.

Middleware: A class of software that is used to connect applications together; it sits between operating systems and applications. Relies on standards to help make sure outputs from one application can be easily consumed by other applications or services.

Multidimensional Online Analytical Processing (MOLAP): A subtype of OLAP using multidimensional databases to support OLAP – fast but sometimes struggles to scale to vast volumes.

Multilayer perceptron: Perceptrons take several inputs and can compute an output based on weighting the inputs and applying some bias to describe when a threshold has been reached. At this point the output is triggered. A multilayer perceptron links perceptrons together into a network (see 'Graph engine') to describe complex real-world models.

Natural Language Processing (NLP): Enables computers to analyse, understand and derive meaning from human language. This approach enable developers to extract, organise and structure knowledge derived from spoken or textual inputs to identify key entities, concepts, taxonomies sentiment and key words.

NoSQL Engines: A NoSQL (or non-relational database) is designed to support different application requirements to traditional relational database management systems (RDBMS). NoSQL databases support the CAP (Consistency, Availability and Partition-tolerance) theorem, which gives rise to a number of significant features that are markedly different to relational databases.

Online Analytical Processing (OLAP): A technology that powers many BI solutions. Enables functions such as report viewing, complex analytical calculations and predictive 'what-if' scenario (budget, sales forecast, etc.) planning.

Ontology: A set of concepts and categories within a particular domain (for example, 'the aerospace industry') and the description of how those concepts and categories are interrelated.

Operational data stores: Data store for analysing structured information that is only lightly transformed and no more than a few days old.

Private cloud: A private cloud is operated solely for a single organisation, whether managed internally or by a third party, and hosted externally.

Public cloud: Public clouds are owned and operated by companies that offer rapid access over a public network to computing resources.

Relational Database Management Systems (RDBMS): Have supported transactions based on ACID (Atomicity, Consistent, Isolation, Durability) principles for many years; examples of such engines are Microsoft SQL Server, DB2, Oracle and open source solutions such as Postgres.

Relational Online Analytical Processing (ROLAP): A subtype of OLPA using Relational databases; slower then OLAP generally *but* can scale to vast volumes.

Representational State Transfer (REST): Basically describes in a simple manner (generally using HTTP) where a particular resource can be consumed or placed; uses a few simple method calls: PUT, GET, POST and DELETE.

REST API: Stands for Representational State Transfer Application Programming interface and is an architecture style that is used for networked applications. It nearly always uses HTTP protocol to define where a resource will reside that can be consumed by a calling application. There are several reasons for using REST, but performance, simplicity, portability and reliability are some of the key ones.

Rulex suite: Is a unique software platform for explainable AI (XAI). Rulex provides powerful proprietary machine learning algorithms.

Sand Boxes: Used for analytics that is exploratory in nature, generally by a Data Scientist. It's a less well governed environment than the central Data Lake, and the Analyst/Data Scientist can use it without fear of damaging the core repository. It is transient in nature and often used to identify new insights which can then be considered for production use if valuable enough to the business.

Shallow natural language processing: Tokenises a sentence to extract nouns, verbs and so on, and possibly semantically tags tokens to higher metadata (semantic) level grouping – for example, [person].Steve [theme].worked with [person,Professor].Tom to [intent]. write a [document].book.

Single sign-on (SSO): A mechanism that provides an authentication service that permits a user to use a single set of login credentials across multiple applications.

Smart factory: A concept driven from the Internet of Things (IoT) which considers how a factory can be embedded with a variety of sensors to understand in detail how it operates and the use of analytics to help optimise processes and machines within the factory.

Software as a Service (SaaS): Refers to a way in which an application can be hosted (and possibly managed) by a third-party provider to make it available to customers over the internet. SaaS is one of three main categories of cloud computing, alongside infrastructure as a service (IaaS) and platform as a service (PaaS).

Systems of Automation (SoA): This is a new domain we are using to describe the data derived by machines, known as the Internet of Things (IoT). This is being driven from the Industrial Internet of Things (IIoT) for manufacturing, sensors and devices that, say, control and monitor factories' production and scheduling and Consumer Internet of Things (CIoT) solutions, such as devices and sensors in the home or wearables.

Systems of Engagement (SoE): These fundamentally differ from the Systems of Record (SoR) as they focus on people rather than transactions. This is where we find the end user-driven data – blogs, web pages, social media.

Systems of Insight (SoI): These bring the data in Systems of Record (SoR), Systems of Engagement (SoE) and Systems of Automation (SoA) together, analyse it, apply business policies and rules to the combined data, derive insight, and make recommendations to improve the quality of decisions.

Systems of Record (SoR): Traditional OLTP systems such as ERP, asset management, financial data and master data, they all reside in this area.

SPRQL: Pronounced 'sparkle', and is a query language from the World Wide Web (WWW) consortium (W3C) for searching data defined in the Resource Description Framework (RDF) format.

SQL Server: Microsoft's flagship relational database.

Support vector machine: is a supervised learning model that is used in regression and classification problems. For a simple problem that has two dimensions (x, y) and that has binary classifications (is/is not), fundamentally a curve is fitted to the data such that the line for the two-dimensional problem is furthest away from all points defined on the graph.

Switching Neural Networks: Is an approach to solving classification problems.

System of Systems (SoS): Is a collection of independent systems that can interoperate together to achieve a desired outcome. Testing of each system, the integration of those systems and the entire SoS is critical to ensure those desired goals are met.

Time Series Analysis: Takes an ordered (by time) set of data and forecasts future values based on previous observations.

Uniform Resource Identifier (URIs): A URI can be classified as a locator, a name or both. The term 'Uniform Resource Locator' (URL) refers to the subset of URIs that, in addition to identifying a resource, provide a means of locating the resource by describing its primary access mechanism (e.g. its network 'location'). In the context of the World Wide Web (WWW) it's the address of a specific page on the web.

Unstructured Information Management Architecture (UIMA): Is an architectural and software framework that supports creation, discovery, composition and deployment of a broad range of analysis capabilities and the linking of them to structured information services, such as databases or search engines. One typical use is the deployment of search engines driven from unstructured information.

Value: Be able to understand the value of the data being used. Its value to the enterprise will dictate how it will be exploited and managed over its lifecycle.

Variety: There is a wide variety of data available for use in today's world, and the enterprise needs to manage this data as is, in its original format, and with extensive transformation tools to convert it to other desired formats for use in analytic solutions.

Velocity: The requirement to handle data arriving in large batches (e.g. sales data from a retailer arriving overnight), right down to low latency streams of data (e.g. stock market data arriving continuously or sensor data from a device attached to a human).

Veracity: Any solution must be able to identify and correct any uncertainty about the data being gathered, or show its results are not biased.

Virtual Machine (VM): Allows encapsulation of an application's needs from the OS upwards over a server or servers that support a hypervisor that manages resources.

Volume: Systems now create and consume more data than ever before (20 years ago a 2TB solution at a large UK retailer was large; nowadays 20 PB at a bank is standard) so the need to handle ever-increasing volumes of data, either at rest or even while in motion, is essential.

INDEX

Druck:
Canon Deutschland Business Services GmbH
im Auftrag der KNV-Gruppe
Ferdinand-Jühlke-Str. 7
99095 Erfurt